BREWING LAGER BEER

BREWING LAGER BEER

THE MOST COMPREHENSIVE BOOK FOR HOME-AND MICROBREWERS

BY GREGORY J. NOONAN

Brewers Publications — Boulder, Colorado

The illustration "Hardness of Ground Water" on pages 26 and 27 is from *Water Atlas of the United States*, by James J. Geraghty and was used with permission of the publisher.

Brewing Lager Beer
By Gregory J. Noonan
Copyright © 1986 by Gregory J. Noonan

ISBN 0-937381-01-2
Printed in the United States of America
10 9 8

Published by Brewers Publications,
a division of American Homebrewers Association
PO Box 1679, Boulder, Colorado 80306-1679 USA
Tel. 303-447-0816

Direct all inquiries/order to the above address.

Cover design by David Bjorkman and Virginia Thomas, *David Thomas and Associates.*

DEDICATION

To the brewing of better beer, and to those who brew it.

CONTENTS

Preface xiii
Acknowledgments xv
Introduction xvii
Outline of Brewing 1
Reference Units 2
Classic Lager Types 3

Part 1: Brewing Constituents

1. Barley 5

2. Malted Barley 11
     Evaluation . . 13
     Carbohydrates . . 15
     Sugars . . 15
     Protein . . 21
     Other Malt Fractions . . 22

3. Water 25
     Water Analysis . . 34
     Turbidity . . 36

pH .. 36
Ions .. 37
Measuring pH .. 42
Specific Conductivity .. 44
Hardness Alkalinity .. 44
Mineral Ions .. 49
Cations—Earths .. 49
Cations—Metals .. 51
Anions .. 52
Other .. 53
Water Treatment .. 53

4. Hops .. 59
   In the Fields .. 60
   In the Laboratories .. 64

5. Yeast 69
   Culturing Pure Yeast Strains .. 75
   Storing Yeast .. 77
   Washing the Yeast .. 78

6. Bacteria 79
   Gram-Positive Bacteria .. 80
   Gram-Negative Bacteria .. 81

7. Enzymes 87

Part 2: The Brewing Process

8. Malting 91
   Steeping .. 92
   Germination .. 93
   Kilning .. 94

9. Crushing the Malt 97

10. Mashing 103
        Doughing-In .. 103
        Mash pH .. 106
        Acid Rest .. 106
        Why Decoction Mash? .. 109
        Three-Decoction Mash .. 111
        First Decoction .. 111
        Protein Rest .. 112
        Saccharification Rest .. 114
        Iodine Starch-Conversion Test .. 117
        Final Decoction .. 118
        Sparging .. 119
        Lauter Tub .. 120
        Setting the Filter .. 120
        Sparge Water .. 122
        Preparing to Sparge .. 123
        Sparging .. 123
        Extract Efficiency .. 125

11. Boiling the Wort 127
        Boiling Hops .. 127
        Hops Rates .. 129
        Evaporation Rate .. 130
        Hot Break .. 131
        Cold Break .. 132
        Finishing Hops .. 133
        Straining the Wort .. 134
        Cooling the Wort .. 135

12. Fermentation 137
        Preparing for Pitching .. 137
        Kraeusening .. 141
        Pitching the Yeast .. 142
        The Fermentation Lock .. 143
        Primary Fermentation .. 144

ix

Temperature .. 145
Temperature Control .. 145
Balling and pH Monitoring .. 146
Primary Fermentation/Lag Phase .. 147
Low Kraeusen .. 151
High Kraeusen .. 154
Post Kraeusen .. 155
Real and Apparent Attenuation .. 156
Racking .. 157
Gauging Yeast Performance .. 158
Yeast for Seed .. 159

13. Secondary Fermentation 161
Lagering .. 163
Fining .. 164
Clarifying with Beech Chips .. 165
Real Terminal Extract .. 166
Bottling .. 167
Imbibing .. 168

14. Planning the Brew 171
A Note on Mixing .. 172
Planning .. 172
Recipes .. 181

15. Brewing Procedure 185
Malt Examination .. 185
Three-Decoction Mash .. 185
Doughing-In .. 186
Acid Rest .. 186
First Decoction .. 187
First Thick Mash .. 187
Second Decoction .. 188
Second Thick Mash .. 188
Lauter Decoction .. 189
Final Rest .. 189

Sparging/Filtering .. 189
Boiling the Wort .. 190
Hot Break .. 193
Cold Break .. 193
Finishing Hops .. 194
Filtering the Wort .. 194
Pitching the Yeast .. 196
Kraeusening .. 196
Yeast Starter .. 197
Primary Fermentation .. 197
Low Kraeusen .. 198
High Kraeusen .. 198
Post Kraeusen .. 200
Secondary Fermentation .. 201
Lagering .. 201
Bottling .. 202
Draft Beer .. 204
Troubleshooting .. 204
Mash .. 204
Wort .. 205
Fermentation .. 206
Bottled or Keg Beer .. 207
Brewing Log .. 209

16. Cleaning and Sterilizing 211
Construction .. 212
Equipment .. 213
Alkaline Cleansers .. 215
Acid Cleansers .. 215
Alkaline Sterilants .. 216
Acid Sterilants .. 216

17. Equipment 217

Appendix A 245

Basic Homebrewing
from Malt Extract Syrup .. 245

Appendix B 251
The Infusion Mash .. 251

Appendix C 253
The Step Mash .. 253

Appendix D 255
Weights and Measures .. 255

Brewer's Glossary 271

Bibliography 279

Index 283

PREFACE

ARE YOU STILL INVOLVED WITH THAT 'BREWING' thing?" people ask.

Once in a while, I see someone I haven't seen in many years and he asks me what I'm doing these days, remembering when I began homebrewing. I tell him I'm still involved full-time with the American Homebrewers Association, and his reaction is usually disbelief. After all, how could anyone make a living homebrewing? "Don't you ever run out of things to write about?" is usually the question that follows.

But just the opposite is true—there is never the time nor the space to fully cover the vast subject of brewing and beer. I had a notion when I first got involved with brewing that this would be the case, and I've been correct.

Since 1978 I've monitored the growth and interest in homebrewing in America as editor of the American Homebrewers Association's **zymurgy** magazine, while at the same time researching my own book, *The Complete Joy of Home Brewing.* I know much more about brewing beer than I did in 1970 when I first began. I feel I have opened a puzzle box, revealing interesting information, old and new, but also a thousand more questions about brewing.

It was not long after my book was released that I met Gregory Noonan at an American Homebrewers Association New England Regional Homebrew Conference. He asked me whether I was interested in reading his manuscript, *Brewing Lager Beer.* Three weeks later a package arrived in the mail. That very evening I read through Gregory's work. Since I had recently completed my own work, I was especially appreciative of Gregory's achievement. The manuscript represented a wealth of information, all in one place—information I had searched through a dozen books to find when I was researching various projects. And Gregory had not only compiled a concise treatise on brewing specifically for the small-scale homebrewer and microbrewer, but also offered exciting information not covered in any modern brewing book currently in print.

As anyone involved in brewing will realize, Gregory Noonan's *Brewing Lager Beer* will become a valuable tool. Yet tools are those helpful items we combine with our own experience in order to build. We can be sure that there will be much more to learn and write about, while continuing to maintain the high quality in our beers we all strive for.

A toast to Gregory Noonan, as he leads us further along.

Charlie Papazian
Publisher, Brewers Publications

ACKNOWLEDGMENTS

Thanks to my wife Nancy, Martha and John Murtaugh, George Fix, Charlie Papazian, Charles Kochenour, and everyone else who contributed to the publication of this book.

INTRODUCTION

BREWING IS EASY. VIRTUALLY ANYONE CAN BREW excellent beer. Only malt, hops, yeast, water, and information are required. Having said this, let me say that my own first brewings were disastrous. I had the first four ingredients, but I lacked information.

When I first set out to brew, I began with a copy of a dubious homebrewing classic. It was ebullient, it was entertaining, but it wasn't very informative. I also had trouble finding ingredients. None of the area supermarkets stocked Blue Ribbon Malt Syrup ("lovely Lena"), and it didn't mention that there existed homebrewers' supply shops. It was only by chance that one day my fingers stumbled over the Brewers' Equipment and Supplies entry in the Yellow Pages.

The very next Saturday I went to the nearest retailer. I bought pale malt, hops, yeast, another book, and some equipment. The proprietor tried to dissuade me from the folly of blindly attacking whole-grain brewing. At that time, his customers used whole malt only as a flavoring adjunct in the kettle. I was unshakable in my resolve. If the breweries could do it, why couldn't I?

Because I didn't know how. I tried crushing the malt with a rolling pin. I borrowed an electric coffee grinder. I got malt flour with chunks. It went into a kettle anyway, along with a lot of water, and onto the stovetop. The strike temperature was 150°F. The actual temperature went from 140 to 165°F, and at any given time, temperatures within the mash varied by as much as 10°F. Starch conversion was abominable. I suspended the grains in cheesecloth draped over a kettle and sparged them with gallon after gallon of hot water.

I tasted the grains. They were still sweet, but since there were pots boiling on all four burners, I stopped sparging. I threw some brown hops into each of the pots. When I got down to what looked to be about five gallons all in one kettle, I stopped boiling. The covered pot went into cold water in the bathtub, and I went to bed. It had been a long day.

In the morning the wort was still only lukewarm. I siphoned it into a crock anyway, along with a considerable amount of the trub, the hops that kept clogging the siphon, and a package of yeast. In due course, it fermented, was bottled and was drunk. It was pretty bad.

I didn't know what I was doing wrong, but I had the glimmer of an idea that a whole lot was wrong. I bought another book. In fact, I bought every homebrewing book in print, but I still faced an information void, especially where lager brewing was concerned. But with reading and my own experimenting, my brewings began to go smoother. My beer got better. I reasoned that others might want to know what I had found here and there. And so I wrote this book.

Consistent brews of impeccable quality and character can be made by anyone who understands the brewing process. Familiarity with the proper procedures—along with understanding the basic chemistry that underlies the brewing process—enables even the most casual homebrewer to produce better beer. For the serious homebrewer and small-scale microbrewer, this information is essential. This is the information I have attempted to include in this book.

This book is just a part of the information explosion occurring in American homebrewing. This flood of knowledge can only help us all to brew better beer.

Greg Noonan
Williamstown, Massachusetts
November 30, 1985

OUTLINE OF BREWING

BREWING BEGINS WITH *MALTED BARLEY,* WHICH is the sprouted, then roasted, barley seed. The malt is coarsely crushed and mixed with water to form a *mash.* During the mash, compositional changes occur, brought about by *enzymes* in the malt. These essentially leach out the contents of the malt into solution and reduce them to more manageable fractions. This *extract* is rinsed from the insoluble malt particles during *sparging,* and the sweet solution yielded is the *wort.*

The wort is boiled with the flower of the *hop vine* for bitterness and flavor and to clarify the wort. Active *brewer's yeast* is added to the cooled wort to ferment it. The yeast forms *carbon dioxide* and *alcohol* from the sugars extracted from the malt; the carbon dioxide carbonates the beer. This fermentation is usually carried out in several stages, and the beer is moved from one vessel to another to separate it from the flavor-impairing, sedimented yeast, malt and hop residues.

The beer is bottled or kegged so that it may be served carbonated.

1

REFERENCE UNITS

VOLUME, TEMPERATURE AND THE DENSITY (weight) of a solution all have various terms in which they are expressed. Throughout this book, the U.S. gallon, degrees Fahrenheit (with degrees Centigrade in parentheses) and density as degrees Balling (with specific gravity in parentheses) have been given. Because the terms original gravity (OG) and terminal gravity (TG) are more readily understood by many homebrewers than wort density and final density, OG and TG have been used where deemed appropriate.

For those more familiar with a volumetric standard other than that used in the United States, tables are provided in the appendix for conversion of the U.S. standards to metric and British units. Other useful tables of measure and conversion formulas for brewing are also found in the appendixes.

2

CLASSIC LAGER TYPES

HE RANGE OF LAGER BEERS IS REPRESENTED by seven recognized types, which are identified by the brewing centers where they evolved. They are:

Pilsner (Pilsener, Pils), Bohemia, Czechoslovakia. 12° Balling (OG 1049). Pale straw color, distinctive hop palate, well carbonated, dry. 4.4% alcohol by volume. After the style set by the classic Pilsner Urquell (Plzensky Prazdroj). Served at 48–50°F (10–13°C).

Dortmunder (Dort, Export), Westfalen, Germany. 12.5–14° Balling (OG 1050–1057). Light, golden-blond color, moderate hop palate; rich, mellow and yet sharp. 5–5.7% alcohol by volume. Served at 48–50°F (9–10°C).

Vienna (Wiener, Spezial, Maerzenbier), Lower Austria. 12.5–15° Balling (OG 1050–1061). Reddish-amber or copper color, lightly hopped; malt-to-roasted-malt flavor. 5.5% alcohol by volume. Served at 50–55°F (10–13°C).

Dark Munich (Muenchener Dunkel), Bavaria, Germany. 12.5–14° Balling (OG 1050–1057). Dark-brown color, well

3

hopped; sweet, roasted-malt flavor. 4.5–5.8% alcohol by volume. Served at 35–45°F (2–7°C).

Light Munich (Muenchener Helles), Bavaria, Germany. 11–12° Balling (OG 1044–1049). Amber color, lightly hopped; slightly sweet, malty character. 4.1–5% alcohol by volume. Served at 45–50°F (7–10°C).

Bock Bavaria, Germany. 16–18° Balling (OG 1065–1074). Light- to dark-brown color; rich and malty, usually having a strong roasted-malt and hop flavor. 6–8% alcohol by volume. Served at 50–65°F (10–18°C).

Dopplebock (Always ends in the suffix *-ator.*) Bavaria, Germany. 18–28° Balling (OG 1074–1112). Dark-brown color, strong, roasted-malt flavor. 7.5–13% alcohol by volume. Served at 50–65°F (10–18°C).

PART 1: BREWING CONSTITUENTS

1. BARLEY

BARLEY HAS BEEN THE BREWER'S PREFERRED source of fermentable extract since prehistory. The kernel is readily malted, contains adequate enzymes to convert the starch to sugars, and upon mashing, yields a very complete, highly soluble extract that is relatively free of unwieldy constituents. It gives beer its characteristic taste, body, head and color.

The barley kernel is the seed of a plant of the grass family (Gramineae). It is one of the hardiest of all the cereal grains and is able to grow under widely varying conditions from Alaska to the equator; it grows best, however, in cool, dry climates.

The seeds grow in two, four or six rows, called *heads*, along a central stem. The number of seed rows is determined by the number of fertile flowers; two-row types have only two of the six flower clusters fertile, whereas all the flowers of six-row barley are fertile. Long, thin bristles protrude from each seed making the "bearded" grain closely resemble wheat.

Harvested when fully ripe, malting barley is dried from a moisture content of 15 to 25 percent down to below 14 per-

Two-Row   **BARLEY**   Six-Row

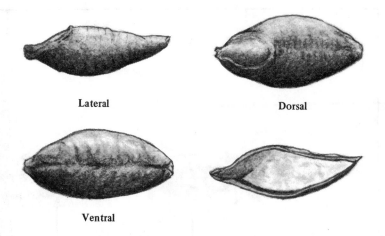

Lateral

Dorsal

Ventral

DEHUSKED BARLEY KERNEL

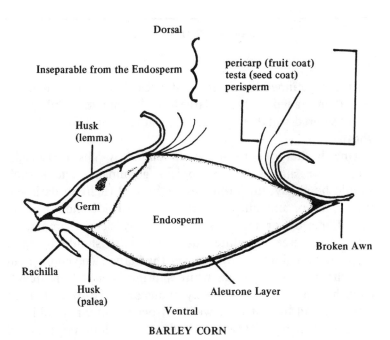

Dorsal

Inseparable from the Endosperm

pericarp (fruit coat)
testa (seed coat)
perisperm

Husk
(lemma)

Germ

Endosperm

Broken Awn

Rachilla

Husk
(palea)

Aleurone Layer

Ventral

BARLEY CORN

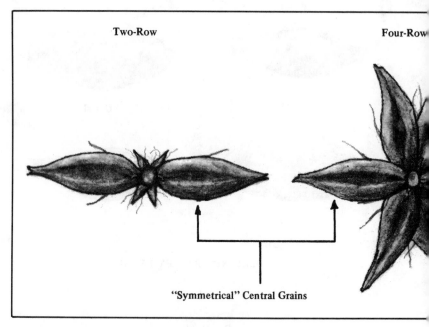

Two-Row   Four-Row

"Symmetrical" Central Grains

BARLEY HEAD, Top View

cent and is binned for six to eight weeks before being malted. It is then graded; only the largest of the four standard grades is considered suitable for malting (more than 3/32 inches in width).

One bushel of brewing-grade barley weighs forty-eight pounds; it should be 95 percent germinant. The kernels should be glossy, uniformly straw colored (light to dark yellow), plump, and smell like clean grain. There should be no rancid, moldy or musty smell, nor any slender, immature grains with greenish-white husks. The husk should be thin, finely wrinkled and tightly jacket the kernel. The endosperm (starch) must be opaque, white and mealy, not translucent, grayish, steely or glassy. Steely grains are excessively high in nitrogen and do not malt well. Nitrogen content should not exceed 1.6 percent. The protein-to-carbohydrate ratio should

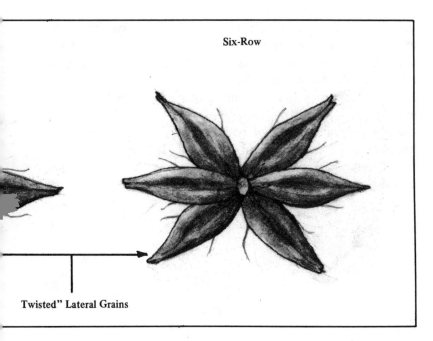

Six-Row

Twisted" Lateral Grains

suit the type of beer being brewed; lighter and well-aged beers require low-nitrogen barley.

European brewers prefer superior two-row, thin-husked, large-berried, high-yield barley, although this type is used less frequently in the United States. It generally malts better than other types, has a more favorable starch-to-protein/husk ratio than other barleys and yields a mellow flavor and good body.

Six-row barley is the most economical to grow because the greater number of rows per head increases the per-acre yield. It is a warm-climate barley and is the type most widely grown in the United States. It is favored by domestic commercial breweries because it is rich in the enzymes needed to convert the adjuncts they employ (adjuncts may account for up to 60 percent of the extract in U.S. brews). Because it is high in protein, it presents problems with clarity and stability. All-malt beers brewed from six-row barley tend to be dark-colored and taste heavy. Its higher husk content improves mash filterability but contributes harsh flavors.

Four-row barley is commonly grown and malted in Northern Europe where it has long been prized for its hardiness in the cold climate. It is not widely used elsewhere, however, because of its steeliness and low yield. It is actually a six-row barley that appears to form four rows rather than six because of its thin, elongated head.

2. MALTED BARLEY

BECAUSE MALT IS ORGANIC, AND SUBJECT TO the meteorological conditions under which the barley type was grown, the same malt types vary substantially in appearance and composition depending on the season and their place of growth. For instance, moist, cool seasons produce a greater amount of starch and less protein and fat, lack of nutrients and minerals affect growth and composition and nitrogen-based fertilizers applied too heavily or too late in the season increase the nitrogen content. Malt quality also depends on the circumstances of its malting and subsequent handling. Furthermore, the different malt types are each composed of several varieties.

For these reasons, it is advisable to ask for an analysis of any malt. Quoted starch and protein content will indicate the potential extract yield, the enzymatic strength and the necessity for (and duration of) a protein-reducing mash rest.

Ultimately, only experience with the particular barley type, its origin, season of growth, age and malting permits finite procedural adjustments.

TABLE 1

Malted Barley, Typical Oven-Dry Analysis

	6-Row	2-Row
Moisture Content	0%	0%
Carbohydrates	82%	84%
Nitrogen-Free Extract	75%	82%
Starch	50%	60%
Husks	20%	9%
Protein	13%*	10%*
Nitrogen	2%	1.6%

*N × 6.2

Dorsal　　　　　　　　　　　Ventral

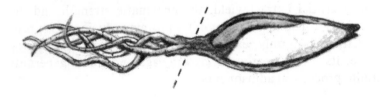

MALT

| 1/8" | 1/2" | 3/4" |

ACROSPIRE GROWTH

Evaluation

Good malt should be plump and firm, even in size and shape, and of a light, straw-colored hue. A sample handful should contain very little straw, rootlets, dust or debris. The malt kernel should be easily crushed between the fingers and uniformly soft from end to end. When broken, the kernel should write like chalk and show no air pockets within the husk.

The portion of the husk covering the *acrospire,* the germinal plant inside the kernel, should be rubbed, cut or peeled away from a sampling of the malted grains; the acrospire length indicates the degree to which the barley has been converted, as well as the uniformity of the malting. Malt to be mashed by only one or two temperature rests must have been uniformly sprouted, and the acrospire must be from three-fourths to the full length of the kernel. Malt that has been roasted when the acrospire is from one-half to three-fourths the length of the grain will yield a greater amount of extract than fully modified malt, but it must be decoction mashed. Malt of widely-varying acrospire growth also must be decoction mashed. Brewing-quality malt should yield no appreciable number of kernels with acrospire growth less than one-third the length of the grain.

The malt should yield 65 to 80 percent sugar by weight after mashing, and test between 1.4 and 2.0 percent nitrogen. Malt of greater than 2 percent nitrogen should only be used when brewing with adjuncts.

TABLE 2

Grading by Size

Grade	Characteristic
1	Remains on 7/64" screen
2	Remains on 3/32" screen
3	Remains on 5/64" screen
4	Falls through 5/64" screen

The two larger sizes will mash well and produce high yields. The small kernels have greater husk content and will give lower extracts.

Grading by Character

Mealy	(mellow, soft)	Will mash well.
Half-Glassy	(semi-hard)	Must employ a longer, more thorough mashing.
Glassy	(hard, translucent, grayish white)	Unsuitable for brewing.

Test malt by floating a handful of grains in water. They should float horizontally; vertical floating indicates air pockets within the husks caused by poor malting; sinking indicates an unmalted grain or malt that is very old.

Avoid malt of very high protein content because it has correspondingly fewer carbohydrates. The protein will retard starch conversion during mashing and increase the likelihood of hazing in the beer. Malt should be selected by its color and modification (gauged by the growth of the acrospire) to suit the type of beer being brewed and the brewing method.

TABLE 3

Degree of Modification

Acrospire Growth	Characteristic of:
0 - 1/4	Cereal malt
½	Dark Munich
1/2 - 3/4	Most lager malt
3/4 - full	British malt, malt for very light beer

Color

Diastatic	Very pale
Lager	Very pale
Caramel-pale	Very pale
Dortmund	Pale
British pale	Pale
Dextrine	Pale
Vienna	Medium
Munich	Medium
Caramel-20	Medium
Crystal	Dark
Caramel-60	Dark
Chocolate	Very dark
Black	Very dark

Carbohydrates

Carbohydrates are compounds formed by molecules of carbon, hydrogen and oxygen. The greatest parts of barley and malt are carbohydrates, as is 90 to 95 percent of the wort extract. The carbohydrate group is composed of insoluble cellulose (the membranes and casing of barley corn) and soluble hemicellulose, starch, dextrins and the simpler mono- and disaccharides that we call sugars.

Sugars

Monosaccharides $(C_6H_{12}O_6)$ are single-molecule carbo-

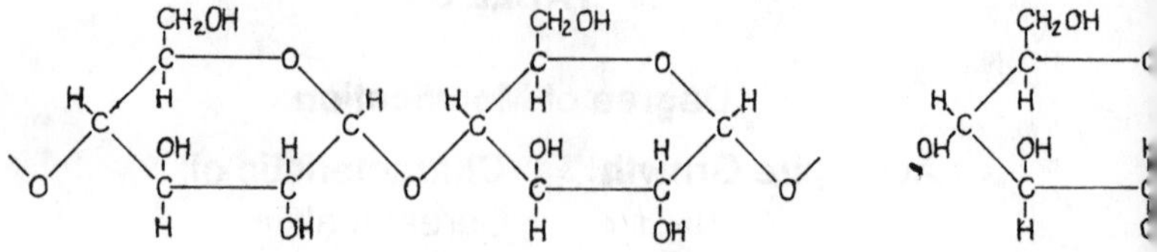

Starch

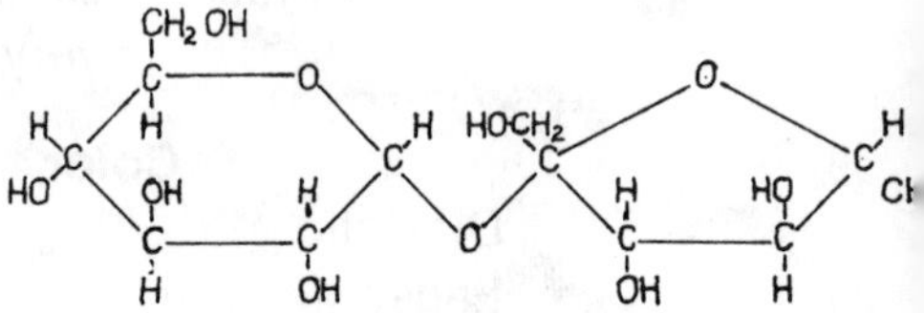

Sucrose

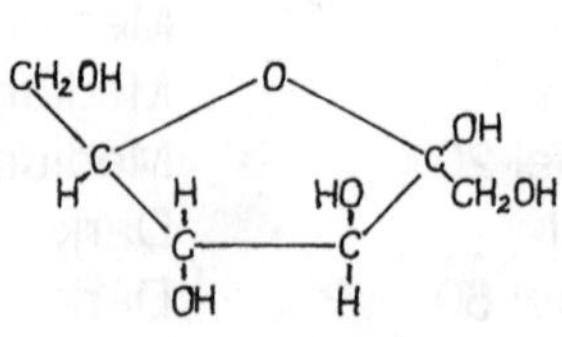

Fructose

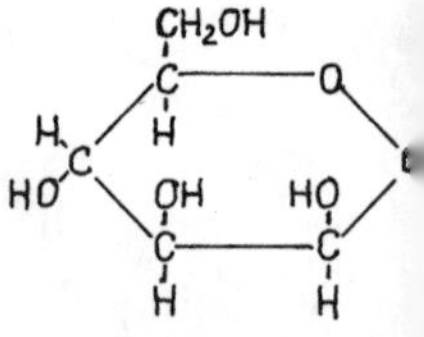

Mannose

hydrates. Glucose, photosynthesized in the leaves of green plants from carbon dioxide and water, is the most common monosaccharide. Fructose (an isomer, or molecular rearrangement, of glucose), galactose and mannose are other monosaccharides. They are all readily and wholly fermentable. Galactose is a constitutent of many oligosaccharides and polysaccharides, occurring especially in gums and pectins.

The disaccharides are double sugars ($C_{12}H_{22}O_{11}$). Maltose, the sugar most closely associated with brewing, is the sim-

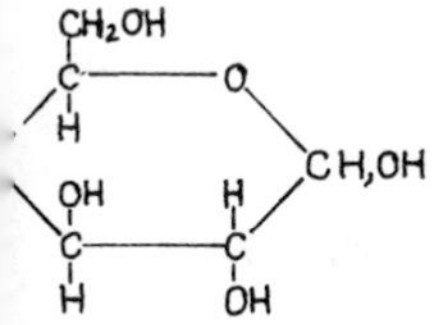

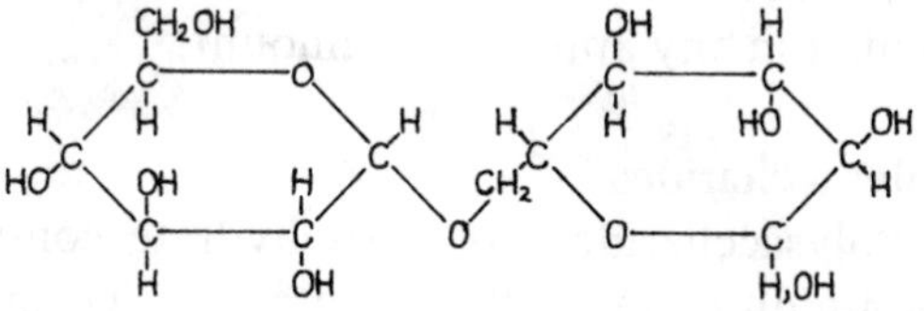

Isomaltose

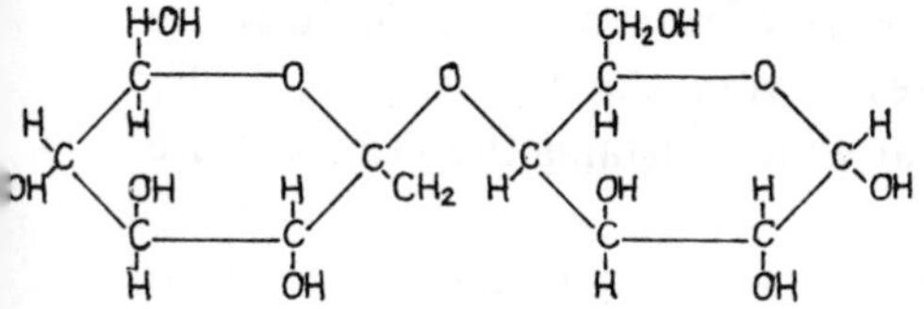

Melibiose

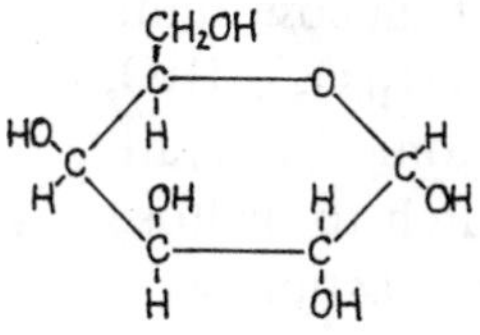

Galactose 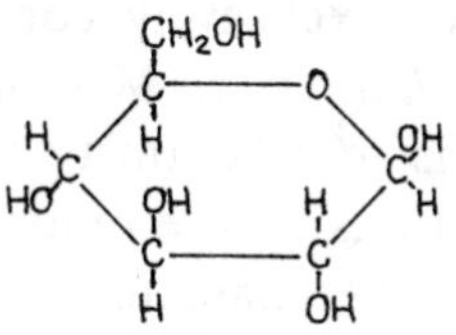   Glucose

plest compound sugar. It is formed by two molecules of glucose, joined together by the removal of a water molecule $(C_6H_{12}O_6 + C_6H_{12}O_6 - H_2O = C_{12}H_{22}O_{11} \cdot H_2O)$. It is the sugar that is primarily derived from the hydrolysis of starch in dilute acids. It is slowly, but very surely, fermentable. Other disaccharides are sucrose (one molecule each of glucose and fructose), lactose (an isomer of sucrose) and melibiose (one molecule each of galactose and glucose). Sucrose is readily fermentable, lactose is unfermentable and melibiose is fermentable only by S. Carlsbergensis. Only sucrose is present in malt in any appreciable amount.

Polysaccharides

Polysaccharides are carbohydrate compounds formed by the union of more than two monosaccharides; the trisaccharides are the most important to brewing. In malt, they are maltotriose, glucodifructose and fructosant; raffinose, which is present in barley, disappears during malting. Maltotriose (three molecules of glucose) is very slowly fermentable by brewing yeast. It is the sugar which sustains the yeast culture during aging.

Polysaccharides of four or more molecules are grouped together as oligosaccharides. Many oligosaccharides, including maltotetraose (and some trisaccharides) are not fermented by Saccharomyces brewing strains (S. Carlsbergensis and S. Cerevisiae).

Oligosaccharides exclusively constructed of glucose units are defined as *small dextrins*. Malt dextrins, $(C_6H_{10}O_5)_n \cdot H_2O$, are glucose chains four to thirty molecules long. They are intermediate fractions in the reduction of starch to maltose and glucose and are characterized by their reaction with iodine. The simplest dextrins do not affect the color of iodine; these are termed *achroodextrins*. Amylodextrins are larger and give a red color with iodine. Erythrodextrins are an intermediate mixture of these and give a violet to red reaction with iodine.

Native starch (in malt, 20 to 400 molecules of $C_6H_{10}O_5$) occurs as granules that are insoluble in cold water. In warm water, amylose, the small fraction of a granule that is water soluble, is diffused out of native starch. In hot water, the starch granule swells until it finally bursts, exposing insoluble amylopectin. If the native starch granule is crushed to flour, it readily combines with moisture to form a paste-like gel.

Amylose is reduced to dextrins, maltose and ultimately

glucose by hydrolysis with dilute acids or diastatic ("starch-reducing") enzymes. Amylose occurs as straight chains of glucose; amylodextrin, on the other hand, occurs as highly-branched chains that are less-readily decomposed to maltose or glucose.

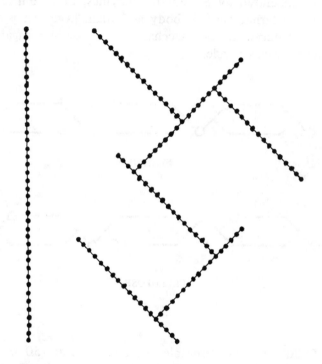

AMYLOSE AMYLOPECTIN FRAGMENTS

Hemicellulose and soluble gums bind the aleurone layer of the barley kernel together and are constituents of the cell walls within the starchy endosperm. They account for about 10 percent of the weight of the barley kernel. They are both polysaccharide mixtures complexed with protein. The malt gums are largely pentosans of xylose, arabinose, galactose and complexed glucose, which may be dissolved at temperatures of 160 to 176°F (71–80°C). Hemicelluloses are more complex and stubbornly resist hydrolysis. In intermediate stages of solubilization, they inhibit filtering and cause hazes; when liberated by proteolytic enzymes, they contribute to a beer's fermentability, body and foam head. They can be fully reduced to oligosaccharides and simpler sugars in a thorough mash cycle.

STARCH

CELLULOSE

Cellulose is an insoluble compound sugar (50 to 5,000 molecules of $C_6H_{10}O_5$) that makes up the barley husks and is irreducible by malt enzymes. It constitutes roughly 5 to 15 percent of the malt by weight. Although it is structurally similar to starch, cellulose does not contribute fermentable extract or desirable flavors to the malt extract, but is employed in the lauter tun to form a filterbed through which to strain the mash extract. However, excessive extraction during low-temperature mash rests and alkaline sparging leaches harsh-tasting tannins and dark-colored melanin pigments from the husk into the extract.

Protein

Carbohydrates alone do not form a satisfactory brewing extract; malt protein is essential as a yeast nutrient and to give the beer body and head. In the barley kernel, protein serves as plant food for the embryo. During malting and mashing, it is reduced by protein-metabolizing enzymes to less-complex *albumins* (an outdated but useful term that groups together all coagulable and water soluble protein fractions) or even simpler amino acids. In solution with mineral salts, some of the protein forms acids, causing the pH of the mash to drop.

The term *protein* strictly defines very complex polymeric coils of amino acid chained together by peptide links (molecular weight 17,000 to 150,000), but in a wider sense, it also includes the products of their decomposition. This reference to protein, on the one hand, as an unwieldy malt constituent (e.g., high-molecular weight albumin and less soluble globulin, glutelin, and hordein), and on the other as a source of a beer's body and head, can be confusing. In fact, the brewer does not strive to eliminate the proteins but to simplify them to a range of colloidable and soluble fractions. Only when an excessive number of complex proteins (mol. wt. 10,000 to 100,000, average 30,000) are carried into the beer will they result in chill haze, an irreversible cloudiness or off flavors caused by oxidation.

The large protein complexes of the malt must be largely reduced to intermediate forms (albumin, mol. wt. 5000–12,000) such as proteoses, peptones and peptides (mol. wt. 400–1500) during mashing, so that they are simple enough to dissolve, or colloid with hop resins, and be carried over into the finished beer. Considerable nitrogenous matter must be present: amino acids, and peptides to sustain culture-yeast activity, and simple albumin to form the body of the beer. Three to six percent of the wort extract is usually nitrogen-based. A beer brewed so that it had little or no low-molecular-weight protein fractions (mol. wt. 12,000 to 20,000) left in it would be unable to form or support a foam head. Generally, 25 to 50 percent of the malt protein is carried into the ferment as simple nitrogen complexes (amino acids, peptides, albumin).

Because enzymes are proteins, the protein content of any malt is an indication of its enzymatic strength. In general, protein-rich, six-row malts are more apt to cloud beer than are other malts, but they do produce stronger enzymatic activity. Low-protein malts are less apt to cause hazing, but are invariably enzyme deficient and must be carefully mashed.

Other Malt Fractions

Peptides, although not true proteins, are intermediate forms between protein and amino acids. They are nitrogen-based, as are vitamins and nucleic acids. Nonprotein nitrogen accounts for up to 10 percent of the total nitrogen-based material in the malt. Peptides, which enhance the beer's viscosity (palate-fullness), may also oxidize to high-molecular weight polypeptides which are unstable and contribute to nonbiological haze formation. The vitamins in malt are principally of the B-complex; they are necessary for yeast growth. Products of the decomposition of nucleic acids account for only .1 percent of the wort extract, but contribute to both yeast nutrition and flavor enhancement.

Polyphenols, phosphates, lipids and fatty acids are other significant malt constituents. Polyphenols from the husk, pericarp and aleurone layers of the malt kernel are acidic precursors of tannins and give beer an unpleasantly bitter, astringent taste and reddish hue. With highly-kilned malt, phenolic melanoids (black pigments) contribute to stale flavors in beer. Complex polyphenol polymers are true tannins and counteract the solubility of otherwise stable proteins. They should be eliminated from the extract by a well-aerated mashing and kettle boil; in the cooled wort and the ferment, the oxidative polymerization of polyphenols to tannins causes medicinal off-flavors and haze formation.

Phosphates in the malt, principally organic phytin, are major factors in the acidulation of the mash. They give up phytic acid (phytate) at high kiln temperatures during malting and by enzymatic reduction in the decoction mash.

Lipids are fatlike substances composing roughly 3 percent of the malt: they range from straight-chain to complex branched-ring hydrocarbons, including neutral fats, fatty acids, alcohols, aldehydes and waxes. About one-third of malt lipids occur as reserves in the embryo, but most are concentrated in the aleurone layer. Triacylglycerol and other triglycerides (triesters of glycerol and long-chain fatty acids) are the predominant neutral lipids in barley. They support respiration of the embryo during malting.

Fatty acids $(C_nH_{2n}O_2)$, or vegetable oils, are fat-derived *(aliphatic)* hydrocarbon chains. In barley malt, these are the relatively-long-chain linoleic $(C_{18}H_{32}O_2)$, palmitic $(C_6H_{32}O_2)$ and oleic $(C_{18}H_{34}O_2)$ acids. Proportionally more of these than other malt lipids are carried into the wort. They are essential in the yeast cell as reserves; in general, however, malt lipids present problems in fermentation. Usually they comprise only .05 percent of the malt extract; however, if excessive amounts of lipids are washed into the runoff by overzealous sparging, they will reduce foam stability and give rise to "cardboardy" and other stale flavors in beer.

Finally, considerable silica and inorganic phosphate are leached out of the malt, along with a wide range of trace minerals necessary for yeast metabolism.

3. WATER

ATER CONSTITUTES 85 TO 90 PERCENT OF THE volume of any beer, and therefore the mineral content of the brewing water has a marked effect on the flavor and appearance of the finished beer—and also on the brewing process. Certain beer styles are suited to waters of very specific mineral composition, and an otherwise well-brewed beer may be ruined by the use of totally inappropriate brewing water.

By looking closely at the geology of any given area, wells, springs, reservoirs or streams might be found that will perfectly suit a given brew. Local, regional and state water departments and services can be very helpful in locating such sources.

Only brackish, polluted and sea water are entirely unsuitable for brewing. Most potable fresh waters, whether too "hard," too carbonate, too "soft," or iron contaminated, may be boiled, aerated, sedimented, filtered or treated with an appropriate mineral salt or acid to be made suitable for brewing almost any type of beer. Practically speaking, however, brewing water should be clear, bright and unpolluted and have agreeable taste and reasonably uniform composition from day to day. It should not be corrosive, have a

25

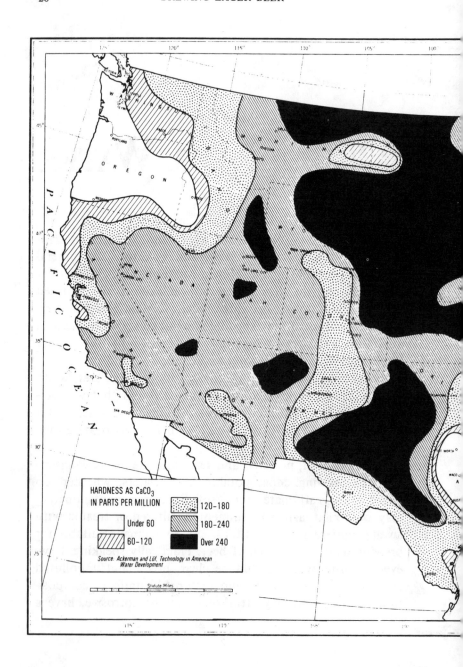

HARDNESS AS CaCO₃ IN PARTS PER MILLION

Under 60

60–120

120–180

180–240

Over 240

Source: Ackerman and Löf, Technology in American Water Development

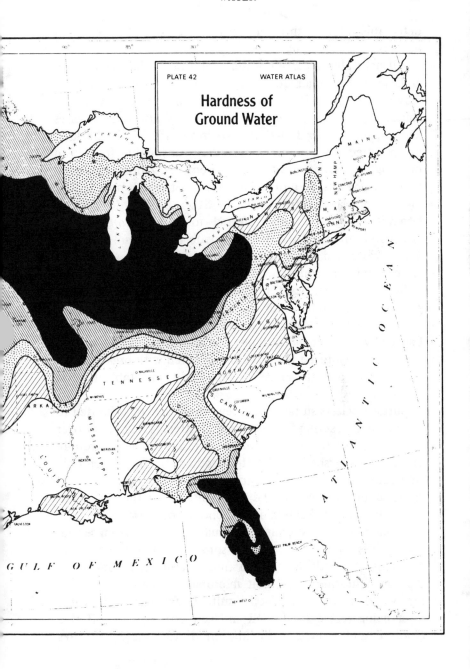

PLATE 42   WATER ATLAS

Hardness of Ground Water

detectable odor, or throw an appreciable amount of sediment upon resting or boiling.

All naturally occurring waters are dilute solutions of minerals in which small quantities of gases and organic matter may be dissolved. Rain water is potentially the purest natural source of water, but because it assimilates atmospheric gases and organic mineral particles wherever the air is the least bit polluted, rain water is absolutely unsuitable for use in brewing. Precipitation in areas far removed from large fossil-fuel burning plants more often than not is still polluted by highly corrosive sulfuric acid (H_2SO_4). Free hydrogen carbonates $(HCO_3$, usually referred to as *bicarbonates)* are also common in rain water. They rob the calcium from the mash, wort and ferment by forming bicarbonate salts that are precipitated from solution during boiling.

Surface waters, besides having the dissolved materials and gases found in rain water, usually contain large amounts of organic matter, vegetable-coloring, soil, silica and clay. Especially in marshy terrains and industrial areas, surface water is likely to be heavily contaminated with organic acids and nitrates and therefore is completely unsuitable for use in brewing.

Surface waters suitable for brewing are generally limited to clear-running, spring-fed brooks and streams that flow over gravel, sand or rocky beds, and deep reservoirs with carefully protected watersheds. Old soft-bottomed streams, which flow sluggishly or carry topsoil and vegetation in suspension, and rivers, ponds and lakes need to be filtered, at the very least, before use and are seldom a good choice for brewing.

Municipal water supplies are usually gathered from several deep wells and reservoirs and sometimes rivers. They are invariably filtered and treated (most commonly with up to 0.5 ppm chlorine) to inhibit microbal contamination. Such tap water is often perfectly suitable for use in brewing, after being rested (or boiled and aerated) to drive off free chlorine and induce sedimentation of carbonates, silicates and incrustants. Chlorine may be removed by activated carbon filtration. Municipal supplies, however, seldom suit the requirements of any given brew quite as well as does a carefully chosen source of ground water, mostly because water departments vary the inflows from several different sources and water composition varies accordingly.

The quantity and composition of underground water at any given location and depth are contingent upon subsurface geological formation. Although the elementary minerals and metals dispersed in the earth's crust are relatively few (rock is largely silica with aluminum, iron, calcium, potassium, magnesium, manganese, zinc and copper), the soluble components (mineral salts) they form yield water of varying composition from place to place. Because of the geological structure of the earth's crust, water rises to different levels at different locations, and its level may be fairly constant or may fluctuate with changing patterns of precipitation.

The value of a spring or well as a brewing source should first be judged by the seasonal consistency of its flow. There is less fluctuation in the composition of any ground water that has a reasonably constant flow year round. Shallow wells and seasonal springs do not usually yield acceptable brewing water. Their composition varies widely, and they often carry soil and other surface contamination in suspension. They commonly yield unacceptable levels of bacterial contamination.

Deep wells originating in large subterranean aquifers and mountain springs percolating up through fissures in bedrock formations without leaching through soil or disintegrated rock are usually of very stable composition and free from surface contamination. Subterranean springs (with the notable exception of mineral springs) emerging from inorganic rock complexes commonly yield water with less dissolved materials than does deep-well water. Deep wells usually tap water sources that have traveled farther than the water of springs, and having contacted more mineral-bearing substrata conse-

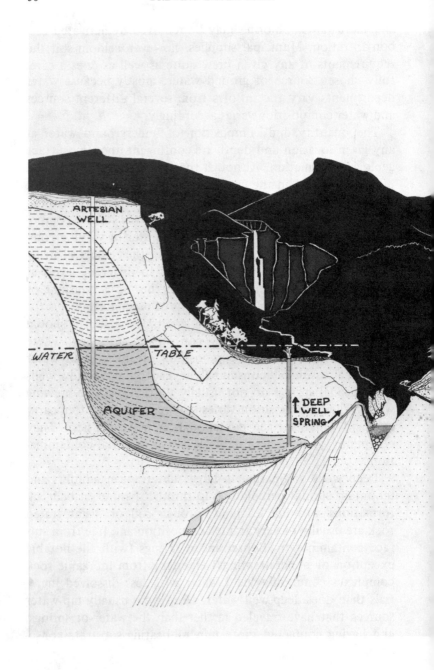

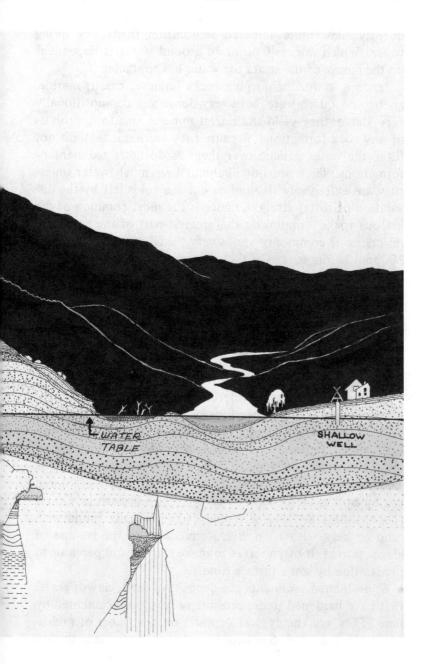

WATER TABLE

SHALLOW WELL

quently have more minerals in solution than does spring water. Which minerals occur in ground water is dependent on the nature of the strata the water has contacted.

Igneous and metamorphic rocks (granite, basalt, marble, gneiss and quartz) are both very dense and compositionally very stable; they yield the fewest mineral ions to hydrolysis of any rock formations. Because they are hard, they do not filter the water passing over them as do most sedimentary formations. They are not likely to bear much water unless they are extensively fissured or enclose voids left by the dissolution of softer strata. Granite is the most common of the igneous rocks, composing the greatest part of the continental plates. It commonly yields very "soft" water of less than 100ppm hardness (as $CaCO_3$), and water of less than 50ppm hardness is not at all uncommon.

These rocks are eroded by freezing, water, scaling, hydrolysis or friction, and the particles are carried away by wind and water and ultimately deposited in topographical depressions. This alluvia forms unconsolidated sediments, often far from the parent rock.

Sand, which is largely silica dioxide split off from quartz, passes water freely while filtering out most suspended solids. Where it lies above impervious bedrock, it yields excellent water. Clay, on the other hand, is impervious and yields very little water, but water pools above it wherever it makes an unbroken sediment. Clay underlies many excellent aquifers. Clay is mostly hydrous silicates of aluminum, often colored red by iron oxide or dark by carbon-based impurities. Gravel (pebbles of 1/8-2 1/2 inch diameter) is usually found with sand or clay, either on river terraces or as the residue of glacial retreat. It often serves to make clay subsoil pervious to penetration by some surface runoff.

Consolidated sediments are deposits of sand, clay or gravel that have hardened under pressure or have been cemented by lime. They are the typical deposits on the floors of prehistoric seas and lakes. Sandstone is very common; it is porous and generally rather coarse. It filters water very effectively, but also gives up its mineral ions to hydrolysis very readily. Sandstone formations yield predominantly "permanent" hardness, but the mineral composition and "total" hardness vary widely from place to place. Water drawn from older sandstone may be soft, but is usually moderately hard, averaging 50–300ppm hardness. New red sandstone usually bears very hard water (150–400ppm); although the hardness is largely sulfate, new red sandstone is often objectionably inundated by iron.

Formed from loose sediment, limestone (calcium carbonate) is not an extremely dense rock, but it is impervious and yields water only if it has been extensively fissured by seismic activity or eons of hydrolysis. The passage of water along joints and bedding plates has carved out huge subterranean caverns and labyrinths in some limestone formations, where abundant water may be tapped. Carbonic acid from the atmosphere readily dissolves calcium carbonate forming very soluble calcium hydrogen-carbonate (bicarbonate) salts and aquifers and springs from limestone tend to yield water high in "temporary" hardness with other minerals in solution. Some limestones are largely made up of magnesia, and may yield considerable sulfate as well. Hardness of 150–350ppm is common.

Chalk formations are very soft, fine-grained limestone from mudlike sea-bottom sediment. They yield from 150–375ppm hardness, largely as calcium carbonate.

Soapstone (talc) is insoluble hydrous magnesium silicate, often found with magnetite (iron oxide) and chlorite. Made of consolidated clay, shale is impervious but may pass water along its bedding plates. Like other sedimentary rock, it commonly contains many minerals. Marl is consolidated clay with sand, and most often calcium carbonate, potash or phosphorus. It is commonly found stratified with sandstone or limestone. Marl generally yields little water, and it is of an undesirable mineral composition. Conglomerates are impervious, hard rocks from lime-cemented gravel and sand; they vary widely in composition, but usually have little effect on the water coming in contact with them.

Using Water Analysis

The source for potential brewing water should be analyzed for organic and inorganic composition and biological purity. Because the composition of any water supply is likely to vary seasonally, and even within each season, it is advisable to analyze it before brewing or when changes in the brew may be due to changes in the water. Where periodic testing is not possible or practical, a simple pH test demonstrates changes in the mineral content.

The standard water analysis identifies the strength of the mineral ions present in the water and also indicates the presence of organics. An actual bacterial analysis may be included or made separately. Analyses for community water supplies are available upon request from local water departments; other sources are analyzed by private labs for a fee. Do-it-yourself kits are also available for identifying the pH, hardness, and presence of various mineral ions (calcium, magnesium, iron, chlorine, nitrate, nitrite); they are easy to use, handy and inexpensive over the long run if analysis would otherwise have to be made by a private lab.

If testing by a lab is necessary, certain procedures for obtaining the specimen are advisable. Rinse a clean quart jar several times with the water to be tested; fill the jar and immerse it nearly to its neck in a kettle of water. Heat and boil for twenty minutes. Decant the water from the jar, invert it on a clean paper towel to drain and then cover it quickly. When cool, fill it with the water to be tested. If it is tap water, allow the cold water to run for a minute before taking the sample to flush clear any mineral deposits jarred loose by the initial release of water from the tap. Cap the jar tightly and rush it to the lab where you have made arrangements to take it. The longer the sample sits, the less

TABLE 4

Typical Analysis
U.S. Public Health Service (U.S.P.H.S.) Units

Turbidity	Color	pH
Sediment	Odor	

Specific Conductivity (micromhos/cm)
Hardness - Total ($CaCO_3$, in ppm)
Alkalinity - Total ($CaCO_3$, in ppm)

Major Constituents
1.-1000.ppm

Calcium (Ca)	Sulfate (SO_4)
Magnesium (Mg)	Chloride (Cl)
Sodium (Na)	Silica (SiO_2)

Secondary Constituents
.01-10.ppm

Potassium (K)
Iron (Fe)
Nitrogen (Ammonia, NH_4)
Nitrogen (Nitrate, NO_3)
Nitrogen (Nitrite, NO_2)

Minor Constituents
.001-.1ppm

Manganese (Mn)
Copper (Cu)

Trace Constituents
less than .001ppm

Zinc (Zn)
Coliform Bacteria (colonies per 100ml)

accurate the analysis will be. Where pollution is suspected, the water must be tested within twelve hours of collection and in all other cases, within 72 hours.

When the brewing water is to be treated with mineral salts or boiled to precipitate carbonates, an analysis after treatment will pinpoint the resultant mineral distribution, but it is hardly necessary. The carefully weighed addition of salts and a simple pH test after treatment are usually adequate indicators of the subsequent mineral distribution.

Brewing with an untreated natural water supply is possible in almost all cases by manipulating the brewing procedure. A water analysis should be made before brewing to determine the formulation and procedure that best suits the particular water composition.

Turbidity, Sediment, Color and Odor

Turbidity and sediment may be caused by suspended clay and other inorganic soil, organic topsoil or waste, colloidal ferrous-and-aluminum-oxides, or manganese and silicon dioxide. Color is usually due to colloidal vegetable pigments, although a yellow to brown hue may be from suspended clay or silt. This sediments out upon resting; particles in colloidal suspension may be eliminated only by filtering. Odor may be from dissolved gases or organic decay.

Overall character may be improved by activated-carbon filtration. Where this is not satisfactory, a clearer water should be found to brew with.

U.S. Public Health Service Drinking Water Standards suggest as limits that should not be exceeded: turbidity—five units, color—fifteen units, odor—threshold number three. For brewing, it is recommended that these all be less than one.

pH

The pH, which indicates acid to alkalinity ratios and also the mineral composition of water, is of utmost importance to the brewer. Appropriate acidity is a prerequisite of a successful brewing cycle. Enzyme activity, kettle break and yeast performance rely upon conducive acidity in the mash, wort and beer. The acidity of the brewing water is therefore of vital concern to the brewer.

pH is the measure of the acidity or alkalinity of a solution. Acid solutions taste sour; alkaline solutions taste bitter and flat. In other terms, acidity is expressed as a greater number of positively charged particles in solution than negatively charged ones; conversely, alkalinity marks an excess of dissociated negative particles.

Ions

All elements are reducible to atoms. Atoms are made up of an equal number of positive and negative charges, respectively termed *protons* and *electrons*. The atoms of each element are distinguished from those of every other element by the total number of protons in their nuclei and the number and arrangement of electrons in orbit. Atoms are chemically inactive because the charges of their protons and electrons neutralize each other. They may, however, be unstable. Only atoms having two electrons in their first orbit and eight electrons in their outermost orbit are stable; only these occur in their true atomic form.

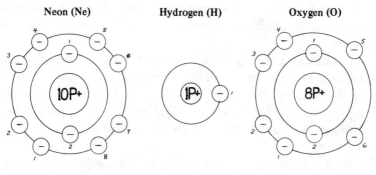

Neon (Ne)   Hydrogen (H)   Oxygen (O)

Stable Element   Active Elements

Hydrogen (H^+)   **Oxygen (O^{--})**

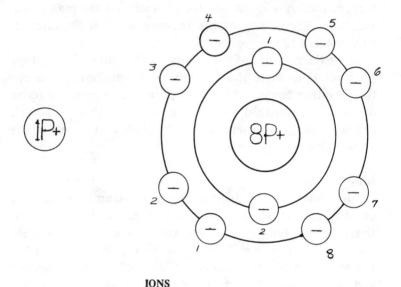

IONS

An unstable atom either gives electrons to or receives electrons from another unstable atom, each thereby forming an *ion* of the element, which has a stable electron configuration. Because this results in an imbalance in the number of positively-charged protons and negatively-charged electrons, all ions have an electromagnetic charge. Ions that have a positive attraction are *cations;* negatively charged ions are *anions.*

Cations and anions combine to form ionic compounds; the strength of their bond and the charge of the compound itself are dictated by the relative electromagnetic attraction of the ions involved. The greater the difference in their charges, the stronger the ionic bond, and the more acid or alkaline their compound.

Ionic compounds are formed by the exchange of electrons. Other compounds are formed by sharing electrons which

Unstable Elements
Sodium and Chloride

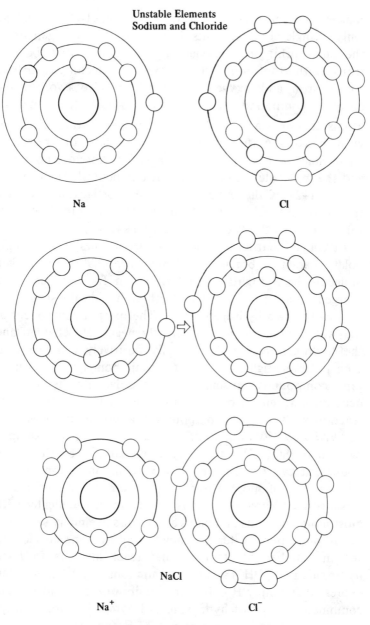

Na

Cl

NaCl

Na⁺

Cl⁻

IONIC COMPOUND SODIUM CHLORIDE

makes them *covalent*. The water molecule, H_2O, is covalent. Only a single electron orbits the nucleus of a hydrogen atom; the outer orbit of an oxygen atom contains only six electrons. Both atoms are unstable, hydrogen needing to give up an electron and oxygen needing to receive two. In the covalent compound of the water molecule, the hydrogen atoms achieve stable single orbits by sharing their electrons with the oxygen atom which then has a stable outer orbit of eight. Since no electrons are exchanged, the bond is nonionic, and the molecule is electromagnetically neutral. The negative valence (-2) of the oxygen atom (O^{--}, or lacking two electrons) is precisely neutralized by the combined positive valence (+2) of the two hydrogen atoms (H_2^{++}).

Although neutral, the water molecule retains a strongly polar character, because the eight protons of its oxygen molecule have slightly more attraction for the negatively charged electrons of the shared orbits than do the single protons of the two hydrogen atoms. The oxygen component of the water molecule is thus slightly negatively charged and the hydrogen component equally positively charged; it is even polar enough to disrupt the ionic bonds of many inorganic compounds, causing them to dissolve into their component ions. When all of the water present is absorbed in the reaction with an ionic compound, that compound is said to be *hydrated by water of crystallization.* For example, gypsum ($CaSO_4 \cdot 2H_2O$) is a hydrated salt. Like other compounds, it can be dissolved into its component ions by the introduction of more water. In fact, water is the most universal solvent known, and it is able to react chemically with most inorganic acids and bases and to dissolve many salts.

Although pure water is characterized as being covalent, a certain number of its molecules react in pairs to form hydroxide ions (OH^-) and hydronium ions (H_3O^+, most often expressed as simply H^+). It is an equilibrium reaction, and the combined number of hydroxide and hydronium ions always remains constant; in pure water at 77°F, the concentration of

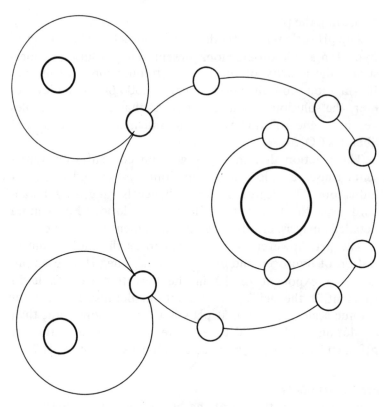

WATER MOLECULE

electropositive hydronium ions and electronegative hydroxide ions are each .000,000,1 moles per liter. When some mineral compounds are dissolved in water, their positive mineral ions bond to the oxygen side of the water molecule, freeing hydronium (H^+) ions, and their negative ions react with the electropositive hydrogen side, releasing hydroxide (OH^-) ions. When an excess of either hydroxide or hydronium ions are released, the ionic equilibrium of pure water is disturbed. Because the combined value of hydroxide and hydronium ions always remains constant, an increase in either always results in a proportional decrease in the other.

Measuring the pH

The pH scale represents the relative molar concentration of hydrogen and hydroxide ions present in any solution by measuring the activity of the free hydronium ions in solution. If this ion concentration exceeds .000,000,1 moles per liter, the solution is acidic; if it is less than .000,000,1 moles per liter, the solution is alkaline and neutralizes acids and liberates CO_2.

The reaction that the hydrogen ion concentration represents causes a color change in litmus paper and other pH indicators. The degree of color change is gauged by a standard scale to identify the pH of any solution. For a more detailed analysis, electromagnetic equipment is employed.

The pH, however, is not expressed as the molar concentration of hydrogen and hydroxide ions. The pH scale simply uses the exponent of 10 in the logarithm (see Table 5) to identify the acidity of a solution. Because it is a logarithmic scale, a solution at pH 4 is 10 times more acidic than a solution at pH 5, 100 times more acidic than a solution at pH 6, and 1,000 times more acidic than a solution at pH 7.

pH Adjustment

All changes in the pH of the brewing water, the mash, the wort, or the beer, whether induced or consequential, are due to the formation, addition or precipitation of mineral ions or organic acids. The pH of the brewing water may be adjusted by precipitating out the alkaline carbonate salts as the result of boiling or by adding organic acids or mineral salts. Salts are added when additional mineral character is also desired. As an alternative to water treatment, the mash may be made more acidic by certain bacteria which cause the formation of organic acids.

The pH of the mash determines its levels of enzyme activity and therefore the acidity of the wort and beer. The pH significantly affects hop extraction and protein precipitation in the kettle and yeast performance and clarification

TABLE 5

Part A.

Moles Per Liter, H^+	pH			Moles Per Liter, OH^-
.1	$1 \cdot 10^{-1}$	1	$1 \cdot 10^{-13}$	.000 000 000 000 1
.000 1	$1 \cdot 10^{-4}$	4	$1 \cdot 10^{-10}$	.000 000 000 1
.000 01	$1 \cdot 10^{-5}$	5	$1 \cdot 10^{-9}$	.000 000 001
.000 000 1	$1 \cdot 10^{-7}$	7	$1 \cdot 10^{-7}$	.000 000 1
.000 000 001	$1 \cdot 10^{-9}$	9	$1 \cdot 10^{-5}$	.000 01

Part B.

Hydrogen Ion Concentration in the pH Scale

4	pH	5	6	7
.000 1	H^+, moles per liter	.000 01		
			.000 001	
				.000 000 1

in the ferment. Because ideal pH levels cannot often be attained, or because the pH at one stage conflicts with the pH optimum of a more critical reaction, concessions are sometimes made; however, shortcomings can usually be overcome by time and temperature manipulation. For example, the enzymatic reduction of proteins in the mash to soluble nitrogen happens most efficiently at pH 5 or below, a level impossible to achieve during mashing. Therefore, it is necessary to make a reasonable rest at temperatures conducive to protein degradation, especially when the mash begins at above pH 5.5.

At above pH 6, the mash suffers from sluggish enzyme activity, and in the lauter tub, troublesome tannins and silicates are leached into the extract. With "soft" water and pale malt, the few acid ions cannot overcome ("invert" buffers leached from the malt, which results in a strong resistance to further acidulation of the mash.

Objectionable sour and harsh tastes are best avoided by mashing at pH 5.2 to 5.5, which should be the target acidity of the saccharification rest in all mashes. This is the level at which enzyme activity, filtering, color, and clarity are best. It can be expected to yield a sweet wort of 5.5 or slightly above, which best serves hop extraction and flocculation of protein in the kettle.

Total Dissolved Solids/Specific Conductivity

The *total dissolved solids* are the mineral ions in solution, which means they have passed through a filter fine enough to screen out all sediments and colloids. They are measured as the residue left after filtered water has been evaporated.

The *specific conductivity* of water measures the mineral ions in solution by gauging the solution's ability to conduct an electric current at 77°F (25°C). Most inorganic acids, bases, and salts are good conductors of an electric current (ions are by definition electrovalent, or charged, particles), whereas organic compounds conduct current very poorly, if at all. Specific conductance therefore, equates to the total dissolved solids in any water.

The specific conductance in micromhos per centimeter *(mho* is the opposite of the basic unit of electrical resistance, the *ohm)* is roughly equatable to the total dissolved solids in solution (in ppm) by multiplying the specific conductance by a factor of .55 (for water of pH less than 7.2 or more than 8) ranging up to .90 (saline water). For most natural waters, multiplying the specific conductance by a factor between .55 and .70 gives a reasonable assessment of the total dissolved solids.

Hardness/Alkalinity

The *hardness* of water is gauged by measuring the dissolved cations of the alkaline-earth elements, most significantly calcium (Ca^{++}) and magnesium (Mg^{++}). These common minerals inhibit the sudsing of sodium-based soap in "hard" water and are precipitated as an insoluble, furry residue.

Alkaline-earth ions are weakly electropositive and give water slight acidity. The polar bonds they form with water molecules are weak and readily broken by strongly basic anions, causing them to precipitate as insoluble salts. Calcium exhibits a fragile solubility. Magnesium is more electropositive than calcium but is not correspondingly less soluble; it is actually more stable in solution. The cations of the larger, less electropositive alkali metals sodium (Na^+) and potassium (K^+) are even more weakly acidic. They are much more stable in water, give an essentially neutral pH reaction, and do not contribute to water hardness.

Calcium is the most widely occurring "metal" found in water, followed by magnesium and sodium, then iron. Potassium and manganese are much less common; potassium is often grouped with sodium and manganese with iron when considering their effects.

The metal cations all occur out of solution bonded to "acid" anions, in crystalline-structured ionic compounds called *mineral salts.* The bicarbonate, sulfate, chloride, nitrate, borate and phosphate ions are all classified as "acids" because they are derived from carbonic, sulfuric, hydrochloric, nitric, boric and phosphoric acids; their effects, however, are decidedly alkaline.

The several salts that may be formed by the acid anions with any one given metal vary in solubility and acid or alkaline reaction according to the electronegative valence of the particular anion involved. A weak metal in solution with a weakly-alkaline anion have very little attraction for each other and stay in solution. The same metal with a moderately-alkaline anion may be precipitated out of solution under certain conditions. With a strong base, the metal may even be insoluble. Thus, calcium chloride is freely soluble, calcium sulfate is of limited solubility, and calcium carbonate is nearly insoluble. Sodium and potassium, because they are only slightly electropositive at best, are freely soluble not only with both chloride and sulfate ions but also with carbonate.

Similarly, the pH of a solution is determined by the relative electrovalence of the several cations and anions dissolved together. Since soluble metals are all only weakly acidic and acid anions range from very weakly alkaline to extremely alkaline, their solution in water may be slightly acidic (calcium and the sulfate ion), neutral (sodium and chloride ions), or very alkaline (calcium and carbonate ions). Mild alkalinity is usually indicative of solutions containing more than one anion (calcium with the sulfate and carbonate ions, for instance).

The anions found in water are almost exclusively sulfates (SO_4^{--}), chlorides (Cl^-), and bicarbonates (HCO_3^-). The sulfate ion is weakly basic, and the chloride ion only slightly more, whereas the unstable bicarbonate ion is a very strong buffer because in its formation from the carbonate ion (CO_3^{--}), it pulls a hydronium ion off a water molecule, freeing hydroxide ions into solution.

Far less common than the sulfates, chlorides and bicarbonates are the weakly basic nitrate, borate, phosphate, and silicate ions; few of their salts are even soluble. In fact, only six salts commonly dissolve in ground water: calcium bicarbonate, magnesium bicarbonate, calcium sulfate, magnesium sulfate, sodium sulfate, and sodium chloride. Only three other salts are occasionally present in significant amounts: calcium chloride, magnesium chloride, and sodium bicarbonate. Potassium compounds are rarely significant.

Water hardness, namely calcium and magnesium in solution, significantly affects the brewing process. If these elements occur primarily with the bicarbonate ion, calcium precipitates out of solution during boiling, robbing the yeast of a ncessary element and causing sluggish pH changes in the mash. On the other hand, calcium in solution with the sulfate ion provides a very stable vehicle for the transmission of calcium into the ferment and aids, rather than retards, mash acidulation.

The bicarbonates (and to some extent the carbonates) constitute most of the alkalinity of natural waters and are of great concern to the brewer. That part of the calcium and magnesium in solution that precipitates out with the bicarbonates during boiling cannot be calculated to support yeast activity. This is known as the *temporary* or *carbonate* hardness of water.

After boiling, the calcium and magnesium ions that remain in solution with the sulfate ion form *permanent* or *noncarbonate* hardness. They are assumed to be in solution with sulfates, although a small number of carbonate ions remain bonded to water molecules. (With magnesium in solution, the number of ions bonded to water is even greater; calcium carbonate is soluble to 20ppm, and magnesium carbonate to 300ppm.)

The hardness of any water is determined by titration, as with EDTA (after addition of a dye), to endpoint. It is expressed as "hardness as $CaCO_3$," although it represents all of the hardness ions in solution.

The alkalinity of water measures the buffering capacity of dissolved anions, especially the bicarbonate (HCO_3). It is also measured by titration. An indicator dye, whose color in neutral and alkaline solutions is known, is added to the water. The number of drops it takes to neutralize the water with a strong mineral-acid solution (such as .02N sulfuric acid) is indicated by the color change of the dye. When multiplied by a certain factor, this yields the concentration of calcium carbonate it would take to produce the same buffering capacity as that actually caused by all of the alkaline ions in solution.

By expressing hardness and alkalinity in the same terms, the two values are readily compared; "as $CaCO_3$" is the accepted standard because its cation is the primary mineral of hardness and its anion is the principal source of alkalinity in most waters.

Hardness and alkalinity roughly define the permanent and temporary hardness of water. *When the alkalinity value exceeds the hardness, the hardness is largely temporary. When the hardness value exceeds the alkalinity, the difference is indicative of unbuffered, permanent hardness.* Especially where the difference is appreciable, the water is eminently suitable for brewing, and responds well to acidulation during mashing.

Temporary hardness, it is well to remember, is always strongly aklaline; permanent hardness is usually only slightly acidic.

Where alkalinity as $CaCO_3$ is unknown, the hardness before and after boiling must be known to define the permanent and temporary hardness. This method is at least as satisfactory an indicator as is the alkalinity reading of a water analysis.

Most water supplies are slightly alkaline due to the buffering of any calcium and magnesium in solution by the strongly basic reaction of even a small amount of bicarbonate. These waters become weakly acidic upon precipitation of their carbonate salts. They react sluggishly to acidulation in the mash and kettle unless the carbonates are sedimented out by boiling or the addition of slaked lime or overcome by the addition of calcium or magnesium as sulfate salts or by the addition or formation of organic acids.

The larger of the two readings, hardness or alkalinity, may also be employed to indicate how much of the total dissolved solids is sodium or potassium chloride or sodium sulfate (salts which contribute to neither the hardness or the alkalinity). This is estimated by subtracting the larger reading from the total dissolved solids.

Where calcium and magnesium measurements are not given in an analysis, dividing the hardness reading by 1.5 and by 3.0 roughly indicates the calcium and magnesium in solution (assuming a 2/1 Ca/Mg ratio).

Mineral Ions Common in Water

Cations—Earths

Calcium (Ca^{++}). Calcium is the principal mineral of hardness, having come from the water's passage over limestone, dolomite, gypsum, or calcified gypsiferous shale. Calcium increases mash acidity and inverts malt phosphate to the precipitated alkaline phosphate by the following reaction:

$$CaH_4(PO_4)_2 \cdot H_2O$$
Calcium Phosphate (Organic)

$+$

$$CA$$
Calcium

$+$

$$3H_2O$$
$\downarrow$
$$2H$$
Hydrogen Ions
$$2CaHPO_4 \cdot 2H_2O$$
Calcium Phosphate (Secondary, Precipitated)

In appropriate amounts, calcium is advantageous to the brew. It stimulates enzyme activity and improves protein digestion, stabilizes the alpha amylase, helps gelatinize starch and improves lauter runoff. Calcium also extracts fine bittering principles of the hop and reduces wort color. A calcium precipitate formed with potassium phosphate improves hot-break flocculation. It is also an essential part of yeast-cell composition; small amounts of calcium neutralize substances toxic to yeast such as peptone and lecithin. During aging, it improves the clarification, stability, and flavor of the finished beer.

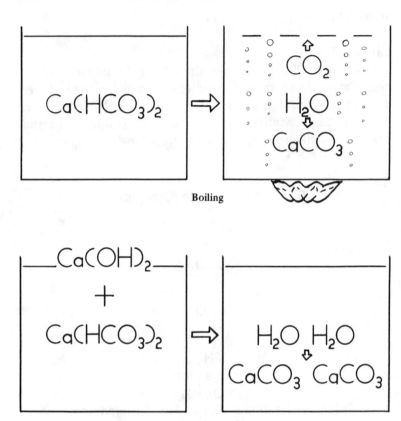

Boiling

Adding Slaked Lime

PRECIPITATION OF CALCIUM CARBONATE

In excess, however, calcium precipitation with organic phosphates interferes with runoff filtering and robs the wort of phosphate, a necessary yeast nutrient. Calcium levels are usually 5 to 200 ppm; its solubility is greatly affected by anions in solution with it.

Magnesium (Mg^{++}). Magnesium is the secondary mineral of hardness. It is essential as a co-factor for some enzymes and as a yeast nutrient. In small concentrations of 10 to 30 ppm, it accentuates the beer's flavor, but it imparts an astringent bitterness when it is present in excess. Over 125 ppm it is cathartic and diuretic. Usually found at levels of 2 to 50 ppm, its solubility is less affected by carbonate anions in solution than is calcium.

Cations—Metals

Sodium (Na^+). The sour, salty taste of sodium accentuates beer's flavor when it is found in reasonable concentrations. It is poisonous to yeast and harsh tasting when it is in excess. Usually found at levels of 2 to 100 ppm, it is very soluble.

Potassium (K^+). Potassium imparts a salty taste. In excess of 10 ppm, it inhibits enzyme activity and acts as a laxative. It is difficult to measure and is usually grouped with sodium. Levels seldom exceed 20 ppm, although potassium is very soluble.

Iron (Fe^{++}). Common in ground water, iron gives an unpleasant, inky taste detectable at levels as low as .05 ppm. Above 1 ppm, iron weakens yeast and increases haze and oxidation of tannins. It blackens porcelain and spots fabrics at .02 ppm, causes white turbidity in water, and corrodes metal. Levels should be less than .3 ppm. Reduce iron content to .1 ppm by aerating and filtering the water through sand.

Manganese (Mn^{++}). Trace amounts of manganese are found in most ground and surface waters. It imparts an unpleasant taste and streaks porcelain at .05 ppm. The manganese level should be less than 2 ppm and optimally below .05 ppm. It can be reduced to .02 ppm by aeration.

Ammonia (NH_4^+). Ammonia is a corrosive ion from microbial activity during organic decomposition. Most volatile of nitrates, it is reduced by oxidation to corrosive alkaline gas NH_3 and NH_2. Always indicative of pollution, ammonia is never present in unpolluted water. Levels of ammonia are normally .00–.03 ppm and should never exceed .05 ppm.

Copper (Cu^{++}). Copper causes yeast mutation and haze formation. It leaves blue-green stains on porcelain. Levels of copper should be less than .1 ppm.

Zinc (Zn^{++}). Zinc is a yeast nutrient when it is found at .1 to .2 ppm, but toxic to yeast and inhibiting to enzymes above 1 ppm.

Anions

Carbonate (CO_3^{--}). Carbonate is a strongly alkaline buffer formed by the reaction of atmospheric carbon dioxide with hydroxides of alkaline-earth and alkali metals. Carbonates go into solution as hydrogen carbonates (HCO_3^-, "bicarbonnates"), which are strong buffers. Bicarbonates form by the reaction of a carbonate ion with a molecule each of carbon dioxide and water.

Carbonate resists increases in the mash acidity by neutralizing acids as they are formed. It also hinders gelatinization of starch by alpha amylase, impedes trub flocculation during the cold break, and increases risk of contamination in the ferment. It contributes a harsh, bitter flavor overwhelming in delicate lagers, and carbonate in excess of 200 ppm is tolerable only when a dark-roasted malt is used to buffer its excessive acidity. Preferably, carbonate should be less than 50 ppm when pale malt or infusion mashing is used.

Sulfate (SO_4^{--}). Sulfate is weakly basic, and its alkalinity is overcome by most acids. It is fairly soluble. It gives beer a dry, fuller flavor, although the taste is somewhat sharp. With sodium and magnesium it is cathartic. Above 500 ppm it is strongly bitter and levels are best kept less than 150 ppm.

Chloride (Cl^-). Chloride is very weakly basic and readily neutralized. It accentuates bitterness, increases stability of any solution, and improves clarity. The "salt" taste of chloride generally enhances beer flavor and palate fullness, but the salt flavor can be reduced with calcium and magnesium. Usually found at levels of 1 to 100 ppm, chloride levels should never be more than 100 ppm for light beers and 350 ppm for beers above 12° Balling.

Silica (SiO_2), silicon dioxide. Originating from sand or quartz, silica is insoluble. As a colloid, it interferes with the filtering of the mash. Under certain conditions, silica forms silicate ($HSiO_3^-$), which causes hazes, precipitating out of boil as scale with calcium and magnesium. Silica levels are usually less than 10 ppm but may be as high as 60 ppm.

Nitrate (NO_3^-). Nitrate is the most highly oxidized naturally occurring form of nitrogen. It may be from geological strata or from contact with sewage or oxidized organic matter. Above 10 ppm, it is indicative of pollution by sewage. An alkaline, nitrate forms strongly alkaline nitrites during fermentation, in the presence of chlorines.

Nitrite (NO_2^{--}). Strongly basic, nitrite originates from nitrates during decomposition of organic matter by coliform bacteria. It rarely exceeds .1 ppm and is always indicative of pollution. Nitrite is toxic to yeast in minute concentrations; as little as .1 ppm may retard or terminate yeast growth.

Other

Coliform Bacteria. This originates from fecal bacteria, such as Escherichia coli, Streptococcus faecalis, pathogenic Salmonella strains, Shigella dysenteriae and Vibrio cholerae. The U.S.P.H.S. standard for drinking water is that there should be less than 2.2 colonies per 100 ml. For brewing water, it is recommended that this be zero.

Where bacterial population is not given in an analysis, nitrate, nitrite, and ammonia values suffice to indicate water pollution.

Water Treatment

Brewing water sources should be chosen first for their purity and second for their mineral composition. In fact, treatment is only necessary when the mineral distribution of any water is unsatisfactory or when accentuation of bitterness or saltiness is desired.

TABLE 6
Hardness

Nature	Hardness as $CaCO_3$, PPM
Very soft	Less than 50
Soft	50-100
Slightly hard	100-150
Moderately hard	150-250
Hard	250-350
Very hard	350 and above

Multiplying the ions below by the corresponding factors yields hardness as $CaCO_3$.

Ca-2.497   Mg-4.116   Fe-1.792   Mn-1.822   Zn-1.531

Total Dissolved Solids/Specific Conductivity

Water low in ionized matter	Below 50 ppm/90 $_m$mho/cm
Range of average water supplies	30-275 ppm/50-500 $_m$mho/cm
Very highly mineralized water	275-550 ppm/500-1000 $_m$mho/cm

pH as a Hardness Indicator

pH	Character
Below 7	Soft and acidic, may be due to dissolved CO_2, as H_2CO_3 (carbonic acid). If pH rises upon boiling, due to mineral acids.
7-7.2	Very hard, sulfate. Reacts positively with acid malt phosphates.

7.2-7.5 — Moderately hard, very alkaline. Some sulfate and chloride, but largely buffered bicarbonate. Reacts sluggishly to acidulation.

7.5-8.0 — Moderately hard, alkaline. Mostly bicarbonates and carbonates. Reacts sluggishly to acidulation.

8 and above — No sulfates or free CO_2. Entirely bicarbonates and carbonates.

TABLE 7
Estimated Character of Certain Brewing Waters

Mineral Origin:	Pilsen	Dortmund	Munich	Vienna
Character:	Soft	Hard	Carbonate	Sulfate
Ca^{++}	7	225	75	200
Mg^{++}	2	40	18	60
Na^+	2	60	2	8
SO_4^{--}	5	120	10	125
HCO_3^{--}	15	180	150	120
Cl^-	5	60	2	12
Total Dissolved Solids	35	1000	275	850
Hardness as $CaCO_3$	30	750	265	750

The most common treatment of brewing water is the elimination of excessive bicarbonate, as a pH correction. This may be accomplished by bringing the water to a boil and aerating it as thoroughly as possible to decompose the bicarbonates and precipitate calcium and magnesium carbonate.

After a brief rest, the water is decanted off of the sediment so that it does not subsequently reabsorb the precipitate.

Where water of less than 50 ppm total dissolved solids and pale malt are to be mashed, treatment of the water by the formation or addition of mild organic acid is more appropriate. Addition of citric or lactic acid to reduce the pH of a brewing water to below 7 gives a satisfactory mash acidity. If the water is hard and excessive amounts of acid are required to alter the pH, the beer will taste sour—with the addition of citric acid more so than lactic acid. Formation of lactic acid by Lactobacillus delbruckii in a carefully controlled mash at 95°F (35°C) achieves similar results with smoother flavor.

The use of naturally-acidic, dark-roasted malt is also a manner of water treatment. This method overcomes the alkalinity of hard water with unprecipitated carbonates.

Ion-exchange water softeners should never be used to reduce hardness. They do not remove the carbonate ion from solution, but precipitate calcium and magnesium while correspondingly increasing the sodium concentration.

Iron, manganese, and colloids that cause hazes are best removed by aeration, followed by filtration or sedimentation.

Mineral salts may be added to the brewing water when additional hardness or other mineral character is desired, or to precipitate carbonates. All salts should be carefully weighed on a gram scale before they are added to the brewing water. Mineral salts cannot be accurately dispensed by the teaspoon. One level teaspoon of finely-powdered gypsum might weigh 3.65 grams. Tightly packed, it weighs 5 grams. A teaspoon of more crystalline magnesium sulfate weighs 4.55 grams, finely-granular potassium chloride 5.05 grams, and sodium chloride 6.45 grams.

It is advisable to mix salts into a small quantity of boiling water and use measured amounts of the solution to introduce the salts to the brewing water. Salts should never be added directly to the mash unless a critical adjustment needs to be made because uniform dispersal is unlikely.

TABLE 8
Mineral Salt Treatment

One gram of a freely soluble mineral salt in one U.S. gallon of water at 68 degrees can be expected to increase the total dissolved solids by 264.2 ppm. The amount of any ion in the salt being added may be estimated from the salt composition percentages given; for instance, one gram of calcium sulfate yields $264.2 \cdot .2328 = 61.5$ ppm of calcium and $264.2 \cdot .5579 = 147.4$ ppm of the sulfate ion. Brewing water profiles in TABLE 7 and the analysis of your water supply may be used to guide salt additions.

Calcium Sulfate (Gypsum) $CaSO_4 \cdot 2H_2O$.

Ca 23.28%, SO_4 55.79%, H_2O 20.93%. To increase content and lower pH. Accentuates bitterness, gives drier and fuller flavor. Soluble to 2650 ppm in cold water, to 2000 ppm upon heating. Apparently most beneficial in concentrations of 150-350 ppm. In excess precipitated with calcium phosphate in the kettle. One gram in one gallon yields 61. 5 ppm Ca, 147.4 ppm SO_4.

Magnesium Sulfate (Epsom Salts) $MgSO_4 \cdot 7H_2O$.

Mg 14%, SO_4 55%, H_2O 31%. To increase magnesium content. Freely soluble. Most satisfactory at 150-300 ppm; reduce when adding with calcium sulfate. Very bitter in excess. Generally avoided in pale lagers. One gram in one gallon gives up 37 ppm Mg, 145.3 ppm SO_4.

Calcium Hydroxide (Slaked Lime, Hydrated Lime) $Ca(OH)_2$.

Reacts with calcium bicarbonate causing both to precipitate as carbonates $[Ca(OH)_2 + Ca(HCO_3)_2 \rightarrow 2CaCO_3 + 2H_2O]$. Also precipitates magnesium bicarbonate. Its calcium ion may replace any magnesium that is in solution with the chloride ion. Addition of slaked lime should not exceed the ppm of alkalinity as $CaCO_3$ given in the water analysis. One gram in one gallon yields 264.2 ppm of the salt.

Sodium Chloride (Common Table Salt) NaCl.

Na 39.34%, Cl 60.66%. To accentuate bitterness and enhance flavor and fullness of beer. Also promotes diastatic enzyme activity and release of acid malt phosphates. Usually less than .75 grams per U.S. gallon (198 ppm) as treatment, or so that neither sodium or chloride contents exceed 100 ppm for light beers, or 250 ppm of each for very dark and full beers. Objectionable in excess. Inhibits or even kills yeast over 850 ppm. One gram in one gallon equals 104 ppm Na, 160.25 Cl.

Potassium Chloride, KCL.

K 52.44%, CL 47.56%. As substitute for part of sodium chloride treatment. In excess of 150 ppm inhibits enzyme activity. One gram in one gallon yields 138.6 ppm K, 125.6 ppm Cl.

Potassium Metabisulfite, $K_2S_2O_5$.

K 35.2%, S 28.8%, O 36%. To remove chloride from solution; in excess antifermentative. Not usually more than 1 to 2 ppm added.

4. HOPS

OPS ARE THE CONELIKE, FEMALE "FLOWERS," *strobiles* of the vining Humulus lupulus. The strobiles are formed by a cluster of petallike, yellowish-green bracts and bracteoles emerging from a central stem. Each bract bears many tiny glandular sacs (trichomes) called *lupulin* at its base. The yellow lupulin is as much as 15 percent of the hops by weight and contains the essential oils, resins, bittering principles, and polyphenols or tannins. It also has some nitrogen, sugars, pectin, lipids, and wax.

The resins are classed alpha, beta, and gamma resins. The alpha and beta are "soft" resins, whereas the gamma resin is "hard" and contributes nothing to the brewing.

The alpha resin has no aroma, but it is intensely bitter and is responsible for the hops' bacteriostatic contribution to the brew. It is the most important hop fraction and the most stable. The alpha resin group is soluble as alpha acids, or as a-acids (humulone, cohumulone, and adhumulone), which are *isomerized* during boiling (their atoms are rearranged) to the even more bitter iso-a-acids.

In contrast, the beta resin group, or b-acids (lupulone,

colupulone, and adlupulone) are far less stable than the a-acids, are extremely subject to oxidation, and are only slightly soluble. They become even less soluble as the hot wort cools and are deposited in the trub as an amorphous yellow precipitate. Very little of their antibiotic, aromatic, and bittering properties are carried into the ferment and the finished beer unless they are oxidized, in which case, they taint the beer with an unpleasant, spoiled-vegetable taste.

Although hops that have high alpha-acid content are preferred as bittering/flavoring hops, aromatic hops are selected for the character of their essential oils. These oils, however, are volatile and are dissipated by boiling, so hops chosen for finishing and aroma are added at the end of the boil. For strong aroma, they are added as an extract even at the point of bottling.

The other major contribution of hops to the finished beer is the tannins they dissolve into the boiling wort. *Tannins* are complex, generally-oxidized polyphenol polymers. When proteins and proteoses come into contact with the astringent-tasting amorphous flakes, they adhere to them and, by virtue of their increased mass, are precipitated out of solution.

Although the bitter flavor and tangy aroma of the hop is now considered an essential complement to the malt sweetness of beer as we know it, hops were first employed in brewing as a preservative. Beer made with hops stored better than beer brewed without them, although the reason why was not understood. Only toward the end of the 19th Century did brewers discover that hops prevented the growth of many water-borne and airborne bacteria. The role of hop tannins in precipitating excess protein, and the role of bitter resins in preserving simple body-forming albumins, also began to be understood.

In the Fields

Hops are grown on perennial vines that trail along wires

HOPS ON THE VINE

strung on trellises fifteen to twenty-five feet overhead. Each year new annual stems twine clockwise around the wire strands supporting the flowers or strobiles. When the strobiles are mature, the plant is cut loose from the trellis, and the clusters of hop cones are stripped from the stems of the plant.

Hops that are of brewing quality must be harvested during the five to ten days of their prime. Immature hops are very green and have a haylike aroma; overripe cones have rusty-colored petals, tend to shatter easily, and have a harsh smell.

The cones, which contain 70 to 80 percent moisture at harvesting, are dried to 8 to 10 percent moisture (usually at 140 to 150°F (60 to 65°C) but below 130°F (55°C) when a very strong aroma is characteristic) over a period of eight to twelve hours. They are sometimes bleached by fuming them with sulfur to lighten their color and give them a softer, silkier, more appealing feel. Dried hops are cured in cooling bins for five to ten days to equalize their moisture content, improve their aroma and appearance, and make the cones more resilient against shattering. They are compressed and baled, each bale measuring approximately 20x30x54 and weighing between 185 and 205 pounds. They are traditionally stitched in burlap hopsack, but modern foil-mylar laminate vacuum-packaging under nitrogen or CO_2 atmosphere is gradually replacing the burlap.

The harvest is purchased by hop merchants, who hold the hops in cold storage until they are sold to the brewer. If the hops have been properly dried and baled, protected from direct sunlight and stored in low humidity and low temperatures [33°F (1°C) is ideal],very little destructive oxidation occurs and the hops will keep for up to two years. Under adverse storage conditions, however, the essential oils are driven off, and many of the alpha-acid resins are oxidized to beta acids or to useless hard resins. Such hops have an "off" or disagreeable aroma and may be yellow or brown. At this point, their bittering strength has been greatly diminished, and their flavor contribution to beer is abnormal.

Brewing hops should be whole cones of a light yellowish-green color, not mottled or spotted, roundish and not elongated in shape, and of less than 6 percent stem and leaf

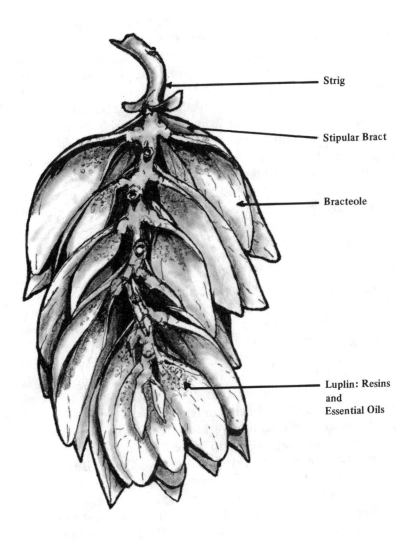

Strig

Stipular Bract

Bracteole

Luplin: Resins
and
Essential Oils

content. They should have a pleasant aroma; it is this bouquet that indicates the condition of the essential oils. The hop cones should be silky, glossy, and springy to the touch. Small hops tend to be of finer quality than large hops.

Two or three small cones should be rubbed in the palm of the hand and sniffed to assess the aroma. The lupulin content can be judged by the stickiness left on the hand. Several cones should be broken lengthwise and the quantity and color of the lupulin assessed. It should be lemon-colored and plentiful. Old, deteriorated hops have powdery, light-brown lupulin, and range in color from green or greenish-yellow to yellow or brownish-green. Usually the discoloration is obvious. Old, dry and powdery hop cones should be avoided, as the alpha-acid content will be considerably reduced. The deterioration of old or mishandled bales may account for a 25 percent or greater loss of alpha-acids. This is also true in the case of lots containing an excessive number of broken cones.

In the Laboratories

An alpha-acid analysis is usually made of samples taken from each hop bale. Alpha-acidity is given as a percentage of the sample, by weight. This is stated by the dealer and is used by the brewer to adjust bittering-hop rates.

Alpha-acids go into solution only after boiling has isomerized them to iso-a-acids. Their bittering contribution is dependent upon isomerization efficiency in the kettle, and the quantity and alpha-acid content of the hops used. Several methods for the quantitative analysis of iso-a-acids make it possible to estimate the hop bitterness in beer; the internationally-agreed standard is Bitterness Units (B.U.). One B.U. equals .0001335 of an ounce (avoir.) of iso-a-acid per gallon of solution, or about one milligram per liter.

Where stated, Bitterness Units are used to target bittering-hop rates, adjusting the amount to reflect the widely varying alpha-acid content of hops from lot to lot and season to season. Dave Line (*The Big Book of Brewing*) devised the Alpha Acid Unit (A.A.U.) to simplify these adjustments. One A.A.U. equals one ounce of a 1 percent alpha-acid hop. Using this system two ounces of a 5 percent a-a- hop gives 10 A.A.U., and so on.

TABLE 9

Color Range

Dark green	
Olive green	Low-quality hops
Pale green	
Yellowish-green	High-quality hops
Greenish-yellow	
Yellow	
Brownish-yellow	Deteriorated hops
Brown	
Brownish-green	

Cone Size

Large	2¼ - 3″ long
Medium	1¼ - 2″ long
Small	¾ - 1″ long

Analysis

M.C.	8-13%
Resins	10-20%
A-acid	5-10%
Essential oils	.2-.5%
Tannin	2-5%
Nitrogen	2-4%

Assuming 30 percent isomerization of the hop resin by a 90 to 120-minute rolling boil, each A.A.U. will contribute 22.472 B.U. to a gallon of wort, or 85 B.U. per liter. Dividing the B.U. given for any beer by 22.472 gives the A.A.U.s required per gallon of wort. The kettle-hop rate is established by dividing the A.A.U.s by the alpha-acidity of the hops being used. Likewise, where Bitterness Units aren't given in a recipe, they can be figured by multiplying the A.A.U.s given (per gallon of wort) by 22.472.

Hop bitterness is accentuated by magnesium, carbonate and chloride ions, and hop rates must generally be reduced

TABLE 10

Part A

Beer Type:	Wort, °B	BU	Hop Type
Pilsener	12	40	Saaz
Dortmunder	14	26-36	Hallertau
Vienna	12.5	24-30	Hallertau/Saaz
Munich, Dark	12.5	22-36	Hallertau/Spalt/ Mittlefrueh
Munich, Light	12	20-28	Hallertau/Spalt/ Mittlefrueh
Bock	16	24-36	various
Dopplebock	18	24-40	various

Part B

Hop type:	Alpha Acid% (av.):	Character:
Fuggles	5	
Hallertau (U.S.)		
Tettnanger (U.S.)		
Hersbrucker (U.S.)		Aromatic, pleasant,
Styrian Goldings (U.S.)		Fragrant, low alpha-acid content.
Willamette		
Cascade	6	

Saaz	7	Aromatic, spicier aroma, medium alpha-acid content.
Savinja/Styrian Goldings		
Hersbrucker/Gebirg		
Tettnanger		
Hallertau		
Spalt		
Mittlefrueh		
Cluster		
Talisman	8	
Columbia		
Bavarian Northern Brewer	9	Markedly bitter, high alpha-acid content.
Brewers Gold		
Bullion		
Northern Brewer	10	
Eroica	12	
Nugget		
Galena		

Part C
Hop Producing Districts

Country of Origin	Hop Type	Grown
Czechoslovakia	Saaz/Zatec Red	Zatec, Auscha, Raudnitz, Dauba
Germany	Hallertau/ Mittlefrueh	Hallertau, Baden
	Tettnanger	Wurtenburg
	Spalt	Spalt
	Hersbrucker/ Gebirg	Hersbruck

Yugoslavia	Savinja/Styrian Goldings	Wojwodina, Slovenia
Belgium	Hallertau/Saaz	Alost, Poperinghe
United States	Various	Yakima Valley (Washington) Willamette Valley (Oregon) Boise and Snake River Valleys (Idaho) Sacramento and Sonoma Valleys (Cal.)

as water hardness increases. Bitterness Units can in any case only be accurately matched if fresh hops are used; with oxidized hops alpha-acidity is diminished and the proper hop rate becomes guess-work.

Hop pellets have gained in popularity with brewers in recent years because they are less susceptible to oxidation during storage, especially under adverse conditions. They are compressed from fresh hops and foil-packaged in an oxygen-free environment. Because they are almost invariably less deteriorated than whole hops, utilization tends to be better.

The most highly prized hops in the world are the mild central-European varieties. Although these and similar types are being more widely cultivated in the western United States, they are not frequently used by domestic commercial breweries. New disease-resistant, high alpha-acid varieties are being developed which also have desirable aromatic qualities; these promise better kettle utilization without forsaking fine hop character, as has been the case with high alpha-acid-percentage strains previously developed for economical use.

5. YEAST

EASTS ARE NONPHOTOSYNTHETIC, RELATIVELY sophisticated, living, unicellular fungi (genus Saccharomyces), considerably larger than bacteria. In an aciduric aqueous solution, they absorb dissolved vitamins, minerals, and simple nitrogenous matter (amino-acids and very simple peptides) through their hemicellulose cell membranes. Then, they employ a structured series of reactions known as *metabolic pathways* to break down these substances into nutrients, mainly amino-acids to nitrogen and sugars to carbon. They obtain oxygen for metabolism from that which is dissolved in the solution, or they split it off of molecular compounds.

Yeast, although living organisms, are actually highly organized enzyme collectives, each and every reaction of the yeast cell being controlled by a separate enzyme. In one reaction, simple sugars are reduced to alcohol and carbonic gas in the presence of a constitutive intracellular enzyme group called *zymase* and a phosphoric co-enzyme. This process is known as *fermentation*. Yeast metabolism directly determines the degree of attenuation of any wort, and its character greatly affects the flavor of the finished beer. In fact, just as every living organism varies from every other, every fermentation has qualities distinctly its own. These depend on a number of factors. Particular strains of yeast produce different flavor characteristics; variations in the pH, temperature, or composition of each ferment results in slight or greater changes in the metabolic products, even in the same strain of yeast:

Although brewing dates back to prehistory, it was not until 1841 that Mitcherlich discovered that yeast were essential to fermentation. Further research by Pasteur and Buchner revealed that yeast produced alcohol only as a by-product of carbon metabolism, and that it was in fact the nonliving zymase enzyme that was responsible for the fermentation of sugar.

Bottom fermenting began with Gabriel Sedlmayer in Munich and Anton Dreher in Vienna in 1841, using mixed strains of yeast that were not purely bottom fermenting. Emil Hanson, working at Jacob Christian's Carlsberg brewery in Copenhagen, set the stage for modern lager brewing by isolating two distinctly different *pure culture* yeasts, that is, strains propagated from a single cell, and therefore all exhibiting the same characteristics. These were the top-fermenting Saccharomyces cerevisiae and the bottom-fermenting Saccharomyces carlsbergensis (s. uvarum). Pure-culture, bottom-fermenting yeast were first employed at Carlsberg in 1883; within the decade, lager culture-yeast was being employed in refrigerated fermentation throughout Europe and America.

Besides their visually different flocculating characteristics, the yeasts operate at different temperatures and ferment different sugars. The top-fermenting yeast strains are only effective at 55 to 70°F (13 to 21°C). They form colonies that are supported by the surface tension of the beer and create a very thick, rich yeast head; in general, they ferment glucose, fructose, mannose, galactose, maltose, sucrose, xylulose, and maltotriose, and partially ferment the trisaccharide

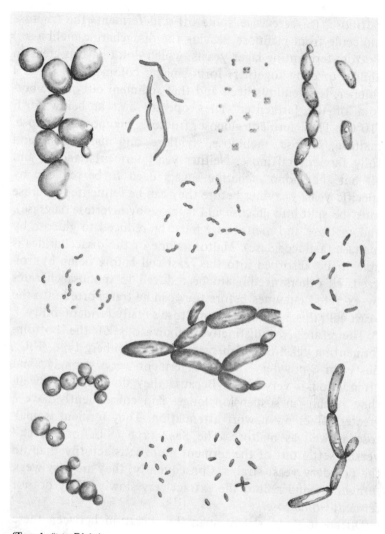

(Top, Left to Right)
Saccharomyces Carlsbergensis, Lactobacillus, Pediococcus, Exiguus
(Middle)
Acetobacter, Acetomonas, Hafnia
(Center)
Pichia Membranaefaciens (wild yest)
 (Bottom)
Tortulopsis (wild yeast), Klebsiella, Zymomonas, Mycoderma

raffinose. (S. cerevisiae splits off and ferments the fructose molecule from raffinose, leaving the disaccharide melibiose.) Bottom-fermenting lager yeasts, which don't have as great an ability to cling together, form smaller colonies that make a thinner, less tenuous head and that sediment out on the bottom of the fermenter. They operate best at below 50°F (10°C). They ferment glucose, fructose, mannose, galactose, maltose, sucrose, melibiose, xylulose, and maltotriose, and fully ferment raffinose. Neither yeast ferments lactose, and all but the monosaccharide sugars need to be reduced by specific yeast enzymes before they can be fermented; sucrose must be split into glucose and fructose by invertase (sucrase), and maltose and maltotriose must be reduced to glucose by maltase (a-glucosidase). Maltose alone of the disaccharides is able to be absorbed into the yeast cell before being hydrolyzed, all others needing to be reduced to monosaccharides by excreted enzymes before they can be transported into the yeast cell; this is the basis of maltose's ready fermentability.

There are two distinctive subdivisions of the bottom-fermenting yeast S. carlsbergensis. The Frohberg type (F.U., dusty or "powdery" yeasts) ferment very strongly, and attenuation is very rapid. Because they do not clump well, they remain in suspension longer and consequently have a greater effect upon wort attenuation. They ferment isomaltose as well as maltose. The Saaz type (S.U., or "break" yeasts) settle out of the ferment more satisfactorily than do the powdery yeast strains. Consequently, they are very weak fermenters and reduce the extract very slowly. They do not ferment isomaltose.

Different yeast strains span the spectrum between these two major classifications, producing very different aspects of taste, body, head, and clarity in the finished beer; the yeasts which ferment the quickest and most completely are not often the yeasts that produce the best beer. Yeast strains are selected for the character of their fermentation, their ability to form colonies, their ability to ferment without forming flavor- and aroma-impairing esters, and their viability rather than their ability to attenuate the wort rapidly.

Chemically, yeasts are constituted of proteins (especially *volutin,* a nucleo-protein visible as small, shiny bodies in the vacuoles and cell plasma), glycogen (a starchlike reserve not usually found in older cells), minerals, enzymes, and vitamins (especially those of the B-complex).

Yeasts require various nutrients to renew these elements of their cellular structure. They absorb simple protein from hydrolytic solution which they refine to a very high-quality amino-acid group that composes roughly half of the yeast cell. Another 10 percent of the cell is calcium-based and requires renewal, as do the minerals and trace elements that account for up to 5 percent of its structure. The minerals, besides calcium, are mostly the inorganic salts of phosphorus and potassium, with some magnesium, sodium, and sulfur. These the yeast obtains from mineral compounds in the ferment, such as calcium and magnesium sulfates. The trace elements, especially zinc, boron, and manganese, are almost always available in small amounts from the malt, hops, or water.

Yeasts reproduce by cell division, known as *binary fission* or budding. They reproduce only in a nutrient-rich environment; one daughter cell emerges and grows to the size of the mother cell in two to six hours in a suitable solution.

There are numerous strains of yeast, and each operates successfully within a very narrow pH and temperature range. It is necessary to carefully control these factors during brewing because the metabolic reactions and the reproduction rate of the yeast greatly influence the nature and flavor of the beer being brewed.

Yeast operate in suspension in a sugar solution, until they clump together and are brought to the surface by attached CO_2 or are sedimented by virtue of their increased mass. They cease to have a considerable effect on attentuation once they have clumped.

As yeast cells age, their previously colorless, homogeneous plasma (protoplasm) becomes bubbly, then separates into solids and liquid substances by forming vacuoles that envelop the liquid plasma secretion; later they become granulated, and gradually the plasma turns to fat (visible as round bodies of varying sizes within the cell walls). Although they are incapable of sporulation, yeasts can be sustained in an unsuitable environment for long periods by these fatty bodies.

In solutions lacking obtainable nutrients, the culture yeast will cease reproducing. When they can no longer sustain their own metabolic functions, albumin-, hemicellulose-, and vitamin-dissolving enzymes are activated, which reduce the yeast cell to amino acids and other simple substances. This autolization releases undesirable medicinal and diacetyl flavors into beer that is not racked off its sediment.

Because a ferment lacks nutrients needed by the culture yeast, or because the temperature or the pH of the ferment does not suit the particular yeast strain, does not mean that wild yeast strains, mutations, or other microbes will not find the conditions ideal. Under normal conditions, one in a million yeast cells spontaneously mutates; under hostile conditions mutations increase dramatically. Either a wild yeast strain or one of these genetically-altered mutations may become the dominant fermentation organism, to the detriment or ruin of the finished beer.

Wild yeast cause spoilage, making the beer taste or smell medicinal or spicy and creating film formation on the beer surface. Because the wild yeast do not cling together as well as culture yeast, and consequently remain in suspension longer, they almost invariably cloud the beer. The offending yeast may even be a wild strian of the domestic S. carlsbergensis or S. cerevisiae, but this does not make their presence any more desirable. Other common spoilage yeasts are Torulopsis, Candida and Pichia species. It is essential to ferment with solely the culture yeast alone, maintaining its purity, ensuring its adequate nutrition, and carefully controlling its conditions through manipulation of the pH and temperature of the ferment.

Culturing Pure Yeast Strains

Pure culture yeasts are strains propagated from a single cell. Yeast from a successful primary fermentation that has exhibited good brewing characteristics are collected and mixed into a small amount of distilled water until the solution just becomes cloudy. One drop of the yeast solution is then mixed into one fluid ounce of diluted wort gelatin (beer wort and sterile water at 4 to 8° Balling (SG 1016–1032) containing 5 to 10 percent pure vegetable gelatin). The yeast is distributed by thorough agitation before the mixture is thinly spread over a clean cover glass, allowed to congeal, and placed in a sterile, moist container. The glass is then fixed to a graduated stage and microscopically examined at powers of 400 to 1000 magnifications and the location of isolated, healthy-looking (white, hemispherical, nonreflective, uniformly sized) cells marked.

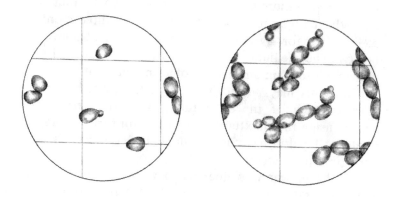

PURE YEAST CULTURE GROWTH

After 24 hours at 68°F (20°C), the glass is reexamined. Colonies should have formed. If they appear healthy, sample yeast cells from several isolated chains that are known to have grown from a single cell are removed with a flame-sterilized platinum or stainless-steel wire loop. (Where a microscope is unavailable, the loop can be used to take a sample directly from the cloudy-yeast solution.)

Each sample is streaked onto the surface of a sterile staining nutrient-agar (W.L. nutrient agar) in a Petri dish. The inoculating streak is cross-hatched to isolate individual cells from it. When visible colonies have formed, an isolated clump is microscopically examined, and if it is uncontaminated, it is used to inoculate an agar wort slant (eight fluid ounces of wort, diluted to 4 to 8° Balling (SG 1016–1032) with sterile water, mixed into five grams of prepared agar or vegetable gelatin at room temperature, heated to boiling after fifteen minutes, and boiled (or autoclaved at 15 psi) for fifteen minutes. This is poured into sterile 20 ml. test tubes tilted 15° from horizontal, capped or plugged with cotton, and allowed to cool.

The temperature is maintained at 50–68°F (10–20°C), until fermentation is apparent (usually two to four days); then the culture may be refrigerated for three months at 39°F (4°C), for lager yeast, or for ale yeast at above 50°F (10°C). The medium can be covered with a layer of sterile mineral oil to maintain an anaerobic environment.

The slants may be recultured by adding one half inch of wort to each of the older tubes, and after fermentation begins, using that mixture to inoculate four freshly prepared slants. All culturing must be done under strictly sanitary conditions using sterile labware.

For the brewer who does not have the laboratory equipment necessary to isolate and incubate pure cultures (basically, a wire loop and the several items of glassware mentioned), purchase of commercially prepared vials or slants is the best source of a yeast culture. Frozen yeast is a reasonable alternative, as are properly handled liquid cultures. Granulated dry yeasts are the least-desirable alternative, as they are likely to contain many dead cells and be contaminated by bacteria during the drying process.

Slants are activated by covering the culture with one half inch of wort. Then in forty-eight hours, that pure liquid-culture is used to inoculate a sterile, narrow-necked eight- or twelve-ounce vessel filled with four fluid ounces of (sterile) aerated wort; this volume can be successfully inoculated directly from the cover glass if slant culturing is to be omitted. The bottle must be capped or covered with a fermentation lock.

After twenty-four hours at 82°F (28°C), each four fluid ounces of wort should yield two to four grams of pure culture yeast. Cooler temperatures, however, are generally employed to retard the yeast's reproduction rate; 50 to 68°F (10 to 20°C) for two to three days is usual. If capped, the lid must periodically be loosened to release pressure. When strongly fermenting, the culture may be roused into one quart of wort and cooled to as low as 39°F (4°C). It is ready to pitch when it comes into active krausen. Each quart of starter will yield sixteen grams or more of pure culture yeast.

Aerate starter cultures often and well, so that the increase in available oxygen will stimulate greater yeast growth. In professional practice, a swab of yeast from the starter is cultured on a slide and microscopically examined for contamination before the parent culture is pitched.

Storing Yeast

Starters may be held at 39°F (4°C) for up to three weeks, or until fermentation subsides. The beer above the yeast should then be decanted, and the yeast covered with cold wort before it is refrigerated again.

For longer storage, after one week at 50°F (10°C), the liquid above the yeast is decanted, and the yeast sediment pressed to remove at least all of the free liquid. The yeast mass is formed into a ball, tightly covered with plastic wrap, placed in chipped ice, and frozen.

Yeast prepared in this manner may be stored for several months. When reactivation is desired, it is crumbled into a quart of well-aerated wort.

Yeast may be collected from each brewing and successively subcultured three to five times before it is necessary to go back to the pure culture.

Washing the Yeast

Usually, yeast requires only to be rinsed before reuse, but periodically cultures should be washed to destroy bacterial contaminants. (This will not, however, destroy wild yeast; only by re-culturing can they be eliminated.)

To wash, decant off the liquid above the yeast cake and rinse it by covering with, and then decanting off, distilled or biologically sterile water. Cover again with a solution of sodium metabisulfite or tartaric (winemakers) acid at pH 2.8, or a .75 percent solution of acidified ammonium persulfate (one teaspoon of tartaric acid with two teaspoons of ammonium persulfate in one quart of water, at pH 2.8), equal in volume to the amount of yeast being washed. Agitate the yeast into temporary suspension. When the yeast have completely settled, or within two hours, decant off the liquid above the yeast, rinse several times, and cover with sterile wort. The yeast will display abnormal characteristics in the first fermentation cycle following an acid wash; they should therefore be cultured through at least one fermentation cycle before being pitched.

6. BACTERIA

SOME BACTERIA (*SCHIZOMYCETES* OR FISSION fungi) are invariably present during brewing, having been transported into the brew by air, water, malt, or the yeast culture. Certain bacteria may be present in small quantities without noticeably affecting the finished beer, but small concentrations of other bacteria can quickly ruin it. There are rare cases where bacteria in the ferment give a beer its particular character, but on the whole, bacterial contamination and growth must be discouraged by strict sanitation. Only where bacteria are cultured to reduce the mash acidity can their effects be tolerated.

The countless types of bacteria oxidize or ferment a wide variety of organic substances. Fortunately, only a relatively few types of bacteria are encountered during brewing and no pathogenic bacteria can survive in beer. They grow on sugar, wort, beer, protein and hop residues, and even on the yeast. By careful control and strict sanitation, flavor and stability problems caused by bacterial contamination of beer can be kept in check. Through cleanliness, it is possible to eliminate the contaminant or reduce it to a level where its growth will not appreciably affect the finished beer.

Because bacteria adapt and mutate so readily (far more so than yeast), they can emerge as the dominant fermentation microbe from a relatively small number of cells. It is also because they mutate so readily that bacteria are so difficult to classify. Although they have a host of characteristics, they are usually categorized by whether or not they are stained by gentian violet (the Gram stain).

Gram-Positive Bacteria

The Gram-positive bacteria encountered during brewing are the Peptococcaceae (family) *Pediococcus* (genus) and the Lactobacillaceae *Lactobacillus*. These are grouped together as *lactic acid* bacteria and were formerly referred to as "beer sarcina" (a term more specifically applied to Pediococcus). Both operate anaerobically and ferment simple sugars to lactic acid; they have inconsiderable effect upon protein.

The several species of Pediococci are strictly anaerobic, globular ("cocci") bacteria occurring singly, paired, or in cubicle packages called *tetrads*. They form inactive lactic acid from amylodextrins, erythrodextrins, and glucose. Heterofermentive strains also ferment maltose, fructose, and sucrose, producing acetic acid as well. In general, the Pediococci produce a disagreeable taste, odor, and turbidity (cloudiness). Contamination is most often from calcified trub deposits on poorly-cleaned equipment.

The Lactobacillus are the single genus of their family. These long, thin, curved rods occur singly or paired at obtuse angles. Microaerophiles, they form lactic acid by the fermentation of carbohydrates in even oxygen-poor solutions. Although they do not cause odor, they may produce a sour taste and turbidity. Several species of Lactobacillus and Pediococcus also cause a *ropy* or gelatinous fermentation or a silky turbulence formed by the excretion of an extracellular slime. It disappears briefly during stirring, but reforms as chains upon the beer surface.

Lactobacillus delbruckii [pH 5.6–5.8, active below 131°F (55°C)] is a heat-tolerant or *thermophilic* homofermentive species that grows on malt. It is especially well-suited to the acidulation of the mash, without producing undesirable flavors or turbidity. It metabolizes glucose and yields only latic acid. Because it is favored by anaerobic conditions, its growth is encouraged by holding a tight, saccharified mash, closely covered, at above 95°F (35°C). This inhibits both aerobic bacteria, which cause oxidation, and nonthermophilic bacteria.

When lactic acid bacteria, and especially thermophilic heterofermentive strains, are active in the mash or its extract, they may spoil it by overacidification and souring. This causes turbidity or the formation of off-flavors, most notably the butterscotch-taste of the diacetyl diketone. The same symptoms in cooled wort, in young beer, and sometimes in aged beer are more likely due to contamination by Pediococcus cerevisiae [pH 5.5, active over a wide temperature range, most active at 70-77°F (21-25°C)] and other nonthermophilic strains.

The thermophilic Gram-positive bacteria are inhibited by isohumulones from the hops and usually will not survive in bitter wort or in beer. Lactic-acid bacteria are often contaminants from pitching yeast or from air. They may be the most significant infectious organism in the fermentation.

The Gram-positive bacteria are rarely a problem in the aged beer because they have highly complex nutritional requirements. During fermentation, the yeast will have absorbed many of the essential amino acids, making them unavailable to the lactic acid bacteria. Only when the proteolysis and precipitation of protein has been poor, when aging beer is not separated from deteriorating yeast sediment, or when temperature shock to the yeast causes it to autolyze will the bacteria be able to obtain enough amino acids to support reproduction.

Gram-Negative Bacteria

The most significant Gram-negative bacteria commonly affecting the lactic-acid mash is the coliform Clostridium butyricum (butyric acid bacteria). These are thick, principally anaerobic rods that putrefy the mash by forming rancid-smelling ethylacetic acid (butyric or butatonic acid). They are inactive above 112°F (45°C) and very active below 104°F (40°C).

Acetic acid bacteria sometimes taint mashes that come in contact with the air below 122°F (50°C) [they are quite active below 95°F (35°C)], but they present a far greater danger to fermenting beer. The acetic acid bacteria are active over the entire pH range of the brewing cycle and are not inhibited by isohumulone from the hops. They are strong oxidizers and are usually responsible for any overwhelming sour-fruit or vinegary taste and odor, and oftentimes turbidity. The surface contamination they cause is often apparent as an oil or moldy (pellicle) film. They are usually introduced to the ferment during racking; aeration of the beer by rousing or splashing provides them with sufficient oxygen for respiration. Active yeast in krausen beer, when added during racking, can consume the dissolved oxygen quickly enough to prevent their growth, but in racking "quiet" beer, it is imperative that all aeration be avoided. Dispensing equipment should be given frequent and complete sterilization, as it is also a point of contamination. Sour-tasting or -smelling draft beer has almost certainly been contaminated by these bacteria.

The lactophilic Achromobacteraceae Acetobacter (significantly A. aceti and A. suboxydans) oxidize ethanol to acetic acid. They are short, chain-forming, ellipsoidal- to rod-shaped, aerobic bacteria. The glucophilic Pseudomonodaceae Acetomonas (Gluconobacter) excrete vinegar and gluconic acid. They are short, rod-shaped-to-ovoid, polarly-flaggelated, aerobic bacteria occurring singly, paired, or in chains. Achromobacter and Pseudomonas are not commonly encountered, and then only in sweet wort because they are acid-intolerant and inhibited by alcohol.

The coliform bacteria (termobacteria) commonly taint the wort by adding a cooked or spoiled-vegetable odor, caused by very rapid fermentation of wort sugars. They are waterborne, nonsporulating aerobes and faculative anaerobes most active at 98.6°F (37°C). Enterobacteriaceae Escherechia are straight rods occurring singly or in pairs. Enterobacteriaceae Klebsiella (Aerobacter) are nonmotile, encapsulated rods occurring singly, paired, or in chains. The cooled wort is an ideal medium for their growth. Aerobacter aerogenes is a commonly encountered source of pungent, vegetable or sulfuric taste and ropy fermentation in both wort and green beer. They adapt and reproduce far more quickly than culture yeast. It is essential that the starter or krausen beer used to inoculate the wort is strongly fermenting and of similar temperature and composition to the wort into which it will be pitched. Otherwise coliform bacteria may become strongly established in the lag phase.

The source of these coliform bacteria is most commonly the rinsing water. Although they are active over a wide temperature range, and are unaffected by hop resins, most are inhibited below pH 4.4 and are not commonly encountered during the later stages of brewing.

Enterobacteriaceae Hafnia (Obesumbacterium) are short, nonmotile, straight rods of variable shape, which commonly taint the early stages of fermentation. Hafnia protea (O. proteus) are fat rods (pH optimum 6.0) that are almost always present in the yeast culture, and only rarely in the wort (other Hafnia strains, acetic and lactic-acid bacteria may also contaminate pitching yeast). They produce sourness and a smell like parsnips or celery. Like others of their family, they are intolerant of very acidic solutions and do not usually affect the aging beer.

Acetic and especially lactic-acid bacteria are the most prevalent contaminants of aging and bottled or kegged beer, but Pseudomonaceae Aeromonas is also encountered. The plump rods of Pseudomonaceae Zymomonas [Achromobacter anaerobium, pH 3.5-7.5, temperature optimum 86°F (30°C), active as low as 40°F (5°C)] are relatively uncommon, but when they are present, they produce an objectionable banana/rotten-egg stench in a very short time. Zymomonas anaerobia or Z. mobilis are then the usual contaminants, fermenting fructose and glucose to ethanol, hydrogen sulfide and acetaldehyde. Ground water or soiled equipment are the usual inoculants.

Bacterial contamination can be assessed both by perceptory analysis of the wort or beer [accentuated by "forcing" closed samples at 85°F (30°C)] and by culturing the wort or beer on a staining or yeast-inhibiting nutrient agar in a Petri dish and estimating the microbial population after several days.

TABLE 12

Brewing Stage	Symptoms	Bacteria Responsible	Solution
Mash, at below 140°F (60°C)	Acidity, sourness, turbidity	Thermophilic lactic acid bacteria	Raise temp. to above 131°F (55°C)
	Rancid odor	Butyric acid bacteria	Raise temp. to above 112°F (45°C)
	Sour, vinegar taste and odor	Acetic acid bacteria	Raise temp. to above 122°F (50°C)
Cooled Wort	Fruity or vegetal odor	Coliform bacteria	Pitch quickly.

Primary Fermentation	Celery odor	Hafnia protea	Go to new yeast culture.
Secondary Fermentation	Sour taste, silky turbidity	Lactic acid bacteria	Lower temp.
	Sour taste, odor and turbidity	Lactic acid bacteria	Lower temp.
Aging/conditioning	As above	Acetic acid bacteria	None
	As above	Lactic acid bacteria	None
	Stench	Zymomonas	None

7. ENZYMES

ENZYMES ARE COMPLEX, PROTEIN-BASED BIOLOGI-cal catalysts that induce reactions between substances, without being changed by the reaction or appearing in its end product. Enzymes may be *constitutive*, that is, normally present within the cell, or *inducible*, formed only in the presence of a particular substrate. They may be *intracellular*, operating only within the cell, or *extracellular*, excreted by the cell into solution.

During the malting and brewing cycle, the barley kernel is decomposed to soluble simple sugars and albuminoids by diastatic and proteolytic enzymes. These sugars are in turn fermented to carbon dioxide and ethyl alcohol by the zymase enzyme group, while other enzymes form organic acids, aldehydes, fusel alcohols, and esters.

The traditional decoction mash is constructed largely upon a series of conditions that reactivate enzyme activity prematurely checked by kilning the green malt. It completes the reduction of the native barley proteins and carbohydrates to a soluble extract.

In the decoction mash, the proteolytic enzymes associated with malting are employed to overcome shortcomings in the malt. Conversely, British malt has been largely saccharified

87

during malting by the diastatic enzymes, which are usually thought of as strictly mash enzymes.

The protoeolytic (peptonizing) group reduces proteins of high molecular complexity to simpler amino-acid constituents through a structured series of interdependent reactions which sever the peptide links (CO-NH) between protein coils and replace them with a water molecule. This restores the amine (NH_2) and carboxyl (COOH) groups of the amino acid

$$NH_2 \cdot \underset{H}{\overset{}{C}H} \cdot CO\text{-}NH \cdot \underset{H}{\overset{}{C}H} \cdot COOH + H_2O \rightarrow PROTEINASE \rightarrow$$

$$NH_2 \cdot \underset{H}{\overset{}{C}H} \cdot COOH \qquad NH_2 \cdot \underset{H}{\overset{}{C}H} \cdot COOH).$$

Protease and then peptase and peptidase solubilize protein and reduce it to proteose, peptones, and peptides; proteinase reduces these to amino acids. Phytase and phosphatase acidify the malt by forming phytic acid, and they are primarily responsible for the acidulation of the mash at 95 to 122°F (35–50°C). They also increase the soluble mineral content of the wort. Cellulase, hemicellulase, collagenase, and pectinate are active within the same temperature range, dissolving the cell walls, endosperm case, gelatin, and pectins.

The diastatic enzymes reduce starch to fractions. Primarily, these are the amylolytic enzymes—alpha and beta amylase. The alpha amylase liquidifies native starch and reduces amylose and amylopectin to a stew of carbohydrate fractions. By randomly separating glucose molecules within the length of polysaccharide chains, it liberates glucose, maltose, maltotriose, oligosaccharides, and dextrins, leaving "a-limit" dextrins wherever it is stopped by branching points in amylodextrin. It reduces complex starch to (at least) achroodextrins very rapidly and completely, so that its solution gives only a faint-red reaction with iodine. Yet it further generates a predominance of maltose only very slowly and ineffectively. It is present in the unmalted barley.

Beta amylase, on the other hand, does not appear until malting. It has no effect on the native starch. In solution it detaches glucose molecules from the nonreducing ends of amylose and amylopectin chains, rejoining them with a water molecule to produce maltose. Alone, it breaks down amylose very slowly and amylopectin very incompletely because it proceeds in a linear fashion and only from one chain end. It is ineffective within two or three glucose molecules of amylopectin's outermost branching points, leaving a very large "B-limit" dextrin that gives an intense blue reaction with iodine. Where alpha-amylase activity splits soluble starch into smaller fractions, beta amylase operates more efficiently, capitalizing upon the increased number of exposed chain ends.

Both amylases are made more effective by the activity of debranching enzymes. A-glucosidase (maltase), limit dextrinase, and pullulanase reduce amylopectin and limit dextrins to amylose by cleaving the linkages at their branching points. The debranching enzymes are most active during malting and at low mash temperatures, whereas the amylases are most effective at hotter temperatures in the mash and during kilning of the malt.

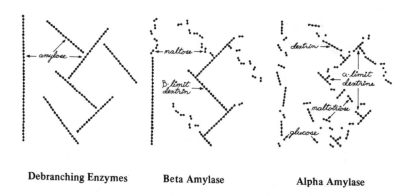

Debranching Enzymes   **Beta Amylase**   **Alpha Amylase**

During fermentation, the zymase enzymes and a phosphoric coenzyme convert glucose to alcohol and carbonic gas; other enzymes are formed during fermentation which split and invert the more complex sugars present in the ferment. Intracellular maltase and glucase reduce maltose to two molecules of glucose; extracellular invertase splits sucrose into glucose and fructose. Finally, proteolytic enzymes within the yeast cell, triggered by a decline in the yeasts' metabolism, autolyze the cell contents to other enzymes, minerals, and vitamins which are slowly released into solution.

It is the enzymatic composition of the yeast cell that determines the nature and vigor of fermentation. Various yeast strains have widely varying enzymatic capability. When the yeast cells do not contain the specific enzymes to reduce the sugars in a wort, they synthesize them. Fermentation lag times, however, are dangerously extended.

8. MALTING

ARLEY MUST BE MALTED BEFORE IT IS MASHED. The starch of unmalted barley is too complex to be readily converted to sugars, and so the grain must pass through a series of steps to activate its constitute enzymes. The first is steeping.

During *steeping,* or soaking, many enzymes in the grains are either formed or activated, and the starchy endosperm mass is solubilized to gummy *polysaccharides.* During sprouting, the hydrolytic enzymes inside the developing plant embryo increase and penetrate the endosperm, reducing proteins and hemicellulose to soluble fractions. The polysaccharides and nitrogen-based protein of the malt are reduced nearly proportional to the length to which the acrospire grew before it was stopped by kilning.

The *acrospire,* or germinal plant of the barley, is grown to the full length of the kernel in British malt, almost fully modifying the endosperm to readily saccharified gum. American and continental malts are less completely modified. The acrospire growth of continental malt is stopped when it is only one-half the length of the grain, in order to minimize

91

the loss of starch by the digestion of the endosperm by the germinating embryo. The lesser degree of conversion is responsible for the lower enzyme strength and greater nitrogen complexity of continental malt. Haze-forming proteins that remain in continental malt must be decomposed during a low temperature mash that is unnecessary when using British malt.

American malts are sprouted only slightly beyond the continental malts. American malts are usually one-half to three-fourths the length of the kernel, but because six-row malted barley is of much higher nitrogen content than traditional lager malt, its enzyme strength is correspondingly greater. Therefore, high kiln temperatures can be held longer than with continental malt without risking a serious depletion of the malt's enzyme strength. Both continental and American malts require the employment of a protein rest to degrade albumin in excess of the amount required for body, head, and yeast nutrients.

Steeping

The barley to be malted should be examined and then if it is judged suitable, steeped to thoroughly wet the endosperm mass and float off dust, debris, and lightweight, unmaltable grains. The kernels are stirred in an aerating fashion into water at 50–65°F (10–18°C) which overflows the steeper and carries off the debris, then soaked for two to four days (preferably in alkaline water) to 35 percent m.c. The water is drained, and the moist grains turned several times during steeping to increase oxygen uptake by the respiring barley. The barley may be aerated for up to twelve hours before it is recovered with water. Kernels should be periodically removed and the extent of the moisture penetration determined; wet endosperm is off-white. The grains will have swollen one and one-third times their original size. Before sprouting, the malt should be of 45 percent m.c.

Steely or nitrogenous barley must be wetted even more completely. The moisture content can be verified by weighing a sample of the moist grain, drying it completely at a low oven temperature, and reweighing the dried grain; the weight loss should generally be 40 to 45 percent.

The white tips of the rootlets may be just emerging (chitting) when steeping is complete.

Germination

Barley may be sprouted in many different ways, but the traditional floor malting produces the most uniform growth, as well as the mellowest possible malt. The grain is laid eight to twelve inches thick (thirty-inch maximum) on waterproof concrete, at an ambient temperature of 45–60°F (7–15°C), for six to ten days. It must be wetted and turned periodically to aerate it and to keep the temperature at an even 50–70°F (10–21°C).

[Cooler temperatures encourage greater enzyme production and soluble-carbohydrate yield by impeding acrospire and rootlet growth. Reducing the initial sprouting temperature to below 55°F (13°C) produces the mellowest and enzyme-richest malt. Temperature control is achieved by lowering room temperature and reducing the depth of the sprouting grain to allow the heat being produced by the respiring grain to dissipate.]

Growth should start during the first day as the embryo internally forms immature rootlets; during the second day, the grains are wetted, then aerated by lifting and turning. This is done regularly thereafter. Growth speeds up, and by the fourth day rootlets usually have appeared.

Generally, the acrospire will have grown to one-half the length of the kernel by the sixth day of germination.

The degree of conversion can be judged with some degree of accuracy by comparing the length to which the rootlets have grown against the length of the kernel, and by cutting through the hull and examining the length of the acrospire.

TABLE 13

Rootlet Length	Acrospire Length
1/2 - 3/4 the length of the kernel	½
1 - 1½ times the length of the kernel	¾
1½ - 2 times the length of the kernel	Full

Generally, the acrospire will have grown to ½ the length of the kernel by the sixth day of germination.

The modification of the endosperm proceeds in the same direction and at approximately the same rate as the growth of the acrospire, although modification tends to exceed the acrospire growth of grain malted at lower temperatures.

The green malt should have a clean, wholesome smell and appear plump, with healthy, unwithered rootlets. The endosperm mass should feel chalky when it is rubbed between two fingers. Hard, watery, or gummy malt endosperm is poorly modified.

Kilning

Kilning dries the malt, facilitates removal of the rootlets and gives malt its character. It also reduces the pH in the mash.

The temperature of green lager malt is generally raised to 90°F (32°C) over twenty-four hours to allow the enzymes to continue starch modification and proteolysis. The lumps of tangled grain are gently broken up after drying has begun, but while the green malt is still moist. The temperature is slowly raised to 120°F (49°C) and held for twelve hours to dry the malt, then raised to roasting temperature. It is essential that the malt be bone-dry before it is heated above 120°F (49°C), so that enzyme destruction is minimalized.

Domestic lager malt may be kilned-off at 130-180°F (55-82°C), while British pale-ale malt is kilned very dry, usually at 200-220°F (94-105°C). Temperatures for Czechoslovakian and Bohemian malts are raised very slowly from 120 to 153°F (49-67°C) to completely dry the malt before it is roasted at 178°F (81°C). Vienna malt is kilned at 210-230°F (100-110°C). Dortmund is roasted at 195 to 205°F (90-95°C), while Munich malts are brought up to 210 to 244°F (100-118°C).

Amber malt is made from well-modified grain that is dried to 3 to 4 percent m.c. and then heated to 200°F (93°C) in fifteen to twenty minutes. The temperature is gradually raised to 280 to 300°F (138-150°C) and held there until the color is satisfactory. It gives a coppery color to beer.

Crystal and caramel malts are fully modified during sprouting and loaded into the kiln at 50 percent m.c. They are heated at 150 to 170°F (65-77°C) for one and one-half to two hours without ventilation (to prevent evaporation). This stewing of the malt more or less mashes it, liquifying and saccharifying it, before it is roasted at 250°F (121°C) or above. These malts in 5 to 15 percent concentrations accentuate the fullness of a beer without substantially increasing color. Dextrine and Cara-Pils malts are similarly treated, but kiln temperatures are kept below 240°F (116°C).

Enzymatic malts are slowly germinated at cooler than usual temperatures from six-row, high-nitrogen malt. They are slowly dried to 6 to 8 percent m.c. and kilned at below 145°F (63°C). Coloring malts contribute little fermentable extract. Black and chocolate malts are undermodified during sprouting, dried to 5 percent m.c., and then roasted at 420 to 450°F (215-230°C) for two hours. At 2 to 5 percent they richen color and contribute a burnt or nutty flavor to beer.

Malts that are kilned over open hardwood fires have

special "smoked" flavors (from phenols released from the wood), which are characteristic of certain beers.

In kilning, the maximum temperature is usually held only until the grains are evenly roasted; then the malt is cooled to below 100°F (38°C). Cleaning removes all rootlets and debris. Care must be taken that the malt is not injured and the husk not broken during cleaning. Rootlets are easily screened from the dried grain.

Weight loss during malting and kilning should be roughly 20 percent. Losses are more extreme where the rootlet growth is excessive or the malt has been caramelized during kilning.

Before being mashed, the malt must be binned for twenty to thirty days in a cool, dry place to mellow it, which will later improve wort clarity.

9. CRUSHING THE MALT

BARLEY MALT SHOULD BE MILLED SO THAT THE husk is not shredded, but is split along its length. In this manner, the contents of the crushed kernel are released, and its maximum surface is exposed to enzyme activity without tearing the hulls. Only reasonably intact husks will form a suitably porous filterbed. Shredded hulls, especially in a decoction mash, contribute a rough, harsh palate in the finished beer. The best grist is obtained from six-roll malt mills, which crush the malt by running it between three successive pairs of rolls ten to twelve inches in diameter, each pair being set closer together and turning faster than the previous pair. Screens are placed between each set of rolls to allow the fine grits to fall through, so that they are not pulverized into flour by further crushing. Over 75 percent of the malt may be reduced to grits in this manner— the remaining part being hulls and flour. More than 10 percent flour is undesirable because it balls or cakes readily. Balled flour results in unconverted starch that is inaccessible to enzymes; some would surely wash into the wort during sparging, causing an irreversible haze in the beer.

Milling equipment other than a six-roll mill may be employed, but none yields as good a grind. Only mills equipped

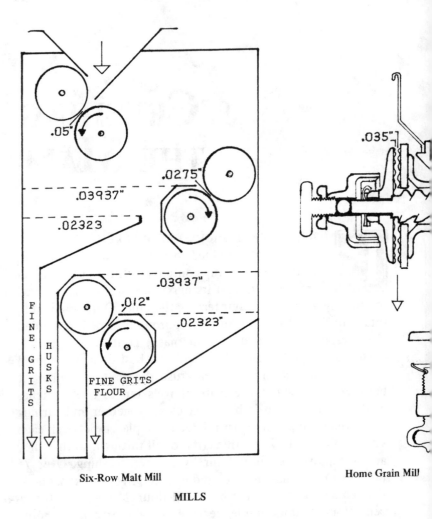

Six-Row Malt Mill   Home Grain Mill

MILLS

with blades that cut the grain are entirely unsuitable, however. Hammer mills and the more commonplace grain mills that employ radially grooved, opposing-face grinding wheels are used, although they tend either to grind grain too finely and shred the husks, or to leave large chunks of the kernel intact. The hard ends of poorly malted grain are particularly subject to being left uncrushed.

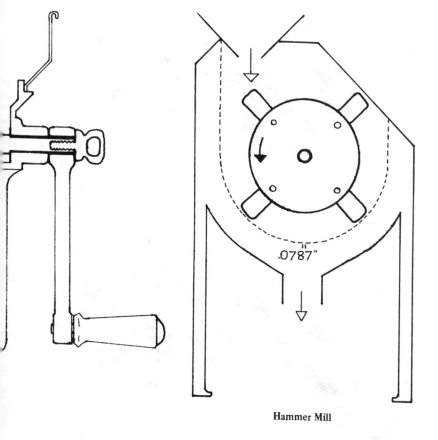

.0787"

Hammer Mill

The resultant heavy, gummy, insufficiently modified starch particles interfere with mash filtering, and like balled flour, undesirably provide a source of unconverted starch to cloud the wort and beer and feed bacteria. Coarsely ground malt also does not yield the extract that it should.

In general, it is better to crush the malt too finely and take extra care doughing-in and sparging very slowly (at the

Well-Crushed

Poorly Crushed

CRUSHED MALT

risk of a set mash) than not to mill it finely enough. Only well-modified malts give up their extract when very coarsely ground—poorly-modified malts especially require adequate milling. If the iodine test after a sufficient mash saccharification rest shows a predominance of very blue-black particles and grain ends (not husk fragments, which always deeply discolor iodine), then crushing was probably insufficient.

Milling for lauter-tub brewing should yield predominantly fine grits.

TABLE 14

U.S. Standard Mesh	Mesh Width	Characteristics	Lauter-Tub Grist Composition
10	.0787 inches	husks held	
14	.05512	husks held	15%
18	.03937	husks held	
30	.02323	coarse grits held	25%
60	.00984	fine grits held	30%
100	.00587	flour held	20%
100	.00587	fine flour falls through	10%

10. MASHING

URING MASHING, THE REDUCTION OF COMPLEX carbohydrates to sugars, and insoluble proteins to simpler amino acid chains, is entirely an enzymatic process. Mashing should yield an extract equal to 65 to 80 percent of the weight of the dry malt (before mashing the malt is only 15 to 25 percent soluble). Not all of this extract is fermentable; in fact, the varying percentages of unfermented "rest extract" give each beer its malt character. The part of any extract that is unfermentable dextrins (sweetness and flavor) and proteins (body) is controlled by manipulation of the times and temperatures of the mash.

Doughing-In

Enzymes act on the malt only in an aqueous solution; water induces the enzymes, encased in the aleurone layer of the malt kernel, to go into extracellular solution with soluble starch and hemicellulose. Because crushed malt, and especially floury malt, tends to "ball" into a dry mass that isolates them from enzyme activity, it is essential to mix the grains with water in a way that does not saturate any part of

TIME/TEMPERATURE GRAPH

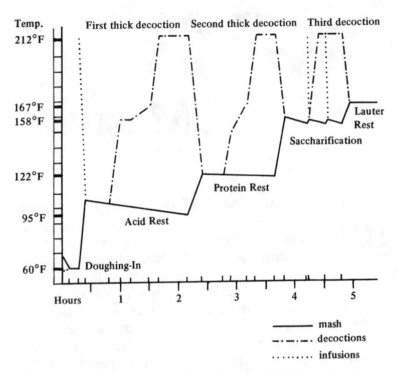

TRADITIONAL THREE-DECOCTION MASH

the mash while another part is still dry. The intention is to create conditions conducive to dissolving all of the endosperm, including the enzyme-rich particles of the aleurone layer, and not to induce enzymatic activity just yet. The even moistening prevents the starch from balling and entirely solubilizes the enzymes.

A successful mixture requires the gradual addition of liquid to the grain which is *doughing-in*. Small amounts of water are sprinkled onto—and then kneaded into—the whole of the grain mass until the crushed malt can absorb no more. Only a small amount of water should be standing free at the bottom of a well-kneaded mash.

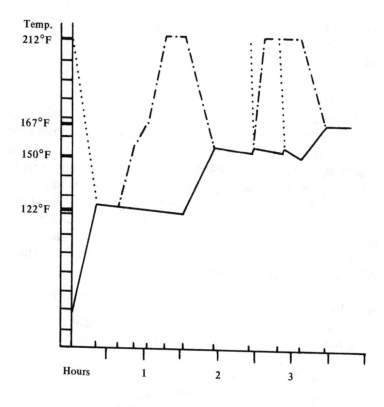

TWO-DECOCTION MASH

Using the least possible amount of water to form a very thick mash improves enzyme effectiveness and simplifies rest-temperature maintenance later on. Liberal infusions of boiling water may then be made during saccharification without overly thinning the mash. In decoction mashing, this is best accomplished by doughing-in the malt with twenty-four to forty fluid ounces of brewing water at 58°F (14°C) (deep-well temperature) per pound of crushed grain.

The doughed-in mash is allowed to stand for fifteen to thirty minutes, the longer time being for malts that are dark, weakly enzymatic, hard-tipped, or poorly malted. At the same time, roughly half the volume of water used to dough-in the malt is brought to boiling. It is infused into the mash to raise the temperature of the whole from 58 to 60°F up to 95 to 105°F (35–38°C).

Mash pH

The correct, initial pH of any mash depends on the type of malt employed, the planned mashing technique, and the anticipated length of time the beer will be aged. It must never be begun at above pH 6.2 or below 4.7. When the mash is from enzyme-poor malt that will be fully decoction mashed and the beer will be well lagered, the mash cycle may begin at pH 5.5 to 5.8. Well-modified malt, such as that of British origin, should mash-in at pH 5.5, or below when infusion mashing. Until the proper initial mash acidity is approximated (within pH 0.2), the mash cycle should not be begun.

Acid Rest

The *acid rest* is solely for correcting the initial mash pH. Very limited bacterial fermentation of glucose to lactic acid, in conjunction with significant phytase activity, acidifies the mash without imparting a harsh flavor to its extract. The rest is most successfully employed when mashing with reasonably soft or sulfate water; it cannot overcome the alkalinity of strongly carbonate waters. Carbonate salts, when present in the brewing water, must first be precipitated by boiling or by adding slaked lime. Otherwise, they must be overcome by the inherent acidity of dark-roasted malt, or by adding acidic mineral salts.

During this rest, the mash should be very tightly covered and aeration avoided to discourage contamination and oxidation by airborne and aerobic bacteria active at these temperatures. The temperature of the mash may be maintained by reasonable dilutions of boiling water; the stiffness of the mash is not nearly so critical as its temperature.

Acidulation of the mash is primarily by the enzyme phytase, active at 86 to 128°F (30–53°C), which dismantles insoluble *phytin*, a salt in which most of the malt phosphate is bound up, to significantly-acidic phytic acid. Generally referred to as an enzyme of malting, reactivation of phytase by the acidic hydrolysis at 95°F (35°C) accounts for a two-fold or threefold increase in the phytic acid in a decoction mash from pale malt. It benefits the mash not only by lowering its pH, but by increasing the mineral content of its liquid extract and producing a rich and accessible source of yeast nutrients, especially myo-inositol, a B-vitamin necessary for yeast growth.

$$Ca_5Mg(C_6H_{12}O_{24}P_6 \cdot 3H_2O)_2$$
Phytin

$+$

$$7H_2O$$

|

Phytase

↓

releases into solution:

$$C_6H_6 [OPO (OH)_2]_6$$
Phytic Acid

$$C_6H_{12}O_6$$
Myo-Inositol

and precipitates:

$$5CaHPO_4 \cdot 2H_2O$$
Calcium Phosphate (Secondary)

$$MgHPO_4 \cdot 3H_2O$$
Magnesium Phosphate (Secondary)

Phytase activity is most dramatic when mashing under-modified malt, less of its malt phosphate having been inverted during malting. Mashes made from highly kilned malts show little pH reduction during an acid rest because phytase is destroyed by the high kiln temperatures. The natural acidity of these malts, however, is usually sufficient for establishing a proper mash pH.

During the rest, the pH of a mash from pale malt drops from 5.5 to 5.8 to pH 5.2 to 5.3. A mash sequence employing an acid rest thus needs to rely less on the brewing water being naturally acidic, or sulfate in character, and begins at a higher pH than an infusion mash.

The rest is not usually held for longer than it takes to boil the first decoction, but when the acidulation occuring within this period is inadequate, some manner of acidifying treatment must be made.

Traditionally, where at mashing-in the pH is above 5.8, a separate "lactic-acid mash" is made prior to the main mashing. A fraction of the mash volume is doughed-in and saccharified, and then rested, closely covered, at 95°F (35°C) for up to several days. The saccharified mash at 95 to 105°F (35–40°C) creates an ideal environment for the fermentation of glucose to lactic acid by Lactobacillus delbruckii [temperature range 86 to 131°F (30–55°C), most active at 107 to 111°F (41–44°C); pH optimum 5.6 to 5.8]. The lactic acid mash is held until its pH drops below 5. It is then intermixed into the main mash to correct its pH.

If the lactic-acid mash begins to smell the least bit rancid, if turbulence or ropiness develops on its surface, or if it is "off" in any way, its temperature must immediately be raised to above 122°F (50°C) to destroy the spoiling aerobic butyric or acetic-acid bacteria. Where thermophilic anaerobes (L. bulgaris, L. brevis, or any of the thermophilic strains of Bacillus) are the source of the spoilage, temperatures may have to go above 140°F (60°C) to terminate the activity. The most common contaminant is the putrefying Clostridium butyricum, which turns the mash rancid and renders it unusable.

Why Decoction Mash?

Although decoction mashing serves to raise the temperature of the mash to the protein, saccharification, and lauter-rest temperatures, its more important function is to cause several significant changes in the boiled portions.

Not even the most thorough infusion mash can eke out the quantity or quality of extract that is obtained by decoction mashing. There are several reasons for this. During decoction mashing, the thick part of the mash passes through the diastatic-enzyme temperature range three times. Also, boiling reduces the size and complexity of malt starch and protein—a process which is absolutely essential when mashing-in difficult malts. Malts such as dark Bavarian, having only one third the enzyme strength of pale malt, cannot be satisfactorily mashed without boiling. Yet infusion mashing never achieves boiling.

Furthermore, decoction mashing also creates a thick mash at saccharification temperature, thus preserving diastatic enzyme strength. Even when a traditional infusion mash is doughed-in thick, so large an infusion of boiling water is required to raise it to saccharification temperature that only a thin mash can be formed, and enzyme viability is drastically curtailed.

Since boiling destroys enzymes, the enzymes in the unboiled mash must be preserved. In a mash that is satisfactorily solubilized during doughing-in, the enzymes are washed into the free liquid when the mash is flooded to raise its temperature to 95°F (35°C). The thickest part of the mash—containing the heaviest and least accessible concentration of native starch and protein—can then be separated out and boiled without decimating the enzyme population.

The heavy decoction is quickly heated to 150 to 158°F (65–70°C), without resting at 122°F (50°C), so that no further enzymatic acidulation of the mash occurs.

There are two good reasons for eliminating this rest and both are based on the pH sensitivity of the diastatic enzymes. First, the dextrinization of native starch by alpha amylase (pH optimum 5.7) is far more effective at the higher pH of this first decoction than later when the whole mash comes into the saccharification range at a far lower pH. Second, the same high pH that stimulates alpha amylase activity retards Beta amylase activity (pH optimum 4.7). Because native starch is far too complex to be successfully reduced by Beta amylase until alpha amylase has reduced it to shorter amylose chains, resting the decoction at saccharifying temperatures is not productive. It is quite enough that the manageable, small dextrins replace the native starch, even when mashing for a high-maltose extract.

Regardless of the diastatic power of the malt, unconverted starch is invariably entrapped within poorly solubilized malt particles after this dextrinization. As the decoction is heated above 167°F (75°C), the particles burst, and their contents are absorbed into the liquid extract. This makes them accessible to alpha amylase activity during the diastatic-enzyme rest of the main mash. This otherwise lost extract increases both the quality and the quantity of the extract yield.

Heating the decoction to boiling reduces the pH of the mash. Boiling it increases mash acidity by precipitating inorganic calcium phosphate.

Boiling also dissolves protein gum. At lower temperatures, protein gum is unaffected by enzyme activity and passes through mashing largely unconverted. Only when thick mash is boiled can the proteolytic enzymes successfully degrade dissolved gum to albuminous fractions; then instead of clouding the beer, the "protein" enhances it. Protein trub precipitated during wort cooling will be dramatically decreased.

Boiling also deoxygenates the mash so that it settles in well-defined layers in the lauter tub. Only the absence of residual protein gum makes this effective filterbed possible; when an infusion mash is employed, such a dense filterbed likely results in a set mash.

In mashing techniques that do not use a decoction sequence, the proteolytic and diastatic enzymes are destroyed before the mash achieves optimum-temperatures for the dissolution of starch particles and protein gum. Then the extract content, clarity, character, fullness, and body of the finished beer are negatively affected. Where the malt is reasonably well-modified and evenly crushed, however, the traditional three decoctions may not be necessary. Doughing-in with boiling water to 95°F (35°C), followed by a second infusion to 122°F (50°C), only a limited protein rest and a single, thick decoction before saccarification may be sufficient.

During decoction mashing, the brewer is at his busiest because he must handle two mashes at the same time with great care. He must be thoroughly organized before plunging into the sometimes hectic decoction mash cycle.

Three-Decoction Mash

First Decoction

The volume of thick mash to be boiled, relative to the volume of the whole mash, is dependent upon mash thickness. A very thick mash requires that only its heaviest one-third part be boiled, along with very little of the mash liquid. Thinner mashes require that proportionally more mash be boiled, along with more liquid. This is because even if all the wet, crushed malt is removed and boiled, it does not contribute enough heat to the resting mash to sufficiently raise its temperature to the next rest.

One pound of crushed malt contributes about the same amount of heat to the mash as does one pint of water; yet it displaces only as much volume as six fluid ounces of water. In a thick mash, the favorable heat-to-volume ratio of the malt is such that the heaviest one-third part can raise the temperature of the whole mash to the next rest. In a thin mash, however, the heat value of the malt is not enough to overcome the far greater amount of water. A greater percentage of the mash must therefore be boiled—but usually not more than 40 percent.

After the decoction has been pulled, the rest mash (cold settlement) is closely covered and held undisturbed, except for occasional mixing to disperse temperature and enzyme activity. Then the mashes are remixed to raise the temperature of the whole to the next rest.

Protein Rest (First Thick Mash)

The stability of the finished beer—its clarity, body, lack of chill haze, and resistance to foreign fermentation and oxidation—is largely established during this protein or "albumin" rest. It "softens" poorly modified malt and improves mash runoff by decomposing heavy, gummy, insufficiently modified malt particles. This rest is essential when the malt is weakly enzymatic in order to allow adequate time under the proper conditions for the fewer enzymes to act.

The strike temperature of the protein rest is 122°F (50°C), although temperatures from 113 to 128°F (45–53°C) won't radically retard enzyme activity. It should be kept in mind, however, that lactic-acid bacteria may be very active at the lower end of this temperature range, and the reduction of large proteins less effective.

The strike temperature must be reached by gradually returning the decoction to the main mash and thoroughly stirring it in. Effective mixing is accomplished by lifting the mash from the bottom of the tub.

The temperature throughout the mash must be regularly monitored as the mixing nears completion. It is essential that the return of the decoction be competently handled so that temperature dispersal is absolutely even. Attempting to correct wide temperature fluctuations within the remixed mash is never easy. In the event that the strike temperature is reached before all the decoction has been returned, the remainder of the boiled mash is force-cooled to 122°F (50°C) before it is returned to the main mash.

It is principally during this rest that complex protein globules are decomposed by proteolytic enzymes to less troublesome fractions. Protease, peptase, and peptidase progressively dissolve the peptide links within the protein coils to liberate coaguable albuminous fractions. These coagulate with the hop resins in the kettle and provide a means for transmitting hop bitterness to the finished beer. It is also albumin, not only protein, that gives beer its body and enables it to raise and support a frothy foam head.

Proteinase dissolves some of the least-complex albumin to individual amino acids, which fuel yeast growth in the early stages of fermentation. Extract efficiency is also enhanced by the protein rest. Extract is exposed by the dissolution of membranous proteins, and complex amylopectin is dismantled by the debranching enzymes (maltase, dextrinase).

Phytase continues its activity during the rest, reducing phytin from the aleurone layer and embryo of the malt to phytic acid. Other acids also rapidly form during the rest, further lowering the pH towards the optimum values for saccharification, the clarification of the wort during boiling, and subsequent yeast fermentation. During this rest, the pH should drop to below 5.4.

Other nonproteolytic enzymes (most notably cytase) actively dissolve pectins and other constituents of the malt hemicellulose during the protein rest.

A thick mash improves enzyme performance. In a thin mash, proteolytic and other heat-labile enzymes are destroyed in the course of the rest; in a thick mash, they may survive into the saccharification range.

The protein digestion can be overdone, however. Devoid of albuminoids, the beer would lack body and a froth head. It would be very stable, but very empty-tasting. Without any coaguable proteins to adhere to, hop tannin would not precipitate from the boil, and the beer would taste "rough."

Reducing nitrogen complexes too far would result in the presence of an excessive amount of simple nutrients in early fermentation, which would encourage bacterial contamination. Later in the fermentation cycle, the yeast would stop reproducing for lack of albuminous matter in suspension from which to extract nutrition.

The degree of protein degradation achieved during this rest may be fairly judged by the thickness and slickness of the protein sludge covering the settled grist in the lauter tub. It should be moderately thick and powdery rather than gummy.

The objectives of the albumin rest should be accomplished within two hours, or the malt is entirely unsuitable for use in brewing. Thirty percent of the malt nitrogen can be expected to have gone into solution at its conclusion. After twenty minutes at $122°F$ ($50°C$), the heaviest part of the mash is again drawn off, to begin the second decoction.

Saccharification Rest

Malt starch occurs as long chains, each link of which is glucose, $C_6H_{10}O_5$. But during the saccharification rest, alpha and Beta amylase reduce starch to its simpler fractions. This yields flavorful dextrins and fermentable sugars.

Alpha amylase very rapidly reduces insoluble native starch to (at least) partially-fermentable polysaccharide fractions (incompletely hydrolyzed starch). Given long enough, the alpha amylase dismantles all these dextrins to maltose, glucose, and small, branched, "a-limit" dextrins, but starch-chain fragments are more effectively saccharified to fermentable sugars by the faster-acting Beta amylase. Beta amylase has no effect on native starch, but in hydrolytic solution, it reduces soluble starch by cleaving glucose molecules from one end of starch chain fragments, and rejoining them in pairs with a water molecule to create maltose, $C_{12}H_{22}O_{11}$.

It is inadvisable to reduce all starch to fully fermentable maltose. Significant quantities of more complex polysaccharides must be carried over into the ferment. Partially fermentable dextrins, oligosaccharides, and especially maltotriose support the yeast during the long, cold aging period, while the unfermentable portions are carried over into the finished beer to give it its desirable special sweetness, richness, and flavor.

The strike temperature of the rest may be from 149 to 160°F (65–71°C), depending on the nature of the beer being brewed. Precisely hitting the appropriate strike temperature is essential, as a variation of two or three degrees for five to ten minutes can dramatically alter the maltose/dextrin ratio of the extract.

Mash thickness also affects the fermentability of the wort. A thick mash (.3 gallons of water per pound of malt) induces the greatest overall extraction. A much thinner mash increases the proportion of maltose, and thus wort attenuation.

The most rapid reduction of the large starch chains in a thick mash occurs at 155 to 158°F (68–70°C), but almost to the exclusion of any maltose formation whatsoever. The richly dextrinous wort produces a sweetness complementary to any darker beer with a contrasting burnt-malt bitterness, such as dark Munich. It is seldom suitable for light-colored beers.

Above 160°F (71°C), strong enzyme action ceases; temperatures below 149°F (65°C), on the other hand, seriously limit dextrin formation while favoring the formation of maltose by Beta amylase. Because starch granules are not gelatinized or dispersed below 149°F (65°C), Beta amylase activity at lower temperatures serves only to eliminate the dextrins formed in the decoction, without further significant starch reduction.

In very light beers, the release of ungelatinized starch into solution at 149°F (65°C) is capitalized upon by raising the temperature of the mash from 131 to 149°F (55–65°C) over fifteen to thirty minutes; this largely eliminates the boiler-mash dextrins, while it softens starch granules. The mash is brought to rest at 149 to 151°F (65–66°C), to gelatinize and dextrinize the starch and produce a maltose/dextrin ratio that favors lightness and rapid maturation.

Full, rich beers require even more careful handling. The decoction must be returned to the rest mash as quickly as possible, but without scalding any part of the main mash or creating wide temperature variations within it. The mash dextrinization strike-temperature should be evenly attained within ten minutes. All of the amber and gold lagers, and even the pale Pilsener/Dortmunder types, rely on the heavier, richer dextrin complement formed at 153 to 155°F (67–68°C).

This is the strike temperature of most "character" beers, with the notable exception of those having a significant burnt-malt palate. Saccharification in this temperature range encourages an alpha/Beta amylase activity ratio greater than 5:1; as a result, the dextrin content of the wort is 25 percent or greater, and the alcohol content by weight of the finished beer is roughly one-third the value of the wort density (°Balling).

As the mash saccharifies, it becomes thicker and browner. The brewer may decide to add brewing water to thin an overly thick mash and to speed up saccharification (Beta amylase is more effective in the looser mash). Caution must be used, however: temperatures above 149°F (65°C) destroy enzymes in a thin mash. Even in a thick mash, Beta amylase is destroyed during a long rest above 149°F (65°C), and alpha amylase is eventually destroyed above 154°F (68°C) in a mash below pH 5.5. This fact must be remembered when mashing to yield a dextrinous wort—a dextrinous wort cannot be formed (and maximum extract yield is not achieved) at below 153°F (67°C).

The mash must be stirred regularly to break up any pockets of unmodified starch and ensure uniform conversion. After fifteen minutes of precise maintenance of the strike temperature, testing for saccharification with iodine should be begun.

Iodine-Starch Conversion Test

Place a small sample of the extract in a porcelain dish. Float common iodine (.02N solution; 1.27g iodine and 2.5g potassium iodide in 500ml water) onto the extract, drop by drop, until a distinct layer of iodine is formed. Note any color change in the iodine at its interface with the mash liquid. Also observe the intensity of the color: is it trace, faint, or strong? Black indicates the presence of native starch; blue evidences gelatinized starch (amylose); red shows amylodextrin. The usual faint purple-to-reddish reaction denotes amylodextrins and erythrodextrins. Total saccharification (a solution of achroodextrins, maltotriose, maltose, and simple sugars) causes no change in the yellow color of iodine.

Iodine is a poison. DISCARD ALL TESTS. Ensure that there is no iodine contamination by immediately washing any article that comes into contact with it. Conduct iodine tests some distance from the mashing, so that no iodine-tainted instrument will be grabbed in haste and contaminate the mash.

It is essential that the starch be reduced to at least achroodextrins (by alpha amylase). Unreduced amylodextrins and erythrodextrins that are carried into the ferment promote the growth of beer "sarcina" (Pediococcus) and the formation of off-tastes, odors, and haze. Even for sweet beers, the reaction with iodine should be no more than faintly red. There should never be a strong color reaction with the iodine; neither, however, should sweet beers be necessarily saccharified to the point where a negative iodine reaction occurs. A very faint reddish reaction indicates an acceptable extract composition for these beers.

The mash should be held at the strike temperature until saccharification is complete. Infusions of boiling water may be made with less regard to enzyme viability as conversion nears completion. The looser mash improves filterbed formation.

Note: Koji or other diastatic enzyme preparations should

not be used to increase enzyme activity. Although they convert hundreds of times their weight in soluble starch to simple sugar, they do not form dextrins.)

If the mash does not saccharify within one hour, it should be stirred, restored to temperature, verified for the proper pH (5.2–5.5), and held for thirty minutes more. If the iodine color is not further reduced, addition of diastatic malt extract is required.

The efficiency of the malt crushing should be gauged at this time. With the back of a spoon, press a sample of the goods until all of the kernel ends and malt particles have been crushed. Repeat the iodine test, as above. If the color at the iodine-mash interface is intensely black or blue, then crushing was insufficient or the malt was poorly doughed-in. (Some faint color from the exposed starch is to be expected; the husk particles themselves will always turn intensely black). Suspicions regarding the efficiency of milling may be verified either by a wort density that is less than predicted or by weighing the dried spent-mash. (See end of this chapter.) If extract efficiency is below 65 percent, the malt has probably been insufficiently crushed.

Final Decoction

When the starch end-point has been verified, the *very thinnest* part of the mash is removed to be boiled. This is usually 40 percent although a very thin mash may require boiling half of the mash. Because there are fewer starch and albuminous particles in the thinner portion, there is less risk of these being decomposed during the boiling and spoiling the runoff. These may remain in the mash tub to be further saccharified. On the other hand, enzymatic reduction of the dextrins in the thin part of the mash will be more quickly terminated as well, preventing oversimplification of the extract.

The lauter-decoction is brought to boiling, while being stirred, in ten to fifteen minutes and is held at a strong boil for a further fifteen to forty-five minutes. The temperature of the rest mash is held at or slightly above the strike temperature during boiler-mash processing.

The boiled extract must be returned to the heavy mash very slowly, pulling the goods up from the bottom of the mash tub to effect a good mix. Care should be taken that the strike temperature of the final rest, 167 to 170°F, (75–77°C) is not exceeded. Temperature adjustments may be made by the infusion of either cold or boiling brewing water, as required.

Exact temperature maintenance is, as before, critically important. Too low temperatures do not terminate enzyme activity nor expand particles of intermediate starch degradation enough to keep them in temporary suspension up and away from the bottom of the mash filter. But at too high temperatures, the starch granules burst, and insufficiently modified carbohydrate and albuminous matter become dissolved and unfilterable. Because the diastatic and proteolytic enzymes have been destroyed by the high temperatures, the starch and protein gum have no opportunity to be reduced to manageable fractions.

The mashing-off temperature may be maintained for up to one-half hour while the mash is roused up. The mixing must be very thorough, so that the mash settles only very slowly and forms a well-delineated filter bed.

Sparging

As the lauter mash rest draws to its conclusion, its temperature should be restored to 167 to 170°F (75–77°C) if it has cooled. The mash should be very thin and very thoroughly intermixed to encourage the absorption of the malt extract into solution and to temporarily force small starches and proteins into suspension, allowing the husks to freely settle. The purpose of sparging/filtering is to rinse the soluble extract free from the malt husks and to trap insoluble, poorly modified starch, protein, lipids, and silicates within the husks. Without adequate filtering, extract is lost, while the mash runoff is clouded by starch, proteins, and husk particles. This produces beer likely to be cloudy, astringent, and unstable.

Lauter Tub

The mash is then transferred to a lauter tub for filtering. The diameter of the vessel should allow the filterbed to form to a depth of twelve to eighteen inches. A filterbed of six-row barley, however, may need to be only six inches thick; the greater percentage of husks in six-row barley increases its filtering efficiency.

The husks accumulate on a false bottom, or filter plate, that fits one-eighth to two inches above the real bottom of the lauter tub. Slots or perforations in the plate allow the sparge water to slowly and evenly filter through the husks. Where a filter plate is not available, a fine-mesh bag can be substituted. The lauter tub itself must be equipped with a spigot located below the level of the false bottom to draw the extract-rich sweet wort off the grain mass.

Setting the Filter

The lauter tub should be filled to one half inch above the false bottom with water 175°F (80°C) to boiling before the hot mash is introduced. This preheats the lauter tub and reduces the amount of debris that is otherwise carried into the space below the false bottom. This practice largely eliminates the need for flushing the space prior to filtering and improves the clarity of the runoff.

The thin lauter mash is quickly added to the tub, given a last thorough stirring, and allowed to settle. An infusion mash does not settle in well-defined stratification as does a decoction mash and tends to "float." The suspended particulate matter somewhat offsets the lack of a clearly defined filterbed, as it entraps less extract. However, it never yields so clear a runoff as does a decoction-mashed filtering. Commercially, false bottoms for infusion mashes generally have larger slots than those used for decoction mashes.

MASH FILTERBED

Within twenty to thirty minutes, the liquid displaced by the settling mash should show clear and black above a nebulous cloud of trub. If it doesn't clear, then filtering efficiency will be very poor. The temperature of the mash is likely to drop during the setting of the filterbed; every effort, however, should be made to limit its heat loss.

The heavy hulls that settle onto the false bottom are covered by a deeper layer of lighter hull fragments and endosperm particles in a well-mixed mash. Until this porous filtermass has formed, tiny, gelatinized particles of starch and protein must remain suspended in the liquid; after, they should settle out, forming the pasty "protein-sludge" or upper dough.

If this trub precipitates too early, and settles within the hulls in any appreciable quantity, it will wash into the sweet wort runoff, inviting bacterial contamination and oxidation in the ferment. It may also cake within the filterbed and cause a set mash that blocks the flow of liquid down through the filterbed. Either a set mash or a runoff that doesn't clear may be due to ineffective crushing and mashing.

Sparge Water

A volume of water roughly 25 percent greater than the mash and extract in the lauter tub should be heated to 170 to 176°F (77–80°C) in preparation for sparging. The temperature of the sparge water is critical because sugars flow more freely in hot solution than in cold. Its temperature must be maintained throughout the sparging to dissolve and rinse free the extract cupped in the hulls or adhered to the malt particles.

Excessive temperatures, however, [above 170°F (77°C)] rupture balled native starch particles and decompose the protein sludge. These are then carried away in the runoff. Because only very simple protein and carbohydrate fractions can be managed by culture yeast, none of these more complex fragments should be allowed in the wort.

If necessary, the salt content or acidity of the sparge water should be adjusted, preferably with calcium salts, to limit extraction of harsh-tasting malt fractions and improve clarity. The pH of the runoff should never rise more than 0.7 during sparging, and at no time should it exceed pH 6. Better results are achieved when the runoff pH does not rise more than .2 to .5.

Carbonate waters in excess of pH 7.5 are not useful for sparging because they induce haze fractions and silicates into solution and may induce renewed enzyme activity. These waters become even more alkaline upon heating. Carbonate salts must be precipitated before the water is used for sparging.

Preparing to Sparge

To set the filterbed and settle the protein sludge, the lauter tub spigot is opened ten minutes after the liquid has cleared. The liquid is run off very slowly over a period of up to two hours until it stands less than one half inch deep above the surface of the mash. This liquid level must be maintained throughout sparging. Draining below the surface level causes the mash to settle too tightly and the protein sludge to cake. Extract efficiency is irreversibly reduced and the potential for developing a set mash increases.

With the spigot closed, the mash surface is carefully leveled and smoothed with the back of a spoon or ladle to fill in all the depressions. The space below the false bottom is purged of particulate matter by flushing it with clear, 170°F (77°C) water, either through an inlet below the false bottom, opposite the spigot, or through a tube thrust down through the mash. The inlet and runoff rates must be carefully matched to avoid disturbing the filterbed above. Flushing can be eliminated only if very little debris has collected above the spigot. A cloudy runoff must be refiltered through the mash until it runs clear.

Sparging

The lauter-tub spigot is opened until a steady trickle runs. The liquid level above the filterbed is maintained by the careful return of the cloudy runoff, until the sweet wort runs clear.

Only runoff that yields a negative (or very faint red) iodine reaction should be introduced to the wort kettle. A sample is taken, and a hydrometer floated in it. The extract content should be twice that expected of the boiled and cooled wort. A beer of 12° Balling (SG 1049) should have a first runoff of 24°B (SG 1098). If the first wort is less than 18°B (SG 1074), too much water has been infused and the clear wort runoff must be recycled until the extract concentration rises. Otherwise, too much wort must be collected, and the boiling unnecessarily extended. As a rule, if more than one and a half quarts of water per pound of malt has been used in mashing, the first runoff must be recycled.

When all the hazy runoff has been returned to the lauter tub, sparging is begun. The 170°F (77°C) spray must be as fine and as evenly dispersed as possible, so it evenly percolates through the mash and diffuses all the extract from it. The sparging rate should be free from surges and matched to the runoff rate, so that the liquid level in the lauter tub is not changed.

The sparging/runoff rate may be gradually increased, but not so much so that turbidity is caused in the run off. Set mashes may also result from too violent a flow rate.

High-husk, six-row barley may be runoff in less than two hours (a six-inch deep bed may be filtered in as little as one-half hour). But maximum extraction is achieved with a very slow runoff rate, a deeper filterbed, and also raking the mash with a knife to within six inches of the false bottom. Restructuring the filterbed ensures even percolation of the water through the grain and complete extraction of the sugars. A mash that is raked, is from finely ground malt, or shows a tendency to set must be run off slowly. Set mashes that don't respond to being stirred must be cut repeatedly during sparging in order to reopen channels of extract flow.

Within one to two hours, the greater part of the extract will have been leached from the malt. Although the maximum yield is obtained by restricting the runoff rate so that it takes four hours to collect the sweet wort, the small percentage of extract gained is usually not worth the effort.

Temperature should be carefully maintained during sparging and filtering, although some drop in the runoff temperature is expected. As soon as the extract has cleared it should be run into a kettle and heated to above 170°F (77°C). Generally, the sweet wort is brought to boiling and hopped as soon as it has covered the bottom of the kettle.

As the color of the runoff pales, its extract content is periodically checked with the hydrometer; when the reading drops to below 2°B [SG 1008, corrected to 60°F (15.56°C)], sparging is discontinued and all the free liquid is drained from the grist.

Below this density, the runoff pH is likely to rise above pH 6, increasing the likelihood that malt tannins, lipids, and silicates will be leached into it. Malt tannins give an astringent taste and are harsher-flavored than hop tannins. They are more soluble and are not as readily precipitated in the kettle. Lipids interfere with foam stability and increase ester-formation giving a cardboardy, stale flavor to the beer.

Extract Efficiency

After sparging, the spent grain can be drained and dried to its original moisture content (determined by weighing, oven-drying and then reweighing a sample of the whole malt) as a method of determining malt extraction. The weight of the dried, spent grain subtracted from the weight of the malt doughed-in yields the extract in the wort. Divided by the weight of the doughed-in malt, this exercise shows the extract efficiency as a decimal percentage. The yield determined by this method is always lower than the hydrometer reading predicts. This is because the extract in solution has water bound to it, causing an increase in the liquid pressure unaccounted for by the weight loss of the spent grains.

11. BOILING THE WORT

VIGOROUSLY BOILING THE MASH RUNOFF PRO-
duces several desirable effects: boiling destroys
mash enzymes, sterilizes the wort, and stabilizes
salts in solutions. It extracts hop resins and tannins, drives off harsh hop oils, and coagulates and precipitates unstable protein. Boiling also evaporates excess water,
lowers the wort pH, and creates a stable medium for controlled fermentation by the culture yeast. Boiling may begin
when enough wort has been collected to cover the bottom of
the kettle. When the sweet wort is from a decoction mash,
the kettle hops are usually added at this time.

Boiling Hops

The hops are broken up into small clumps and scattered
over the surface of the violently boiling wort. They may be
added all at once, but more commonly, they are meted out in
portions throughout the boil. The actual sequence is determined by the character of the hop that is meant to be carried
over into the finished beer.

Hops added early-on in the boil ensure a more complete
precipitation of proteins, hop tannins, and hop particles,

thus providing a cleaner fermentation. Their longer boil also succeeds in isomerizing alpha resins and in bonding 25 to 30 percent of the iso-a-acids to the wort. This results in a greater percentage of the hops' bittering and preservative qualities being carried into the finished beer.

Most of these hop resins are transported into the ferment in combination with simple albumins, forming tiny substances-in-solution known as *colloids*. This colloidal matter is not significantly precipitated by hop tannin and is largely responsible for forming the body and head of the finished beer. Because their surface area is disproportionately greater than their volume, colloids do not normally settle out of solution. Consequently, their contribution to the beer's body is not offset by inherent instability, as is the case with non-colloidal protein.

When the wort is the product of an infusion mash, it should be boiled vigorously for fifteen to thirty minutes before the hops are added to decompose and precipitate some of the proteins. If this is not accomplished before the hops are added, then most of the sticky hop resins will combine with the coarse protein flocks and precipitate out of solution. Even this intense initial boil, however, does not eliminate the large proteins as effectively as do the processes of decoction mashing. Although the proteins can be precipitated, they cannot be dissolved into less troublesome albumin, peptides, and amino acids because all enzyme activity has been terminated by the boil.

When the wort is the product of a decoction mash, excessive complex proteins aren't usually a problem. The several boilings and restings largely reduce or eliminate them. Decoction-mashed wort can therefore be hopped more conservatively than infusion-mashed wort, simply because the hops need not overcome a great amount of protein.

All of the aromatic hop character of the finished beer is lost during a long boil. These volatile, essential oils and esters can be preserved by adding a portion of the hops later in the boil. It is usual, in fact, to add the loose hops in two and sometimes three portions. Only decoction-mashed beers that employ hops for their preservative contribution rather than for their flavor and aroma fully extract the entire quantity of hops during a ninety-minute or longer boil.

Beers that are heavily hopped in the beginning of the boil exhibit a cleaner kraeusen fermentation head and are more stable than beers hopped either lesser or later. It is essential that most of the hops should be vigorously boiled in the uncovered wort for ninety minutes to isomerize alpha acid, precipitate tannin and proteins, and drive off harsh-tasting essential oils from the bittering hops. Generally, the largest portion of the boiling hops are added to the kettle with the first mash runoff; then the smaller portion is cast into the wort thirty minutes before the boil ends. *Finishing* hops, which give the beer a sharp hop flavor and bouquet, may be added within the last minutes of the boil, as the wort is struck from the kettle, or as an extract during fermentation.

Hop Rates

The quantity of hops is determined by several factors: the desired strength of hop character in the finished beer; the alpha-acid content and condition of the hops; the quantity of protein that must be precipitated from the wort; and the efficiency of the hop extraction.

However, hop acids have limited solubility and they precipitate out of the wort during cooling when they are in excess. Extravagant hop rates are thus pointless. Lower hop rates also produce fewer oxidized hop resins and particles that must be skimmed from the fermentation head.

Usual lager hop rates are approximately .2 to .35 ounces of dry hops per gallon of cooled wort, but they may be as low as .15 ounces or as high as .55 ounces per gallon. This depends on hop quality and alpha-acid content and the beer type and its density. Contrary to what might be expected, hop acids become less soluble as wort density increases. Kettle-hop rates are not increased to reflect the density of strong beers; rather, finishing-hop rates may be increased so that hop flavor, not bitterness, balances their sweetness.

Establishing the Evaporation Rate

As soon as all of the sparging runoff has been brought to a full boil, its extract content and volume are measured. With the hops fully submerged, correct to 60°F (15.56°). Correct the volume to 60°F by multiplying volume at full boil by .9615. These figures establish the evaporation rate necessary to evaporate the wort to the desired volume and concentration within the prescribed parameters of the boil. The usual evaporation rate in an uncovered boil is at least 10 percent per hour.

Never proceed with a boil that would yield less wort than is needed to satisfy fermenting, priming, topping-up or kraeusen, and yeast culturing requirements. If a correction must be made, then the extract content must be allowed to vary from what was expected. Too great or too small a volume of sweet wort is of less concern; it can be reduced by a longer boil (at the cost of darkening the beer), or increased by brewing-water infusions or covering the kettle for part of the boil. Where extract-poor malt, inefficient mashing or sparging, or miscalculation results in a wide disparity between the density that was expected and what occurs, a lighter beer must be accepted. The only alternative is to increase the extract content with malt-extract or wort, should any be available.

Never boil for less than the prescribed time. Overpressure boiling can reduce kettle time, but it alters the beer flavor. The kettle may be covered for part of the boil to control evaporation, but the wort must be vigorously boiled, uncovered, for the final thirty minutes to drive off harsh, volatile, boiling-hop and malt oils, sulphur compounds, ketones, and esters.

Never simmer the wort in lieu of a vigorous boil. Efficient albumin/resin bonding and protein/tannin precipitation is achieved only through the agitation of the boil. In fact, a violent boil has the greatest influence on the stabilization of the wort. If movement cannot be induced by the circulation of thermal currents in the wort (heating in an angular-shaped kettle improves circulation), then agitation becomes increasingly important. Oxygenation improves flocculation, but at the cost of oxidizing and discoloring the wort. Aeration of the mash, wort, or beer at any time except during wort cooling should be avoided.

Once adjustments to the volume of the wort have been made, the evaporation rate should be established and maintained for the duration of the boil.

Finally, the pH of the boil should be checked in a sample cooled to 60°F (15.56°C). Optimum protein flocculation occurs at above pH 5.5, and an initial pH of 5.5 to 5.8 is usually appropriate. Lower pH values produce fewer, smaller flocks; below pH 5.0, the protein does not coagulate. Whenever the pH is less than optimal, agitation and movement within the kettle become increasingly important to flock size.

The pH of the wort drops during boiling as calcium phosphate is precipitated out of solution (sodium and potassium phosphate are unaffected by boiling); usual pH reduction is approximately 0.2 for a sweet wort of 5.5, and .3 for a pH of 5.8 or so.

Hot Break (Kettle Break)

Samples periodically taken from the wort and viewed in a glass container should reveal the progressive flocculation of albuminous protein with hop tannin (polyphenols). Invisible in suspension, they first appear as a mist of tiny flakes that cloud the wort soon after boiling commences. The rolling motion of the boil causes the malt proteins to collide with and adhere to the sticky hop polyphenols. The particles rapidly coagulate into a much smaller number of larger flocks one-eighth inch across, roughly composed of 50 to 60 percent protein, 20 to 30 percent polyphenols, 15 to

20 percent resins, and 2 to 3 percent ash. Upon resting, these large flocks should readily precipitate, leaving the sample brilliantly clear.

Cold Break

As the end of the prescribed boil approaches, the samples taken should be force cooled to below 50°F (10°C) and examined. The wort that showed clear when it was hot should cloud slowly as it cools, as previously invisible coagulum loses its solubility in the cooler solution. This cold break should settle, again leaving the wort clear, bright, and sparkling.

The wort must be boiled past a positive cold break in the sample, and flavoring hops should not be added until after the break has been achieved. It is very important that the break samples be evaluated; however, boiling should not be extended beyond the recommended time even when the break is poor. The scarcity of flocculum in a well-agitated, strong boil at the proper pH may be caused by malt of poor quality or by an excessively long or insufficient albumin rest. In the first case, almost all the albumin has been reduced to amino acids or retained in the spent grain and the beer is thin. In the latter case, the protein is too complex to coagulate, and the beer lacks stability and suffers serious oxidation and taste impairment.

In any case, no correction is possible if temperature, pH, and movement of the wort are all satisfactory. The boiling should not be extended unless it is subsequent to a pH or temperature adjustment to the wort.

If a satisfactory break cannot be established because proteolysis has been insufficient, the only recourse is to rack the beer off its sediment several times during fermentation and lagering to separate it from decaying proteins in the trub. Even so, the beer will invariably be cloudy, bitter, and astringent.

Finishing Hops

Finishing hops are usually the very finest hops and are chosen for their flavoring or aromatics. Generally they are only a small fraction of the quantity of boiling hops employed. Fragrant hops are broken up and added to the kettle, or an extraction of their hop oils is infused into the kettle, cooled wort, or fermented beer.

The later in the brewing cycle that finishing hops are added, the greater their bouquet will be. When whole hops are added after the wort is struck from the kettle, however, there is a greater risk that excessive tannin, oxidation of hop particles, or microbial contamination may ruin the flavor and stability of the beer.

Flavoring hops are commonly added ten or fifteen minutes before the end of the boil, so that they are effectively extracted as the wort is filtered through the hop bed. They contribute no bitterness to the beer, and little aroma, but give the beer a crisp hop flavor.

Later addition of hops is made only when a distinctive hop aroma is desired. Traditionally whole hops were added even up to the point of bottling, but a hop extract may be substituted. The extract is made by steeping aroma hops for ten minutes at pH 5.5 or above in four fluid ounces of wort per each half ounce of hops. This extract is strained through the hops, and the hops sparged. The extract is not usually added until after the wort has been strained, so that none of it is lost in the hop and trub residue. This achieves a cleaner kraeusen head than adding loose or bagged hops post-kettle, and therefore less risk of contamination. The aromatic character of an extract varies some from that achieved by dry-hopping: boiling drives off some volatile essential oils while extracting others. Overall, aroma from an extract is milder.

The hop nose and flavor characteristic of most lagers is obtained by adding loose hops or extract to the wort at or shortly before the conclusion of the boil. Later additions can produce a strong (often vegetative) aroma that is usually complementary to or characteristic of only very strong, dark beers. The sharp hop nose and flavor of some light lagers is more often attributable to liberal kettle finishing-hop rates.

Hop nose and flavor are matters of personal preference; finishing-hop rates may be adjusted to suit the brewer's preference, as well as to reflect the aromatic quality of the hops being used.

Straining the Wort

At the end of the recommended boiling period, the wort should be at its desired volume and concentration (both corrected to 60°F (15.56°C). It should be well-agitated for several minutes, then be covered and allowed to rest without heat until the spent hops and the trub settle out of the wort. The wort should show clear and bright within thirty minutes. It should be filtered before it cools below 170°F (77°C).

The hot wort may simply be siphoned off its hop and trub residue, but this causes an unreasonable amount of extract to be lost. It is more efficient to strain the wort through a loose bed of hops two inches thick in a large strainer or on a false bottom perforated with 1/16-inch holes on 1/8-inch centers (or slots .062 inches wide covering 30 percent of the surface). The extract is run off very slowly at first to settle the hops. Then it is returned to the liquid above the filterbed until it runs clear.

The first clear runoff may immediately be force cooled and mixed with the yeast starter to facilitate adaptation of the yeast upon pitching. When all of the clear wort has been run off, the hops should be slightly sparged with up to eight fluid ounces of boiling water per ounce of hops, or until the density of the runoff drops below 5°B (SG 1020). The extract still retained by the hops is insignificant—never attempt to press or wring out the last of it. Great care should be taken to see that only clear runoff is run into the wort cooling vessel.

Cooling the Wort

The clear runoff must quickly be cooled to separate the cold break trub from the wort. Fast cooling is essential; the more slowly the wort cools, the more protein is trapped in suspension, giving rise to chill haze and harsh, sulfurlike aftertastes in the beer. The cold break should be roughly 10 to 20 percent of the volume of the hot break sediment, and be much less coarse.

Cooling in lager breweries traditionally took place in shallow, open coolships to present maximum surface for air cooling. Better flocculation is achieved, however, by force cooling the wort and employing a deeper settling tank, closely covered against contamination. Below 145°F (63°C), care must be taken to prevent contamination of the wort by airborne wild yeast and bacteria or unsterilized equipment. The wort must be force cooled to below 50°F (10°C) to secure a satisfactory break. Complete precipitation of tannin/proteins—and thus brilliantly clear beer—is achieved by cooling the wort until it becomes slushy. But cooling to 39 to 43°F (4–6°C) before racking the beer off of its settlement is generally sufficient.

Since boiling the wort drives its oxygen out of solution, it must be aerated to force oxygen back in. Yeast require considerable (4 to 14 ppm) molecular oxygen during respiration; without it, they autolyze. Cells that survive an oxygen-starved respiratory phase taint the ferment with abnormal, estery flavors. Their lag phase is characteristically shortened, and their fermentation sluggish.

In an oxygenated wort, the yeast splits the sugar molecule in such a fashion that it produces more CO_2 than alcohol. The carbonic gas rising to the surface quickly forms a blanket above the ferment which insulates it from airborne infection. It may also carry with it a film of debris that can be readily skimmed from the head during the kraeusen stage of fermentation.

Aeration by rousing the wort when it is hot saturates the

wort more completely than does aeration of the cooled wort. The risk of airborne contamination is less while the wort is above 145°F (63°C). Also, aeration of the hot wort causes some of the oxygen to combine with protein fractions, improving the cold break. However, oxidative polymerization of polyphenols to tannins, and oxidation of hop resins and other wort constituents, is greater. The color darkens when the hot wort is aerated and flavor oftentimes suffers irreversible damage.

Very pale, very dark, or full-bodied worts should never be aerated while hot; dark-colored and malty beers are perilously subject to oxidation. Aerating the cooled wort (at 60°F (16°C) or below) yields satisfactory oxygen dissolval (up to 8 ppm), but the atmosphere must be essentially sterile to preclude contamination of the extract. In all cases, the wort should be conservatively aerated unless experience shows that the subsequent yeast lag phase will be unreasonably brief or fermentation weak.

The cold break should be well-settled before the wort is racked into the fermenter. The pH of the wort must be 5.0 to 6.0 for fermentation to be successful. With infusion-mashed and ale worts, a pH of 5.2 is usual, but for lager beers a cooled-wort pH of 5.3 to 5.5 is normal.

12. FERMENTATION

NY SUCCESSFUL FERMENTATION PROCEEDS along a predictable course dictated by the composition of the wort. The amount of extract, its dextrin/maltose ratio, the amount and complexity of the nitrogenous matter, the availability of yeast nutrients, the pH, and the oxygen saturation and biological purity of the wort are values that have been fixed by mashing a particular malt, and boiling, cooling, and aerating the wort.

The only significant influences upon the fermentation that can be manipulated by the brewer are those of the yeast—its character, purity, vitality, quantity, and its rousing—and the temperature and duration of the ferment. Changes in any one of these can affect the residual-sugar, mouthfeel, clarity, aromatic esters, acids, and aldehydes of the beer.

Preparing for Pitching

The fermentation cycle should never be started with a weak yeast; it will only be made weaker upon being diluted into the wort. The yeast to be pitched should have been cultured in a wort similar to that being brewed. Yeast that must undergo significant adaptation suffers a high rate of mortality

137

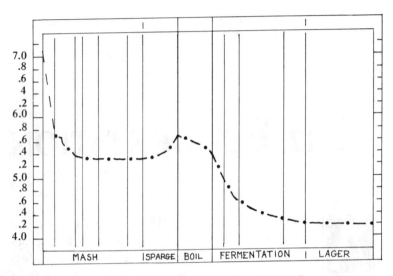

pH in TYPICAL LAGER BREWING

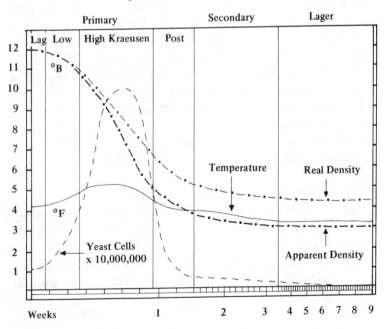

causing fermentation to start slowly and be relatively weak. The likelihood of contamination dramatically increases and decomposition of dead yeast cells mars the beer flavor.

Sugar solutions should not be used to culture yeast. When yeast is cultured in solutions lacking maltose, it loses its ability to absorb maltose and suffers from unreasonably long periods of adaptation upon being diffused into the wort.

The culture should yield approximately .5 to .6 fluid ounces (10–14 g.) of a pasty, thick yeast sediment per gallon of wort to be pitched. Up to one fluid ounce (21 g.) of yeast is necessary for each gallon of wort when a very strong start is needed or when the yeast is a weak fermenter. The greater amount of yeast is also needed to ferment a wort of very low or high extract content. In the first case, more yeast ensure an adequate start in the nutrient-poor environment, and in the latter case are needed to ferment the greater amount of extract.

Pitching too much yeast, however, overtaxes the supplies of dissolved oxygen, simple sugars, and yeast nutrients. This causes *autolysis,* or self-digestion, of the yeast resulting in beer with yeasty, sulfur-like flavors. Less yeast than the amount recommended above should be pitched when the yeast strain has proven to be a very strong fermenter. A good culture should require only .4 fluid ounces (8.5 g.) of yeast slurry per gallon of wort. Conservative pitching rates of healthy yeast produces more aromatic beers and are the rule unless experience dictates otherwise. Conservative pitching rates should not be confused with inadequate pitching rates. Too few yeast result in long lag phases, slower reproduction, retarded growth rates that taint the beer with estery aromas, less overall attenuation of the wort, and increased risk of contamination.

The pitching yeast should be clear, its sediment thick and rich, and its aroma pure and pleasant. If the culture is collected from the parent ferment at the height of kraeusen, the sediment will be composed mainly of healthy yeast. Then regular rousing of the culture produces more yeast and a richer sediment. Dusty yeast that remains suspended and does not form a rich sediment by the time it has thrown up a rocky foam-cover is unsuitable for pitching.

The yeast culture is the most significant source of microbial infection to the ferment. A culture that smells, tastes, or looks contaminated will produce disastrous results if pitched. Yeast must be handled carefully, so that the brewing strain is cultured, and not wild yeast or bacteria.

If a dry yeast absolutely must be pitched, then slurry two grams of granulated yeast per gallon of cooled wort into twice its volume of sterile 120°F (49°C) water. After twenty minutes, mix it into four fluid ounces of wort at room-temperature to minimize shock-excretion while the dessicated yeast resuscitates. Rouse it by pouring it back and forth between two sterile vessels, allowing it to splash freely into each until the solution forms a frothy head. Cover it and rest it for thirty minutes. It should be visibly fermenting before it is further diluted and slowly cooled to pitching temperature.

(A note of caution: granulated dry yeast may be contaminated by significant quantities of bacteria. It is probably the least viable and most-often contaminated source of brewing yeast. Subculturing from a slant, frozen, or liquid culture, or kraeusening from a healthy ferment, is more likely to produce a satisfactory fermentation cycle.)

Before pitching, the yeast is forcefully roused into the first clear runoff from the kettle (force cooled to the pitching temperature and racked off of its sediment). The purpose is to aerate and evenly distribute the yeast, and allow it to adapt to the extract while the rest of the wort is being force cooled and sedimented. The solution should be kept covered until it is used for pitching.

Cooled wort in excess of that to be fermented is poured into the containers in which it will be stored. It is heated in a boiler (or steamed) until it comes to a boil, then capped and cooled. The containers should be of a suitable size for further topping-up and priming or kraeusening, and for yeast culturing. The amount of wort removed should at least be equal to the requirements listed in Table 18. Refrigerate the tightly capped containers until needed; they will keep for at least six months at 33°F (1°C).

Kraeusening

Kraeusen is the German word used to describe the infusion of a strongly fermenting young beer into a larger volume of wort or an aged beer that is past the stage of strong fermentation. Kraeusen beer introduces vigorous yeast in its own sugar-rich substratum. It is characterized by the active raising of a tightly-knit or rocky foam head. Visible yeast colonies should be suspended in the liquid below.

Kraeusen beer should be taken only from ferments that exhibit textbook characteristics. Although successive kraeusening may encourage the culturing of wild or dusty yeast, it still remains the best method by which fermentation may be induced in the cooled wort.

The culture must be strong, so that it is not overwhelmed by the larger volume of wort or unable to renew active fermentation in a well-aged, extract-depleted beer. Kraeusen was traditionally obtained from a strong primary fermentation, but it may be made from wort and a yeast culture. In fact, this is known as a *yeast starter*. Sterile wort is pitched with a culture, and its volume is increased to at least 5 percent of the wort volume by doubling. (The starter volume is built by adding wort in up to a 10:1 ratio when fermentation becomes apparent.) It should be in full kraeusen when it is pitched.

When 10 percent new beer (just coming into high kraeusen) is used to induce fermentation in the cooled wort, yeast lag-phase is virtually eliminated. The yeast, having adapted to the solution, require no respiratory phase to develop a cell membrane and enzymes appropriate to the given wort. Initial fermentation is stronger. Employing kraeusen beer to top-up the secondary (lager) fermenter induces a strong temporary fermentation and reduces the risk of oxidation and contamination at racking.

When wood chips (see p. 165) are used to clear the lager beer, *aufkraeusening* is absolutely necessary. That is, there must be movement of the aged beer so that every part comes into contact with the latticework of chips. Introducing kraeusen beer at a temperature 5°F (3°C) warmer than the aging beer creates the necessary movement of the whole volume of beer. The chips alone could not otherwise clarify an aged beer.

Krauesening also reduces lagering time by introducing vigorous fermentation capable of more rapid metabolism of the small amount of fermentable sugar in the aging beer than the few yeast cells already in the solution.

Introduction of 10 to 15 percent new beer at bottling produces a smoother beer with finer bubbles than other means of carbonation. It more completely bonds carbonic gas to the beer so that carbonation is less apparent. This is the only means by which a truly smooth beer can be brewed.

The kraeusen-beer head should be skimmed free of particulate matter before use. Good sanitary procedures are an absolute necessity. Whether it is being mixed with wort or with aged beer, the new beer should be well-roused in.

Pitching the Yeast

As soon as the first part of the wort is cooled, the pitching culture is forcibly roused and then uncovered. It is diluted into up to five times its volume of cooled wort, then further roused, covered, and left to rest.

When the wort temperature reaches 39 to 43°F (4-6°C), it is allowed to rise freely as it is racked off its cold-break sediment by siphoning or decanting, so that it runs into the primary fermenter at the same time that the yeast culture, starter, or kraeusen beer is added. Going into the fermenter it should be at 42 to 47°F (6-8°C); the pitching solution may be up to 5°F (3°C) warmer than the wort. Gentle rousing should be continued throughout the transfer to achieve an intimate admixture.

Care should be taken that the wort's trub sediment is not disturbed, especially as its draining nears completion. Good hot and cold breaks are meaningless if a significant amount of trub is carried into the ferment. Racking should cease as soon as the runoff shows the least bit cloudy; trub carried into the ferment taints the beer with objectionable flavors and aromas.

Proteinaceous precipitate from the hot and cold breaks forms the greatest part of the trub. Although amino acids are absolutely necessary for yeast metabolic functions, yeast react to an excess of simple protein by generating aromatic fusel alcohols. Even more of these volatile carbonyl compounds are excreted when the wort has been underoxygenated. Fusel alcohols are subject to esterization, which produces bananalike or solventlike odors, and to oxidation, which forms aldehydes, that taste stale.

Trub also contains polyphenols, ketones, and sulfur compounds from the hops, which may be absorbed into the ferment. Ketones and polyphenols give astringent-tasting, mouth-puckering flavors. Volatile sulfur compounds (H_2S, DMS, thiols and mercaptans) produce skunky, onionlike, rubbery, burnt-match flavors and odors.

The Fermentation Lock

Although the release of carbonic gas from the fermentation gives it some measure of protection against oxidation and contamination, covering the fermenter immediately after pitching and fitting it with a fermentation lock is advisable. The airlock allows the pressure created by the carbonic gas to push past the liquid in the lock without allowing air in. This prevents the reverse passage of airborne wild yeast and bacteria into the culture-yeast fermentation. Oxygen trapped within the fermenter by the lock is readily driven off by the rising blanket of heavier carbon dioxide produced by the ferment.

The liquid in the lock should be maintained at a constant level, not so deep that it puts the fermenting beer under any appreciable pressure. During the primary fermentation, it is essential that virtually no carbon dioxide remain in solution, since it carries malt and hop debris, albuminous matter, and harsh esters out of the ferment.

The purpose of the fermentation lock is to prevent infection. It must be kept perfectly clean and should be changed regularly. The trap can be filled with an antiseptic solution in which microbes cannot exist, a practice which is advisable duing primary fermentation. Of course, this solution must not contact the ferment either by splashing caused by excess pressure or by careless handling. Common antiseptic solutions may be found under sterilant solutions.

Primary Fermentation

Five to twelve days may elapse from the time that the yeast is pitched until vigorous fermentation abates; six or seven days is usual. In general, high maltose-content worts are fermented at higher temperatures over a relatively shorter period of time. Dextrin-rich worts are suited to lower temperatures, which retard fermentation times.

The duration of the primary fermentation is also subject to the strength and reducing characteristics of the pitched yeast strain. Nonselective strains that completely ferment the extract work very quickly but produce a thin, inferior-tasting beer. Temperamental strains such as Saaz incompletely convert the extract during a relatively long, weak ferment, but produce a richer-tasting and fuller beer.

Normal primary fermentation is verified by its characteristic low, high, and post-kraeusen stages. Where deviations are encountered, the source of the irregularity must be investigated, identified, and corrected as soon as possible.

Temperature

The temperatures quoted here apply to dextrin-rich worts of 10°B (SG 1040) or greater, producing full-bodied beer. If a high-maltose wort relatively free of haze-forming protein fractions is being fermented, or if a top-fermenting yeast strain is used, temperatures should be higher by six to eight degrees F (or three to four degrees C). Fermentation times will be correspondingly foreshortened.

Do not, however, exceed the recommended temperatures when fermenting a dextrinous wort with lager yeast. The yeast requires the longer fermentation at the lower temperatures to break down and convert the less readily fermentable dextrinous sugars.

Temperature Control

Fermentations generate heat. The temperature of any ferment must be closely monitored, and the excessive heat drawn off by lowering the ambient temperature. In no case should the internal temperature exceed 60°F (15°C), and it should be limited to a cumulative increase of 7 to 14°F (4–7°C) over the starting temperature. Higher temperatures result in the formation of fusel alcohols and esters, and consequently solventlike and fruity odors.

Ideally, the maximum temperature should not rise above 47 to 52°F (8–11°C). As soon as this is reached, the ferment should be attempered by lowering the ambient temperature. The maximum temperature may be maintained through high kraeusen until the yeast nutrients subside, yeast activity slows, and heat generation ends. But the fermentation temperature is usually lowered soon after the maximum temperature is reached.

Temperature changes at any stage of the fermentation should not exceed 5°F (3°C) daily. Abrupt reduction in temperature will shock the yeast and may arrest fermentation completely. The sudden death of many yeast cells deleteriously affects flavor, releasing nutrients into the beer that may consequently encourage lactic-acid bacteria. Moreover, yeast mutations tend to adapt to a sudden temperature change more readily than culture yeast. Temperature maintenance and modification must be handled carefully.

Convection currents within the ferment (formed by assymetrical cooling of the fermentation vessel) improve temperature distribution and yeast performance, producing a more even fermentation.

Balling and pH Monitoring

The acidity of the ferment increases during fermentation as the yeast adapt and respire glucose to succinate and other organic acids. With top-fermenting yeast, the pH drop during respiration is dramatic; it falls .4 to .6 within twelve hours of pitching and to 4.0 within twenty-four hours, before it levels off as fermentation begins in earnest. With lager yeast,

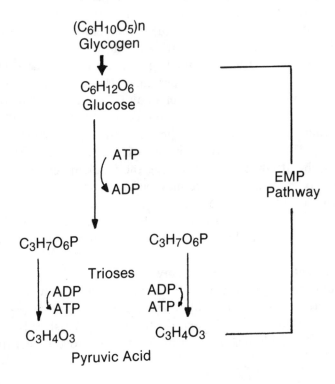

the pH drop is much less precipitous; for a wort of pH 5.5, a .5 drop requires 48 hours, and the pH only falls to 4.5 or so by the end of primary fermentation. One measure of consistent yeast performance is its effect on the pH of the extract solution. To this end, monitoring the pH is critical during the lag phase of a top-fermenting culture, and at the low, high, and post-kraeusen stages of a lager ferment.

The liquid pressure of the fermenting beer also makes its most dramatic drop during primary fermentation and should be regularly checked and logged to define yeast activity and pinpoint racking time.

Primary Fermentation: Lag Phase

After pitching, yeast take some time adapting to the conditions of their new environment. During this "lag" phase, there is little visual evidence of their activity. How successfully the yeast culture adapts to the wort depends upon the number and condition of the yeast cells and the nature of the wort itself. Temperature, density, glucose/maltose content, amino acid availability, and the level of dissolved oxygen all influence yeast behavior.

At pitching, yeast rely on glycogen, a carbohydrate reserve, to provide energy for the synthesis of enzymes and a permeable cell membrane. Glycogen is structurally similar to the amylopectin of malt starch, but with a greater number of shorter branches. Without adequate glycogen reserves, the pitched yeast cannot survive until they can develop the ability to absorb and metabolize wort sugars and nutrients.

During the lag phase, yeast employ a complex enzyme system to hydrolize the polymeric glycogen to glucose. The glucose molecule is phosphorylated and its carbon links broken (glycosis) to yield two triose phosphates. These simpler three-carbon compounds are oxidized to pyruvic acid (pyruvate, an important yeast oxo-acid) with the release of energy by formation of energy-rich ATP, adenosine triphosphate, from energy-depleted ADP).

An inadequate starch reserve may be characteristic of a

particular yeast strain, but often this is due to depletion of glycogen from storing a culture for too long or at too warm a temperature. A culture that survives glycogen deprivation produces abnormal levels of vicinal diketones (VDK, especially diacetyl), marring the beer flavor. This causes fermentation to take longer and be less vigorous because there are fewer cells and consequently slower yeast growth.

Yeast cells also store simple acids, alcohols, nitrogen, and phosphates catabolized from compounds assimilated during culturing. At pitching, yeast employ other enzyme groups to combine these simple chains, synthesizing many of their complex structural and metabolic requirements. Pyruvic acid is reduced to oxaloacetate, from which amino acids and proteins may be synthesized, or to acetyl Co A, an Acyl Co A, or acetic-acid-related compound that can be oxidized to a host of fatty acids, triglycerides, and lipids required for cell-membrane synthesis. Molecular oxygen is required for these reactions. Unless there is sufficient dissolved oxygen in the wort, the formation of a cell wall able to react to and regulate uptake of the particular sugars and nutrients in that wort will cease. Unable to selectively absorb nutrients from solution, many yeast cells will autolyze, and surviving cells will not develop normally. Both scenarioes produce off-flavors in beer.

Lacking dissolved oxygen, acetyl Co A esterifies fusel alcohols. These solventlike and fruity-tasting "higher" alcohols are intermediate products of amino-acid metabolism and are normally oxidized back to organic oxo-acids. When respiring yeast lack oxygen, fusel alcohols may be excreted or dehydrated by acetyl Co A to esters. The principle ester formed is ethyl acetate, which irreversibly taints the beer with a bananalike aroma.

Inadequate oxygenation also causes pyruvic acid, fatty acids, and amino acids to be decarboxylated to aldehydes. These too are normally metabolic intermediates, but without enough oxygen, they are excreted. They may be reabsorbed by the yeast during fermentation, but they are just as likely to be further decarboxylated to fusel alcohols or remain after fermentation ceases. Acetaldehyde, the aldehyde of pyruvic acid, usually predominates, giving an odor like green apples.

As the yeast depletes its glycogen reserves, it is manufacturing the enzymes and permeases necessary to reduce wort sugars. Only the monosaccharides and sucrose in wort can be absorbed by yeast that have not adapted to the solution into which they have been pitched. *Permeases* are enzymelike transports that carry specific compounds through the plasma membrane and into the yeast cell. The yeast must synthesize permeases to absorb maltose and maltotriose, and the enzyme a-glucosidase to hydrolyze them to glucose. Other inducible enzymes are formed and secreted to the yeasts outer cell-membrane surfaces. These dismantle oligosaccharides and dextrins so that their fermentable fractions can be absorbed.

The lag and respiratory phases are generally longer when yeast have not been cultured in a solution similar to the wort

into which they will be pitched. Prolonged adaption, common with granulated dry yeast, can lead to the increased formation of fusel alcohol and ester. Culturing in solutions that contain a high percentage of corn sugar or glucose blocks the formation of maltose permeases. This is the reason why worts high in corn sugar often suffer from a second lag phase just as fermentation seems about to start.

The first evidence of yeast activity is usually the formation of wisps of lacy white foam on the surface of the beer eight to twenty-four hours after pitching. Gradually this foam forms a wreath at the rim of the fermenter, and the beer below is milky-white from the haze of suspended yeast colonies. Carbon-dioxide production is prodigious, although attenuation of the wort slight. CO_2 is being released as a by-product of pyruvic acid decarboxylation to acetyl Co A and oxo-acids; the carbon source for this reaction is glycogen, and only very little of the wort sugar is being metabolized.

If the yeast lag-phase extends beyond twenty-four hours, and the wort and yeast starter were originally well roused and oxygenated, then more yeast should be pitched. Rousing the quiet beer (actually it is still a wort) may cause the yeast to

start fermenting, but as a rule, more yeast should be pitched. If the extended lag phase appears to be characteristic of the yeast strain, it should not be recultured; excessive respiration produces undesirable flavors.

Low Kraeusen

As they deplete the molecular oxygen, the yeast begin anaerobic wort metabolism. Within twenty-four to thirty-six hours of pitching, the foam wreath should begin to migrate toward the surface center; this marks the commencement of the *low kraeusen* stage of primary fermentation. It characterizes the start of intense anaerobic catabolism of maltose, the uptake of a wide range of wort amino acids, and a period of exponential yeast growth.

As the head rises to form low rich mounds and curls of foam, it carries with it protein, hop residues, and degenerated yeast cells which are visible as a brown scum that collects on the head and at the surface edge. In closed fermentations, the scum is eliminated by being "blown off" along with some of the liquid supporting it; in open systems, it must be eliminated from the fermenter by skimming. If the scum is allowed to harden on the sides of the vessel or fall back into the ferment and oxidize, it will impart harsh, bitter taste to the beer and provide an exposed nutrient source for bacterial contaminants. Care must be taken that the fermentation is not contaminated if it is exposed for skimming. A low humidity improves atmospheric purity, reducing the likelihood of contamination.

Throughout fermentation, the ferment may be topped-up with boiled wort, brewing water, or distilled water to compensate for evaporation and blow-off or skimming losses. This prevents residues from caking on the sidewalls of the fermenter as the volume recedes.

At this point, the yeast have completely adapted to the conditions of the ferment and are rapidly multiplying. Extract reduction should be about .5°Balling (SG 1002)

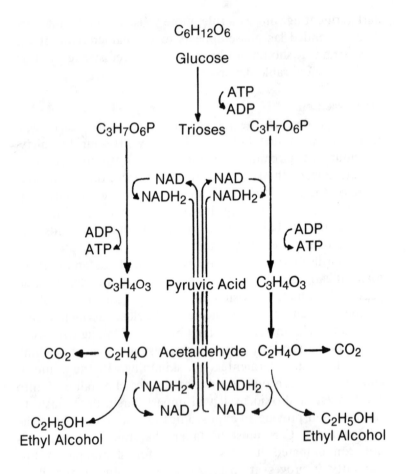

Anaerobic Glucose Fermentation

daily during this brief low-kraeusen phase. The pH also declines as organic acids are released as byproducts of the yeast metabolism of amino acids.

The major fermentation products are ethyl alcohol (ethanol) and carbon dioxide, but even during a normal fermentation cycle, other compounds are excreted by the yeast. The metabolism of the yeast is fueled primarily by the hydrolysis of carbohydrates, but amino acids and fatty acids from the wort also serve as energy sources.

Normal carbohydrate metabolism follows the EMP pathway to pyruvic acid so that ATP may be regenerated to fuel continuing biosynthesis of the yeasts' metabolic requirements. The ADP-ATP cycle, however, cannot continue if pyruvic acid buildup is left to block it. Pyruvic acid in excess of that required for acetyl Co A and oxaloacetate synthesis is metabolized to CO_2 and acetaldehyde by the yeast enzyme pyruvate decarboxylase. The CO_2 is excreted. Acetaldehyde is hydrated to ethyl alcohol by the enzyme alcohol dehydrogenase so that hydrogen buildup blocking the ADP-ATP synthesis can also be eliminated.

Nitrogen metabolism is closely related to glucose hydrolysis. The yeast enzymatically split amino acids in the wort and separately absorb the nitrogenous amino groups (NH_2) and oxo-acid skeletons. These can be reassembled as amino acids or as proteins appropriate to the yeasts' requirements. Oxo-acids necessary for amino acid synthesis may also come from carbohydrate metabolism, and similarly there are several other ways in which oxo-acids are used with consequences affecting beer flavor. They may be decarboxylated to aldehydes, and the aldehydes hydrated by the enzyme

alcohol dehydrogenase to form fusel alcohols. Lack of dextrinous sugars, trub in the yeast cake, and elevated temperatures all contribute to the formation of piquant, fruity-smelling, harsh-finishing fusel alcohols.

Oxo-acids may be metabolized to acetohydroxy acids, which are not metabolized by the yeast and are therefore expelled by them. During low kraeusen, this provides for the elimination of oxo-acids (primarily from pyruvic acid), which carbohydrate metabolism is producing in excess.

Excreted into solution, acetohydroxy acids can be oxidized to vicinal diketones, principally diacetyl (dimethyl diketone, $C_4H_6O_2$). Diacetyl has a perceptible buttery flavor, which is objectionable in amounts above .15 ppm; during low kraeusen it may be as high as .35 ppm. That there is some oxygen in the ferment during low kraeusen and that the temperature is not unreasonably depressed are both important to diacetyl control, because after yeast growth has slowed, healthy cells reabsorb vicinal diketones and metabolize them to harmless diols. When the acetohydroxy acid is not oxidized to vicinal diketones during vigorous fermentation, later diacetyl formation irreversibly mars beer flavor.

High Kraeusen

With top-fermenting yeast, a thick head of clumped yeast covers the beer soon after intense fermentation becomes apparent. At their normal operating temperatures, top-fermenting yeast have largely metabolized the sugars in solution at a time when lager yeast are still undergoing exponential growth. Not until forty-eight to seventy-two hours after the mounds of foam begin to form (three to five days after pitching) do the lager yeast weave a tightly knit cover over the surface of the beer. This cover rises further and finally breaks into cream-colored, less dense, "rocky heads."

Extract reduction approximates 1°Balling (SG 1004) daily over the two to five days of high kraeusen, while the yeast are reproducing logarithmically. The temperature must be exactly controlled.

Although 60°F (15°C) may be quoted as the maximum allowable temperature, every effort should be made to hold it to 47-52°F (8-10°C). When this temperature is reached within the ferment, the ambient temperature can begin to be lowered; in no case should the maximum temperature be held for longer than 72 hours. The temperature should not be lowered more than 5°F (3°C) daily and should be reduced to 38 to 40°F (3-4°C) over several days. The temperature at the conclusion of kraeusen fermentation is usually about 45°F (7°C).

The continued release of organic acids during high kraeusen reduces the pH to 4.5 to 4.8. If the pH drops too rapidly, the yeast will settle out of suspension prematurely; if the pH drops too slowly, it will prevent the beer from clearing properly.

Post Kraeusen

The extract is largely metabolized by the yeast during high kraeusen. As the yeast activity slows, carbonic gas production slows and consequently the agglutinated yeast colonies sink out of suspension and the foam head is no longer formed.

At this point, all of the head is usually floated, siphoned, or skimmed off, even as more is forming, so that it does not fall back through the beer. The only exception is when a low-extract, quickly-maturing beer is being brewed. Such a beer requires the albumins from clean foam for yeast nutrients and for body. The increase in the alcohol content of the beer induces the reabsorption of the albuminous matter into solution. Then, only a clean head should be allowed to fall back through the ferment. The final dirty-brown, spotty, foam cover should always be meticulously separated from the beer. This residual scum would give the beer a harshly-bitter background flavor. The stability of this beer is invariably less than if the head had been removed, and the beer should not be lagered.

Generally, four to six days after high kraeusen begins (six

to twelve days after pitching), the formation of the foam cover ceases. As the availability of fermentable extract drops during the post-kraeusen stage, the yeast adapt to changing conditions by accelerating their secretion of extracellular enzymes capable of splitting off the fermentable portions from dextrins in solution. Reasonable levels of diacetyl and the related diketone 2,3-pentane dione are also absorbed and metabolized by the yeast. It is important that the fermentation temperature is not prematurely lowered and that the beer is not racked off its yeast sediment until the diacetyl has been reabsorbed. It is usual for the beer to be held in the primary fermenter for two or three days after the kraeusen head has fallen, with the temperature being lowered from $45°F$ ($7°C$) to 38 to $40°F$ ($3-4°C$). The extract drop over the final twenty-four-hour period of primary fermentation should be about .5°Balling (SG 1002), and the density should be about one-third what the wort density (OG) was.

It is relatively common in modern fermentation cycles to raise the temperature of the post-kraeusen beer to $52°F$ ($11°C$), and to hold that temperature for two to seven days. This is the *diacetyl rest*. It encourages oxidation of yeast-excreted acetohydroxy acids to vicinal diketones, and it reinvigorates the yeast culture so that it metabolizes diacetyl, thereby removing it from solution.

Because fermentable extract is rapidly consumed at the higher temperatures of the diacetyl rest, subsequent conditioning can be foreshortened. Secondary fermentation will be both subdued and brief, and lagering may require only seven to fourteen days to achieve the same clarity and flavor stability that would be expected with the usual five-to-seven-week secondary fermentation and lagering.

Real and Apparent Attenuation

Normal primary fermentation ends when head formation ceases; this may take as few as five days when the wort is below 10°Balling (SG 1040), or eight to ten days for a very rich and dextrinous wort. Roughly 50 to 65 percent of the extract will have been converted to alcohol and carbon dioxide, although the hydrometer may show only a 65 to 80 percent reduction in density ("one-third gravity"). The difference between the real attenuation of the beer and the apparent attenuation as gauged by the hydrometer is usually about 15 percent. This phenomenon occurs because the hydrometer measures liquid pressure and does not reflect the fact that this pressure has been reduced by the formation of alcohol as well as by the reduction of the fermentable extract. Because alcohol is far lighter than water (the liquid pressure of pure water is SG 1000; of alcohol, 798), the hydrometer sinks further into a solution in which alcohol is present, and the hydrometer reading is lower than the extract loss alone can account for.

But the real attenuation may easily be determined. First, a volume of beer is measured at the temperature the brewer's hydrometer is calibrated to, usually 60°F (15.56°C). This volume of beer is raised to a temperature of 173°F (78°C) or slightly higher and roused for several minutes to drive off the alcohol. Then it is cooled to 60°F and topped up to its original volume with distilled water. The volume of water required to replace the lost volume of beer is equal to the alcohol content (by volume) of the beer. The hydrometer reading of the dealcoholized sample, after topping-up, accurately reflects the real extract content of the beer. The real attenuation is measured by subtracting this reading from the original °Balling (OG) of the wort.

Racking

The beer is carefully racked off its settlement when its density is one third or less of the wort density (OG) and its drop over the preceding twenty-four hours is .5°Balling (SG 1002) or less. A reducing-sugar analysis usually shows less than 5 percent. The beer should be free of any foam cover. The transfer to a closed secondary fermenter should be done under antiseptic conditions and all equipment should be sanitized before use.

The purpose of racking is to separate the beer from decaying yeast cells and flavor-impairing precipitates. Care should be taken that no yeast sediment or trub is carried along into the secondary fermentation. Siphoning or decanting must be terminated just as soon as the runoff becomes the least bit cloudy. The fermenter should be topped-up with boiled wort, or if necessary with sterilized and deaerated brewing water, leaving only a minimal amount of head space to allow for moderate foaming.

Employing up to 5 percent strongly-fermenting kraeusen beer at racking produces a stronger start of secondary fermentation and a better overall fermentation. This absolutely must be done when yeast performance during primary fermentation has been poor, as it replenishes the degraded culture.

Racking must be done without rousing or splashing to prevent oxygen entering the solution. Oxygen in beer past early kraeusen poses serious consequences to the beer flavor: oxidation of acetohydroxy acids in the secondary fermenter produces diacetyl that the yeast cannot reabsorb; fatty acids may be oxidized to aldehydes; amino acids may be oxidized to fusel alcohols and esters; and phenolic material may polymerize and become haze fractions. It is also important that the secondary fermenter be topped up with kraeusen beer or deaerated wort or water so that only enough airspace remains to allow for very mild foaming.

Gauging Yeast Performance

A sample of the beer at racking should show very clear, bright, and black. It should demonstrate a good break. When held up to the light, it should show clear. When agitated, distinctly visible suspended yeast colonies should float about and then, upon resting, settle out rapidly and firmly. Such a yeast is satisfactory for collecting to be repitched and for employment in a long secondary and lager fermentation.

Only "break" or *Bruchhefen* sedimentary yeast forms

colonies as the yeast nutrients in the beer diminish. Powdery or dusty *Staubhefen* yeast do not sediment in so clean a break and are likely to form a troublesome foam cover on the beer surface even after attenuation drops daily below .1° Balling (SG .5).

Dusty yeast ferment more of the extract than do break yeast, and do so more quickly. Beer brewed with dusty yeast is unsuitable for long secondary fermentation and lagering, because the yeast have largely eliminated the less-readily-fermentable extract necessary to support aging. Secondary fermentation should be conducted at lower temperatures [as low as 30°F (−1°C)] to increase sedimentation and retard fermentation. The beer should be racked into the secondary fermenter before the density has dropped much below one-third that of the wort (OG).

The appearance of dusty yeast in a ferment is probably due to the propagation of an inferior strain; it should not be used for repitching. Any seed yeast may also need to be replaced and should be evaluated before it is used again.

Yeast for Seed

Fermentations displaying normal characteristics are the sources of yeast suitable for culturing. If the yeast have deteriorated (the beer is tainted with fruity or sulfury esters or fermentation is sluggish), are unable to reabsorb diacetyl (buttery taste and aroma), or are contaminated by wild yeast (cloudy beer after kraeusen) or bacteria (abnormal, sour, medicinal taste and aroma), they are not suited for repitching or culturing.

Seed yeast for subsequent brewings, culturing, and bottle priming should be collected only from the middle layer of the primary- fermentation sediment. The yeast cake should be relatively clean and composed of three distinct layers. Two very thin, dark layers of dead, inferior cells, trub and possibly wild yeast and bacteria sandwich between them the active, healthy, white yeast, or *barm*. Barm has the best fermenting qualities—strong cells, with good agglutination, that settle out properly. Where an open fermenter is used, all of the top layer is scraped aside with a long-handled spoon before the middle layer is gathered up and spooned into a sterile glass container. Where a closed fermenter has no yeast-collection system at its base, the entire sediment is washed out and the barm separated from the trub by several rinsings, which float off the dead cells and organic residues.

Yeast collected for seed is covered with very cold, biologically-clean water and agitated into suspension. When most of the yeast has settled, the water is decanted off, taking with it dead cells and trub. The rinsing is repeated. A subsequent acid wash with ammonium persulfate solution (p. 78) destroys any bacteria, but the yeast culture still has to be recultured to restore its normal fermentation characteristics.

Yeast covered with sterile wort (or water) in a glass container with a fermentation lock can be stored at 32 to 40°F (0–4°C) for up to seven days without significant deterioration—however, the yeast need to be rinsed again before use. If the seed yeast will not be pitched within twelve days, they must be frozen.

Under sterile conditions, yeast may be subcultured through as many as twenty successive brewings, if they are repitched within twenty-four hours of collection. If the period before repitching is longer, the culture is usable for only four or five intermittent brewings. As a general rule, the greater frequency of use, the more times a strain may be directly subcultured.

13. SECONDARY FERMENTATION

HETHER OR NOT A BEER WILL BE LAGERED, A secondary fermentation in a second, closed fermenter allows for the slow reduction or *conditioning* of the remaining fermentable extract. In secondary fermentation, the beer is free from the flavor impairment of degenerating yeast cells. Seven to twenty-one days may be required for the yeast to deplete the fermentable sugar left after the kraeusen period has ended. Traditional lagering requires that the beer be held for a further five to seven weeks for clarification and stabilization.

During secondary fermentation, the beer is slowly attenuated, beginning at 39 to 41°F (4–5°C), to clarify and chillproof it. It is slowly cooled to 33 to 37°F (1–3°C) [or to as low as 30°F (–1°C) to settle dusty yeast] to allow the yeast to settle thoroughly and to reduce the activity of any microorganisms possibly contaminating the ferment.

Because the potential risk of airborne contamination by wild yeast is greatest during the slow, cold ferment, the beer absolutely must be protected from contact with the atmosphere by being fermented in a closed vessel fitted with a fermentation lock. Contamination is the major risk at this point: yeast activity is slow because the beer no longer

161

contains abundant extract and nutrients, yet dormant bacteria may be capable of significant dextrin, protein, or yeast-waste fermentation or oxidation. Even though the pH is below the optimum, given a warm enough temperature, even a few wild yeast, acetic, or lactic-acid bacteria might rapidly propagate and ruin the beer.

Reproduction by the culture yeast will have entirely ceased during this stage of fermentation; further attenuation relies solely on the metabolic activity of the relatively few remaining yeast cells. It is imperative that conditions are conducive to the continued metabolism of the fermentable extract by these yeast cells and that they are not subjected to temperature shock. If the yeast culture needs regeneration, then an active starter culture or 5 percent kraeusen beer is added.

The duration of the secondary fermentation and the temperature at which it should be conducted are determined by the maltotriose and dextrin content of the post-kraeusen beer. If its density has not dropped more than .5°Balling (SG 1002) over the twenty-four hour period preceding racking and the hydrometer reading is still one-third of the value of the original wort reading, then the beer is rich in dextrins. It should be fermented out in the secondary at 33 to 34°F (1°C) for at least fourteen days. When the density at racking is much less than one-third the value of the wort density, it indicates that the beer is lacking in dextrins, has less than 1°Balling (SG 1004) of fermentable extract left in solution, and should undergo a secondary fermentation at 34 to 37°F (1–3°C) for not more than ten days before the temperature is reduced for lagering. Lagering times will also be foreshortened.

Long fermentations often darken the color of the beer by the oxidation of phenols. Consequently, when lagers are brewed for paleness, secondary fermentation must be carried out at higher temperatures [36 to 39°F (2–4°C), but not above 40°F (5°C)] over the shorter time period.

Since beer for draft need not be brewed to give a long shelf life, it is also fermented at higher temperatures [34–37°F (1–3°C)], and for a shorter period of time. When the hydrometer reading drops less than .2°Balling over a twenty-four-hour period, it can be assumed that there is just enough yeast and fermentable extract left in solution to support cask carbonation. Then the beer is racked into a keg or cask.

Lagering

A long, cold, post-fermentive rest is usually employed when the wort is from a decoction mash. It yields a more stable beer with a smoother flavor.

Lagering mellows harsh flavors by the combined effect of the falling rate of yeast metabolism, increased acidity, and low temperatures. These factors cause harsh malt tannins to coagulate with haze-forming proteins, precipitating these and other sulfurous compounds out of solution.

Yeast cells are not usually decomposed during lagering, but the culture becomes progressively dormant as fermentable extract and finally glycogen reserves are depleted. With the decline in available carbohydrates, the yeast reabsorb some of the esters and sulfur compounds from yeast-cell decomposition in the warmer primary ferment and from inadvertent oxygenation or light exposure.

Successful lagering requires that the beer not be subjected to either temperature fluctuations or oxygenation. Oxygen in nearly-fermented beer causes the formation of diacetyl and the oxidation of fusel alcohols from amino acids and malt polyphenols, especially where dark-roasted malt has been used. Where lagering temperatures are too warm, aldehyde formation is accelerated.

Aldehydes give beer stale flavors reminiscent of cardboard or paper. Where higher temperatures decompose yeast cells, solventlike esters, sulfury, stale, and soapy flavors arise.

When the kraeusen tradition is being followed, a lattice of beech chips is laid on the bottom of the secondary fermenter

$$C_2H_5OH$$
Ethyl Alcohol

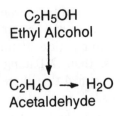

$$C_2H_4O \rightarrow H_2O$$
Acetaldehyde

and covered with the nearly fermented or *ruh* beer. From 5 to 15 percent new beer at up to 39°F (4°C) is roused into it. Where fermenter construction permits, it is common to lager the beer under +.2 to -.3 atmospheres (4.4 lbs./sq. in.) of pressure, after the fermenter is purged of the atmosphere in the headspace. This can be accomplished by various pressure-regulating arrangements.

The lagering period is determined by referring back to the hydrometer reading of the cooled wort. Dextrinous beer from a decoction mash undergoes a secondary fermentation and lagering period of seven to twelve days at 33 to 34°F (1–2°C) for each 2°Balling (SG 1008) of cooled-wort hydrometer reading (OG). Lighter beer lacking dextrins is not usually held for more than seven days for each 2°Balling of the wort density. Very strong, kraeusened beer, on the other hand, may be stored for six to eight months before it is bottled.

Reducing the temperature to near freezing several days after secondary fermentation falls off reduces lagering time; in fact, the decrease in the solubility of body-forming colloids at 30 to 33°F (–1 to +1°C) necessitates a briefer lager period.

Fining

Whether or not the beer is being fully lagered, fining improves its clarity and reduces aging times. As a rule, brilliantly clear beer can only be achieved by fining. It precipitates degenerated yeast cells, proteins, and tannins out of the beer. Used as a fining substance, gelatin combines with tannic acid forming an insoluble precipitate with haze proteins and yeast. Either brewer's gelatin or unflavored pure-vegetable gelatin may be used, so long as it is dry, smooth, pale-colored, and odorfree. Gelatin that has absorbed moisture during storage is spoiled. Use only gelatin to fine lager beer; isinglass and other preparations do not clear lager beer and may even damage it.

When the beer has fermented out, it is ready for fining. A sugar analysis should show less than 2 percent. The beer must be colder than 50°F (10°C) for the gelatin to react with the ferment; the closer to freezing temperature that the beer is, the more efficient the action of the gelatin finings.

The dissolval of the gelatin with beer, wort, or water must be meticulously handled, so that the finings are completley liquified and then evenly dispersed into the aged beer. The finings will not combine with culture yeast and albumins unless they come into intimate contact with them. To accomplish this, the gelatin must be diffused throughout the entire volume of beer.

If a very strong hop aroma is desired, liquid hop extract may be added with the gelatin finings. Hops for strong aroma should never be added after fining, as they will sour the bouquet and first-taste of the beer. Hop extracts, when added with the finings, are less harsh and may even improve the clarification of beer from a well-mashed and boiled wort by increasing the polyphenols available for coagulation.

If the bottled beer lacks a good foam head or is thin, then the amount of finings should be reduced in future batches. Experience with a particular malt and brewing technique may even preclude the need for fining.

Clarifying with Beech Chips

Beech or hazelnut chips one-eighth inch thick by one-half inch wide are laid on the bottom of the lagering vessel to form a loosely-woven lattice. Extract coats the many surfaces of the chips, bonding weak yeast cells to them, and thus clearing the beer.

The chips are first soaked and then boiled for twelve to twenty-four hours in a sodium bicarbonate solution (1 1/2 lbs/gal) before being rinsed. The process is repeated, sometimes substituting bisulfate of lime. Finally, the shavings are rinsed in a cold-hot-cold water cycle. The pH of the last rinse should be neutral, indicating that all of the bicarbonate has been washed from the chips. They may be washed and reused until they crack from age.

Real Terminal Extract

When the aged beer is ready to be bottled, its real-extract content can be determined by boiling off the alcohol from a measured volume of the beer, topping it up to its original volume with distilled water, and gauging its density with a hydrometer. The liquid pressure exerted by the fully fermented beer (sugar analysis less than 2 percent) is due to unfermentable dextrins, oligosaccharides, and soluble nitrogen. Taking a hydrometer reading of a dealcoholized sample is the only means by which the "body extract" may be accurately measured, that is by removing the "apparent density" effect of alcohol from it.

The amount of unfermentable extract remaining in the finished beer is the direct result of the duration and effectiveness of the proteolytic, alpha-amylase, and beta-amylase mash rests. Other influencing factors are the amount and nature of malt used, the effectiveness of protein/resin bonding in the boil, and the ability of the yeast to ferment maltotriose, maltotetraose, and isomaltose. Typical bottled lagers have a real density of 3.0 to 5.0°Balling (SG 1012–1020); richer types average 5.5°Balling (SG 1022). Darker lagers range to 6.5°Balling (SG 1026), and bocks are even higher. The real density of a fully fermented beer is generally 40 percent greater than its apparent density.

Dark and full-bodied beers should show 45 to 60 percent real attenuation, light to pale beers up to 70 percent. Apparent attenuation is usually 60 to 75 percent in the first case and up to 85 percent in the latter.

Bottling

The aged beer must be racked off its sediment into a sterile, closed fermenter and mixed with a quantity of actively-fermenting kraeusen beer or priming solution sufficient to produce the desired bottle pressure (see Table 27). When dextrose is used to carbonate the bottled beer, it should be made up into a solution and pitched with yeast one or two days before bottling. Dry primings should not be used. High-quality dextrose should be the only sugar employed for bottling.

Whether kraeusen beer or sugar provides the conditioning extract, measurements must be exact, and mixing with the aged beer very thorough, or inconsistent results will follow. The character of the finished beer can be greatly influenced by the degree of carbonation.

Mixing the kraeusen (or priming solution) into the aged beer cannot be done in an aerating fashion but should raise a foam head. This greatly aids in the prevention of oxidation and contamination of the beer at bottling by forming a protective blanket of carbonic gas above the beer and driving atmospheric from the neck space above. The colder the beer is at bottling, the more CO_2 it retains in solution and the greater is its ability to drive off oxygen. It also resists contamination by virtue of its cold temperature.

The bottles into which the beer is siphoned must be biologically, as well as physically, clean. They should be washed with 3 percent caustic soda, rinsed and then sterilized at above 170°F (77°C) in a 1 percent chlorine bleach solution, drained, and thoroughly rinsed. Clean bottles may be "pasteurized" by soaking them for at least 30 minutes in clean water at above 140°F (60°C) or placing them wet in an oven at 200°F (93°C) for twenty minutes before being inverted to dry. All bottles should be inspected; any with chipped rims must be rejected.

Any type of bottle neck may be used, so long as it can be sealed and can withstand the pressure of bottle fermentation. Carbonation in excess of three atmospheres requires the use of a heavy-gauge bottle. Under carefully controlled conditions, thin-walled, "non-returnable" bottles are sufficient when brewing lager beer of normal carbonation.

Each bottle should be filled to within three-quarters of an inch of the top and be left to rest, loosely capped, for several minutes before the caps are secured. This allows air trapped in the neck space to be driven off by the release of carbonic gas. Any oxygen that is not released will be absorbed into the beer and will diminish its stability and mar its flavor. Oxygenation at bottling from splashing the beer or from trapping air in the neckspace is a problem as serious as contamination.

The bottled beer should be held at 45 to 50°F (7–10°C) for several days to allow strong fermentation to be established within the bottle before lowering the temperature. Temperature reduction should never exceed 5°F (3°C) daily. Bottle conditioning should take place away from direct sunlight, and the bottles should not be subjected to temperature fluctuations caused by drafts.

The beer should be aged in the bottle for an absolute minimum of ten to fourteen days, and more likely thirty days, before serving. Lagered beers usually keep for several months. There is an optimum storage period for every beer when chemical changes within the bottle produce the best taste and aroma, and this should dictate the length of the bottle-aging period.

Imbibing

When bottle-conditioned beer is ready for drinking, it should be carefully poured so that the yeast sediment is not disturbed; a good yeast strain cakes solidly on the bottom of the bottle. Hand-crafted beers are not usually consumed with the same carelessness as a can of beer at a ball game. They are brewed to be drunk at the right temperature, with discernment and appreciation for the subtler aspects of their character.

A beer is judged by its flavor, aroma, body, head, color,

and clarity. All of these values are subjective and various standards depend on the type of beer being brewed, the balance of one characteristic against another, and the predisposition and preference of the consumer.

Color, clarity, and head are assessed before the beer is even tasted. The aroma is usually sampled by swirling the glass and holding it under the nose. The cleanliness and sharpness of the hop bouquet are the major criteria by which aroma is judged. Odor may be characterized as being ethereal, aromatic, malty, yeasty, fruity, vegetative, or musty.

Flavor is evaluated by the first sensation, the taste, and the feel while swallowing, and then by the aftertaste. The body of beer is judged by its fullness, texture, or "mouth feel."

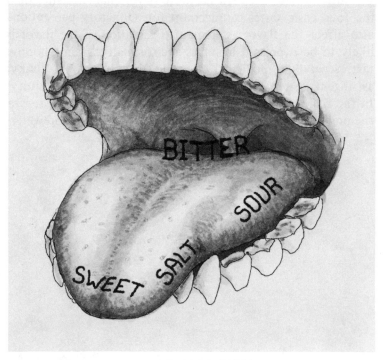

AREAS FOR TASTE

The palate fullness of beer is mostly due to the low molecular weight albumins carried over to the finished beer and to dextrins.

Taste is generally classified as sweet, sour, bitter, or salty. *Sweetness* is produced by unfermentable sugars and simple dextrins. *Sourness* (acidity) is directly affected by the pH of the beer and below pH 4.0 becomes both noticeable and objectionable. *Bitterness* is due to the iso-alpha acids from the hops and from the roasted malt and probably generates more controversy than any other criterion. The hop taste is usually judged too strong only if it lingers after the beer is swallowed. *Saltiness* is formed by the mineral content of the wort and generally accentuates bitterness and dryness.

Because our taste perceptions are highly sophisticated, we can differentiate between far more flavor characteristics than the four basic tastes can account for. Olfactory perceptions also affect the flavor assessment. Evaluation of the flavor is likely to be expressed in terms such as malty, grainy, hoppy, tart, vegetative, medicinal, metallic, dry, sulphury, skunky, astringent, watery, burnt, nutty, yeasty, buttery, and fruity. In the final analysis, the character of the beer should cater to the preferences of the ultimate consumer—the homebrewer.

14. PLANNING THE BREW

EFORE EACH PHASE OF THE BREWING CYCLE IS begun, prepare everything that will be needed so that the operation may proceed smoothly and without interruption.

Ideally, begin each brewing by bottling any aged beer and freeing up the primary fermenter for use during water treatment. Yeast can then be collected from the primary and mixed with wort saved from a previous brewing to create a strong yeast starter/kraeusen for pitching.

Select a mash tun with a spigot, or fit one to it, so that it may be used to dispense the sparging water. Also fit a spigot to the kettle, so that the bitter wort may be filtered through the hops without requiring any extra equipment.

Note the quoted temperatures at which pH estimates are made. Readings of extract solutions may vary with temperature changes, so that the hotter the mash or wort sample is, the lower the pH appears to be. The pH and density should both be gauged at the standardized temperature of 60°F (15.56°C).

Where periods of time are quoted, the longer times generally suit full-bodied, fully-lagered beer, or the mashing, sparg-

171

ing and boiling of difficult malts. The shorter times favor light, quickly-maturing beer, or well-modified pale malt.

If you have not read the whole text, do so before beginning to brew. The procedural outline immediately following is inadequate by itself; the brewer should be familiar with the wider scope of information found elsewhere in the text.

A Note on Mixing

Whenever two substances are to be mixed, mixing must be done gradually to ensure even distribution. When one of the substances is liquid, and the other is dry, the dry substance is gradually and evenly moistened before it is flooded with the liquid. Unless this precaution is taken, dry "balls" may become isolated by being encased in paste.

Always mix by the gradual dilution of the smaller amount of any two substances into the larger. Always mix liquids into dry substances.

To oxygenate any solution, rouse it splashingly and force air into it, as by pushing downward with an inverted spoon. To rouse a solution without aerating, very gently rock the vessel or stir slowly, pivoting the spoon at the surface level of the solution.

Planning

The size of any brewing is predetermined by the capacity of the closed fermenting vessel(s), since to discourage oxidation and contamination during lagering, the secondary fermenter must be filled nearly to capacity (some head space may be allowed for foaming).

Table 18 is provided to determine bottling volume and the necessary capacity of fermenters, kettles, and the mash and lauter tubs, relative to the capacity of any-size closed fermenter. Quoted volumes should be adjusted to reflect actual brewing experience; for instance, the amount of malt to be doughed-in and the mash-tub volume are subject to the wort density (and character of the beer) that is desired, or the sparging water and boiling volumes may vary according to actual sparging efficiency.

Following the worksheet, examples are given based on using five-gallon carboys for closed primary and secondary fermenters.

TABLE 18

Worksheet

The worksheet is provided for the calculation of capacity requirements of equipment, relative to the size of the closed fermenter(s). Use the worksheet to design brewings of any size.

To Calculate Fermenter Volumes:
1. **Capacity of Secondary**   ____ gal.
   Fermenter:
   Line 1 should be actual capacity. For
   example, 5 – gallon carboy filled to the
   neck = 5.125 gal.

2. Kraeusen beer for secondary fermenter
   (usually 5-10% of fermenter capacity), wort
   or water to replace racking loss: – ____ gal.

3. Racking loss, primary to secondary
   (usually 3-5%; blow-off losses
   approximately 5% for lager yeast, 10% for
   ale yeast):   + ____ gal.

4. **Primary Ferment** (lines 1-3):   = ____ gal.

5. **Pitching** (kraeusen/yeast starter, usually
   10% of primary ferment volume)   – ____ gal.

6. Wort being removed, bottled and refrigerated; (line 6 must be equal to lines 2, 5 and 25);   + ____ gal.

7. **Cooled Wort** (lines 4-6):   = ____ gal.

To Calculate Extract/Malt Requirements:
8. **Density of Wort** desired: ____ °B

9. Pounds of **Extract** required to yield one gallon of wort at this density; see table 19:   ____ lbs.

10. **Extract** required (multiply line 7 by line 9):   ____ lbs.

11. Yield expected from extract source; see table 20:   ____ %

12. **Malt** (or **Malt Extract**) required (divide line 10 by line 11):   ____ lbs.

To Calculate Mash and Kettle Volumes:
13. Displacement of malt (multiply line 12 by .05):   ____ gal.

14. Water for doughing-in; usually 24-40 fl.oz. per lb. of malt, infusion mashing 20 fl.oz. (multiply line 12 by .18-.32, infusion .16);   + ____ gal.

15. Mashing-in; usually 12-20 fl.oz. of boiling water per lb. of malt, infusion mashing 48 fl. oz. (multiply line 12 by .09-.16, infusion .38):   + ____ gal.

16. Boiling water to thin a thick mash/ maintain temp. during saccharification rest (multiply line 12 by .04-.18):   + ____ gal.

17. **Mash, Lauter Mash** (add lines 13-16): = _____ gal.

18. **Decoction** (thick mash multiply line 17 by .33-.4, thin mash by .4-.5): _____ gal.

19. **Sweet Wort** (runoff); usually 112 fl. oz. per lb. of malt (multiply line 12 by .88): = _____ gal.

20. Spent mash, displacement; approx. 4 fl. oz. displacement per lb., and 2 fl. oz. per lb. of trapped extract (multiply line 12 by .05): – _____ gal.

21. Sparging water (subtract line 20 from line 17. Subtract this figure from line 19): = _____ gal.

22. Wort volume at full boil (multiply line 19 by 1.04): = _____ gal.

To Calculate Bottling Volume:
23. **Capacity of Lager Fermenter:** _____ gal.

24. Racking/bottling loss (usually 2%): – _____ gal.

25. Bottle priming. See table 27. Multiply the given volume of kraeusen beer or dextrose by line 23 (for dry primings, dissolve sugar into a given volume of water). Divide the fl. oz. of solution by 128 to convert to "gal.": + _____ gal.

26. **Bottling Volume** (lines 23-25): = _____ gal.

EXAMPLE 1
Decoction Mashing, 5-Gallon Carboy Fermenters

- °Balling of wort: 12°B (SG 1049)

- Extract required: 6.3 lbs.
- Mash extract-efficiency: 70%
- Malt required: 9. lbs.

- Displacement 9 lbs. of malt: = .45 gal.
- Water at 60°F (15°C) for doughing in: + 7 qts.
- Boiling water infusion to 95°F (35°C): + 3 1/2 qts.
- Thinning a thick mash: + 1 1/2 qts.
- Mash, Lauter Mash: = 3.45 gal.
- Mash Kettle = 1.5 − 2.5 gal.
- Sparging water: + 5 gal.
- Spent mash volume: − .45 gal.
- Sweet Wort runoff: = 8. gal.
- Wort volume at full boil: = 8.32 gal.
- Cooled Wort: = 6. gal.
- Wort removed, bottled and refrigerated: − 5 1/2 qts.
- Pitching, Kraeusen / yeast starter: + 2 qts.
- Primary Ferment: = 5.125 gal.
- Blowoff and racking loss: − 1 qt.
- Kraeusen for secondary fermenter: + 1 qt.
- Secondary Ferment Lagering: = 5.125 gal.
- Racking / bottling losses: − 1 pt.
- Kraeusen beer for bottle pressure of 2.5 atm.: + 2 1/2 qts.
- Bottling Volume: = 5.625 gal.

EXAMPLE 2
Step-Mashing, 5-Gallon Carboy Fermenter

- °Balling of wort: 12°B (SG 1049)
- Extract required: 1.05 lbs. per gallon
- Mash extract-efficiency: 65%
- Malt required: 10 lbs.

- Displacement of 10 lbs. of malt: .5 gal.
- Water at 60°F (15°c) for
  doughing in: + 2. gal.
- Boiling water infusion to 95°F
  (35°C):   + 1 gal.
- Mash, Lauter Mash: = 3.5 gal.
- Sparging water: + 5.8 gal.
- Spent-mash left after sparging: – .5 gal.
- Sweet Wort runoff: = 8.8 gal.
- Wort volume at full boil: = 9.2 gal.
- Cooled Wort: = 6.25 gal.
- Wort removed, bottled and   – 6 1/2 qts.
  refrigerated:
- Pitching yeast starter: + 2 qts.
- Primary Ferment: = 5.125 gal.
- Blow-off and racking losses: – 2 qts.
- Wort for topping-up fermenter: +2 qts.
- Secondary Fermenter: = 5.125 gal.
- Racking/bottling losses: – 1 pt.
- Kraeusen beer for bottle
  conditioning, 2.5 atm: + 2 1/2 qts.
- Bottling Volume: = 5.625 gal.

TABLE 19
Extract Content

A.

The amount of extract that is needed to produce a gallon of cooled wort at any given density (°B), is determined by the formula $\frac{(259 + °B)°B}{3100}$

1. °Balling of cooled wort desired: 1. _____ °B

2. Add line 1 to the weight of one barrel
   of water at 60°F: 1. _____+259 lbs.:   2. _____

3. Multiply line 1 by line 2:   3. _____

4. Divide line 3 by 3100:   4. _____ lbs.

Line 4 is the lbs. of extract, as cane sugar, that is needed to produce one gallon of wort of the given extract content.

Example: $\dfrac{(259 + 12°B)12°B}{3100}$ = 1.049 lbs. extract per gal at 12°B

Divide line 4 by the yield of the particular extract source (see table 20) to determine the pounds of that extract source required to yield one gallon of wort at the given liquid pressure.

Example: 6-row pale malt, poorly modified, decoction mash: 75% yield. 1.049 ÷ .75 = 1.4 lbs. malt required, per gal. of wort.

B.
Lbs. of Extract Per Gallon of Solution, for Various Densities:

°B of Wort	OG	Lbs. Extract Per Gallon	°B of Wort	OG	Lbs. Extract Per Gallon
0.5°	1002	.04	12.0°	1049	1.05
1.0°	1004	.0837	12.5°	1051	1.095
3.0°	1012	.25	13.0°	1053	1.14
5.0°	1020	.425	13.5°	1055	1.19
7.0°	1028	.60	14.0°	1057	1.23
8.0°	1032	.69	14.5°	1059	1.28
9.0°	1036	.78	15.0°	1061	1.33

$10.0°$	1040	.87	$15.5°$	1063	1.375
$10.5°$	1042	.91	$16.0°$	1065	1.42
$11.0°$	1044.5	.96	$18.0°$	1074	1.61
$11.5°$	1047	1.00	$20.0°$	1080	1.81

TABLE 20
Extract Yield from Various Sources

Source:	Modification:	Mash:	Extract Potential by Weight:	Color °L 1 lb. in 1 Gallon:
Diastatic	moderate	multi-rest infusion	75% 74%	1.5
Lager 6-row	moderate	multi-rest	73%	1.7
Lager 2-row	moderate	multi-rest infusion	75% 72%	1.7
British pale	full	multi-rest infusion	74% 72%	3.0
Cara-pale	moderate	multi-rest	72%	2.0
Wheat	full		80%	2.0
Dextrine	full		72%	4.0
Vienna	moderate		72%	6.5

Munich	moderate	72%	13.0
Caramel	moderate	70%	20-120
Amber	full	70%	30.0
Crystal	full	70%	55.0
Chocolate		60%	400.
Flaked Barley		55%	1.5
Roasted Barley		55%	500.
Black Malt		45%	550.
Rice		80%	
Corn Flakes		80%	
Malt Extract	(average)	65%	
Glucose		80%	
Dextrose	(corn sugar)	70–80%	
Sucrose		100%	

The quoted extract potentials represent maximum brewhouse yields. In practice yields may be less than those given, due to inefficient crushing, mashing or sparging. Unless experience proves otherwise, a homebrewer should expect yields to be approximately 5% lower. For example, 70% for two-row lager malt in a three-step mash, or 65% for caramel malt.

To formulate recipes:

1. Determine what the O.G. of the wort will be.

2. Multiply the extract required per gallon (table 19) by the amount of cooled wort the brew-length requires.

3. Multiply 2 by the percentage of extract that each source will contribute.

4. Divide 3 by the extract potential (column 4) for each source. This is the weight, in lbs., for each extract source.

RECIPES

Recipes are for five-gallon carboy "closed" fermentation. 5½ gallons of cooled wort should be present after boiling, of which 3 quarts should be bottled for topping-up to replace blow-off or racking losses and for use in yeast culturing. Pitch with a two-quart yeast starter.

Pilsener

OG 12°B (SG 1049)
TG 3.0°B (SG 1012)
Color 4.5°Lovibond
40 Bitterness Units
Soft water
4.8% alcohol by volume
6½ lbs. two-row lager malt
1 lb. Munich malt
½ lb. Cara-pale malt
Doughing-in 6 quarts of water
Mashing-in 3½ quarts
Saccharification strike temperature 153°F (67°C)
Temperature maintenance 1½ quarts
Sparging 4½ gallons of water
9.8 AAU Saaz Kettle hops
½ oz. Saaz finishing hops 15 min. before strike
½ oz. Saaz aroma hops at strike

Dortmunder

OG 13.5°B (SG 1055)
TG 3.2°B (SG 1013)
Color 5°L
30 BU
Very hard, high-sodium water
5.4% alcohol v/v

7 lbs. two-row lager malt
1 lb. Munich malt
1¼ lb. cara-pale malt
Doughing-in 7 quarts
Mashing-in 1 gallon
Strike temperature 153°F (67°C)
Temperature maintenance 1½ quarts
Sparging 4½ gallons
7.3 AAU Hallertau/Perle Kettle hops
½ oz. Hallertau finishing hops
½ oz. Tettnang aroma hops

Vienna

OG 12.5°B (SG 1051)
TG 3.3°B (SG 1013)
Color 8.5°L
26 BU
Hard water
4.9% alcohol v/v
5.5 lbs. two-row lager malt
2.5 lbs. Munich malt
.25 lb. cara-pale malt
.25 lb. caramel–20°L malt
Doughing-in 7 quarts
Mashing-in 1 gallon
Strike temperature 156°F (68.5°C)
Temperature maintenance 1½ quarts
Sparging 4¼ gallons
6.4 AAU Hallertau/Perle Kettle hops
½ oz. Hallertau finishing hops

Munich Dark

OG 13.4°B (SG 1054)
TG 3.5°B (SG 1014)

Color 16.5°L
28 BU
Carbonate water
5.2% alcohol v/v
5 lbs. two-row lager malt
3¼ lbs. Munich malt
1 lb. caramel–40 malt
Doughing-in 2 gallons
Mashing-in 1 gallon
Strike temperature 155°F (68°C)
Temperature maintenance 1½ quarts
Sparging 4½ gallons
6.9 AAU Hallertau/Perle Kettle hops
¼ oz. Hallertau finishing hops

Munich Light
OG 11.5°B (SG 1047)
TG 3.0°B (SG 1012)
Color 5°L
23 BU
Carbonate water
4.5% alcohol v/v
5½ lbs. two-row lager malt
1¼ lbs. Munich malt
1¼ lbs. cara-pale malt
Doughing-in 6 quarts
Mashing-in 3½ quarts
Strike temperature 155°F (68°C)
Temperature maintenance 1½ quarts
Sparging 4¼ gallons
5.6 AAU Hallertau Kettle hops
¼ oz. Hallertau finishing hops

Maibock
OG 16.5°B (SG 1067)
TG 4.0°B (SG 1016)

Color 10.5°L
25 BU
Various water types
6.6% alcohol v/v
7.5 lbs. two-row lager malt
2.5 lbs. Munich malt
1 lb. cara-pale malt
.5 lb. caramel–20 malt
Doughing-in 2½ gallons
Mashing-in 5½ quarts
Strike temperature 155°F (68°C)
Temperature maintenance 1½ quarts
Sparging 6 gallons
6.2 AAU Perle Kettle hops
½ oz. Hallertau finishing hops
¼ oz. Tettnang aroma hops

Dopplebock
OG 18.5°B (SG 1076)
TG 4.5°B (SG 1018)
Color 18.5°L
28 BU
Various water types
7.5% alcohol v/v
7.5 lbs. two-row lager malt
3.5 lbs. Munich malt
1 lb. cara-pale malt
1 lb. caramel–40 malt
Doughing-in 2½ gallons
Mashing-in 1½ gallons
Strike temperature 155°F (68°C)
Temperature maintenance 2 quarts
Sparging 7½ gallons
7 AAU Perle Kettle hops
½ oz. Hallertau finishing hops
½ oz. Tettnang aroma hops

15. BREWING PROCEDURE

 OLLOWING IS A STEP-BY-STEP GUIDE TO THE process of brewing. For any clarification needed, refer to the textual explanation for why certain brewing effects occur.

Malt Examination

Peel the husk away from the dorsal side of twenty or so kernels of malt to expose the acrospire. Unless the acrospire has been uniformly grown to from three-fourths to the full length of the kernel, the malt must be fully decoction mashed. This is also true of any malt that has been kilned to a dark color, that is of either questionable enzymatic strength or very high in protein, or that is steely or poorly malted.

Three-Decoction Mash:
Three and a Half to Nine Hours

Crush the amount of malt called for in the recipes above, or from the worksheet. The malt need not be weighed; it may be measured assuming that one pound equals 4.25 cups, U.S. liquid measure.

Doughing-In

Dough-in the crushed malt by sprinkling it with small amounts of brewing water at roughly 58°F (14°C) until 24 to 28 fluid ounces of water per pound of malt has been kneaded in. For a thin mash, when brewing light, quickly-fermenting beer, 32 to 40 fluid ounces of water per pound are required.

Hold the temperature relatively stable for fifteen minutes (or for up to thirty minutes for dark-roasted or enzyme-poor malt). Mix regularly and thoroughly to distribute moisture evenly throughout the mash. The malt should be uniformly and universally solubilized. Check for successful moisture penetration of the coarser grits and hard ends of the kernels by pulverizing several between the fingers. Make sure there are no dry pockets or balled flour.

Acid Rest

Bring 12 to 14 fluid ounces of brewing water, per pound of malt doughed-in, to a boil. For a thin mash, 16 to 20 fluid ounces are required. Sprinkle and knead it into the grain to raise the mash temperature evenly to 105°F (40°C). After twenty minutes, check the mash pH; if it is at or below 5.8, proceed with the first decoction. Otherwise, acidifying measures must be taken before mashing should proceed.

The mash acidity can be reduced by adding acidified mash from a "lactic-acid mash." One or two days before brewing, mash-in 5 percent of the malt to 155°F (68°C) with boiling water. Rest for at least one hour and then bring this well-saccharified mash to boiling to deoxygenate it. Cover and cool, undisturbed, down to 125°F (52°C). Add a small amount of dry crushed malt (to introduce Lactobacillus delbrueckii) and cover. No airspace should be left above the mash.

After twenty-four hours at 95–120°F (35–49°C), the pH will drop to 5. After two days, it will be at 4.5 or so. Five percent acidified mash at pH 4.8 will reduce a mash at pH 6 to 5.8. At pH 4.5, it will lower the mash pH to about 5.6. A lactic-acid mash is most effective when the brewing water is relatively soft.

More commonly, the pH of an overly-alkaline mash is corrected by decanting all the free liquid off the grist and cautiously mixing gypsum or lactic or citric acid into it until its pH drops to 5.5, and mixing it back into the grist. If the pH of the brewing water exceeds 7.2, in future brews adjust the pH of the brewing water, rather than the mash, using proportionally similar treatment.

First Decoction

Pull the heaviest one-third part of the mash to the side of the tub and withdraw it to the decoction kettle. When dealing with a thick mash, return any free-standing liquid that settles above the boiler mash back to the main mash. The decoction for a thin mash may need to be 40 percent of the mash volume, and consequently must take some free liquid along.

Closely cover the cold settlement and maintain its temperature at 95 to 105°F (35–40°C); mix occasionally.

Heat the decoction to 150 to 158°F (66–70°C) in ten to fifteen minutes and hold for ten minutes to dextrinize. Heat to 167°F (75°C) over fifteen minutes. Bring to a boil in ten to fifteen minutes, while frequently lifting the grain up and away from the bottom of the kettle. Cover and boil vigorously for fifteen minutes (up to forty-five minutes for dark-roasted or enzyme poor malt).

First Thick Mash

Return the darkened decoction to the starchy cold settlement by degrees, while lifting and breaking up the mash, over a period of ten to twenty minutes, to evenly raise the temperature of the whole to 122°F (50°C) [or within the range of 118 to 128°F (48–53°C)]. Check the temperature throughout the mash, making sure that it is even.

Monitor the mash pH; it should drop to pH 5.2 to 5.3. The usual rest period is only twenty minutes before the heaviest part of the mash is drawn off for the second decoction.

Second Decoction

Withdraw the heaviest 40 percent of the mash to the boiling kettle (as before, adjust the decoction volume to reflect consistency). Cover both mashes. Heat the decoction to 150°F (66°C) in ten minutes, to 167°F (75°C) in fifteen to twenty minutes, and to boiling in ten to fifteen minutes. Boil vigorously for twenty minutes, stirring frequently.

Second Thick Mash

Return the boiler mash to the rest mash evenly, so as not to scald any portion of the rest mash. Temperature dispersal must be absolutely uniform. The strike temperature, usually 153 to 155°F (67–68°C), should be reached within ten minutes when the beer is to be fully lagered. (Returning the boiler mash very slowly to raise the mash temperature to 149 to 151°F (65–66°C) over a period of fifteen to thirty minutes favors maltose production for brewing light beer.)

Hold the saccharification temperature for fifteen minutes; the mash will darken in color.

Test for successful starch conversion. Float tincture of iodine (.02N solution; usual medicine-cabinet variety) drop-by-drop above a small sample of the mash in a porcelain dish. Check the color at the interface of the iodine and the mash. Continue mashing until there is no color change, or for a sweet beer until the reaction is only very-faintly reddish. Disregard discoloration caused by husk particles; it in no way indicates lack of conversion.

Use Caution. Iodine is a poison. Do not let it inadvertently taint the mash. Discard all samples and rinse the dish and any equipment that has been contaminated by the iodine.

The precise saccharification strike temperature must be maintained. This may be simply accomplished by infusing small amounts of boiling water into the mash. Because the mash liquid absorbs a great deal of extract during saccharification, it may become too thick to satisfactorily settle into a well-stratified filterbed. These temperature-maintenance infusions serve to improve filtering of a heavy mash and are generally necessary when less than one and one half quarts of water have been used to mash-in each pound of malt. Thinning a thick mash assures that its viscosity does not interfere with filterbed settlement in the lauter tub.

Lauter Decoction
When starch end-point has been verified, rack off the very thinnest 40 to 50 percent of the mash. Bring it to a boil in ten to fifteen minutes. Boil vigorously while stirring for fifteen to forty-five minutes.

Final Rest
Remix the mashes slowly and thoroughly, evenly raising the temperature to 170°F (77°C) or slightly above. Rouse and mix the mash for ten to thirty minutes while maintaining the strike temperature to force the insoluble mash particles into a temporary suspension. This causes a clearly-stratified settlement of first the hulls, then the unmodified starch particles, and finally the protein haze to be formed in the lauter tub.

Sparging/Filtering
Fill the lauter tub to one half inch above the false bottom with brewing water at a temperature of from 175°F (80°C) to boiling. Give the mash one final stirring and transfer it to the lauter tub. Maintain the temperature at as close to 170°F (77°C) as possible for fifteen to forty-five minutes while the filterbed forms undisturbed.

In the meantime, bring the appropriate volume of sparging water to 170 to 176°F (77–80°C).

Ten minutes after the malt particles (husks, acrospires, and any starch granules) have settled and the liquid above the protein coagulum has cleared, set the filterbed by opening the draincock until a steady trickle of runoff forms. Drain the mash until the protein has settled and the clear liquid lies only one-eighth to one-half inch deep above the sludge. Smooth and level the mash surface after the draincock is closed.

Flush all debris from the space below the false bottom. Carefully balance the inlet and outlet flow-rates so that the liquid level above the mash is not disturbed. Close both petcocks when the runoff is free of debris.

Reopen the spigot until a steady flow emerges. Maintain the liquid depth above the mash by returning the runoff to the lauter tub until the wort runs perfectly clear.

Collect the sweet wort and immediately begin heating it to boiling. When all the cloudy runoff has been returned to the lauter-mash, open the sparging-water tap, matching the trickle of fine 170°F (77°C) spray to the runoff rate. Manipulate the flow, balancing the sparging rate to the runoff, so that the filtering takes two hours to complete. (Divide the amount of sweet wort to be collected by 120 minutes to define the required runoff flow-per-minute.) Six-row barley with a high husk content may be run off in as little as thirty minutes. During a slow filtering, the mash may be carefully raked to within six inches of the false bottom to improve extract yield.

Smooth the surface as any cracks appear. Sparge until the density of the runoff drops below 2.5°Balling [SG 1010, corrected to 60°F (15.56°C)]. Discontinue sparging and allow the mash to drain.

Boiling the Wort

Add the loosely broken up boiling hops to the sweet wort as soon as all of the extract has been collected.

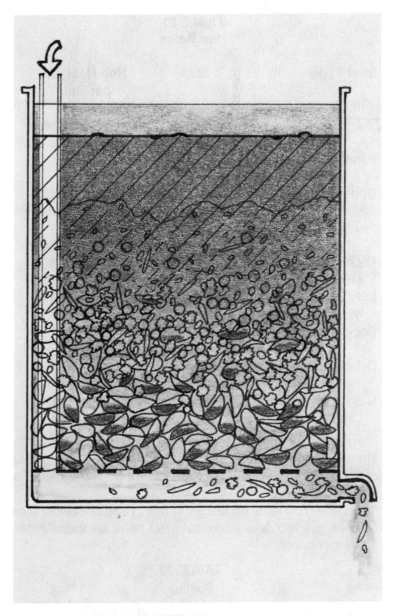

LAUTER TUB

TABLE 21
Hop Rates

Beer Type	°B	B.U.	Hop Rate, oz per Gal.	
			Boiling Hops A.A.U.s	Finishing Hops
Pilsener	12°B	40	1.75	.1-.15 Saaz
Dortmunder	12.5-14°B	26-36	1.15-1.6	.08-.15 Hallertau
Vienna	12.5-15°B	24-30	1.05-1.35	.04-.1 Hal/Saaz
Dark Munich	12.5-14°B	22-36	1.-1.6	.1-.18 Hallertau
Light Munich	11-12°B	20-28	.9-1.25	.08-.12 Hallertau
Bock	16-18°B	24-36	1.1-1.6	.15-.25 Various
Dopplebock	18-28°B	24-40	1.1-1.8	.15-.3 Various
U.S./Light Lager	10-12°B	10-20	.5-.9	.03-.04 Various

To determine the required hop rate, divide the A.A.U.s by the alpha-acidity of the hops being used. For example, using hops of 7% a.a.: 1.75 A.A.U. ÷ 7% a.a. = .25 oz. hops per gallon of wort.

Increase hop rates up to 25% to reflect age or deterioration of hops; discard discolored, oxidized hops, as these impart off-flavors to beer.

TABLE 22
Boiling

Wort Character: **Boil For:**
Decoction mash, 12°B (SG 1049)   1-2 hours

or less
Decoction mash, above 12°B   11/2 - 21/2 hours
Infusion mash, 12°B or less   11/2 - 21/2 hours
Infusion mash, above 12°B   2 - 3 hours

Check the wort acidity. It should be pH 5.5-5.8. If it is below pH 5.2, protein precipitation will be retarded; adjust with a carbonate salt if necessary. Measure and record the density, corrected to 60°F (15.56°C).

TABLE 23

pH Reduction During Wort Boil

If pH at Start of Boil Is:	Then pH at End of Boil Is:
5.7-6.0	5.4-5.7
5.2-5.6	5.0-5.4
5.0	4.9

The pH at the conclusion of the boil should be 5.2-5.5

Hot Break

Agitate the wort regularly. Periodically examine samples to assess flocculation. Remove a glassful of wort. The tannin/ proteins that mist the boiling wort should coagulate into a much smaller number of flakes one-eighth inch long or longer as the boil progresses. Check the pH. It should drop during the boil. The reduction can be expected to approximate that quoted above.

Cold Break

As the end of the boiling period draws near, the flocks in the hot sample should precipitate and leave the wort clear. Force cool the sample; it should slowly cloud as it cools. This cold break should settle out from the wort, leaving it clear, bright, and black. If a clean break cannot be established during the designated boil, and the intensity of the boil and wort pH are acceptable, the beer must be quietly racked off its sediment several times during the secondary fermentation and lagering. Do not exceed quoted boiling times, especially when brewing light beers.It is not likely to improve clarification and increases oxidation and discoloration of the wort.

Finishing Hops

Add finishing hops ten to fifteen minutes before the end of the boil, as the heat is shut off or when the wort is being run from the kettle. The later the addition, the lesser the flavor and the greater the aroma.

Filtering and Cooling the Wort

Agitate the wort thoroughly and cease heating. Cover, and allow the hop and trub residue to settle (up to thirty minutes). The hops should settle on the false bottom or in a filterbag at least one to two inches thick. Run off the extract from a tap below the filterbed, slowly at first, to set the hop filter. Return the runoff to the kettle until it clears. Where hop pellets are substituted for whole hops, siphon the wort off its trub.

The wort must be cooled to 39 to 43°F (4–6°C) to precipitate the cold break. Force cooling the wort gives a more complete break than does passive attempering. A wort cooler should always be employed to properly clear the wort. Where an immersible cooler is employed, the wort can be cooled in the kettle before it is filtered. Otherwise the filtered wort is run through a counterflow chiller and into an enclosed settling tank. Allowed to rest undisturbed, the wort precipitates a sediment equal to 10 to 20 percent of the hot-break trub.

Rack off the first 2 to 5 percent of the filtered and chilled wort and mix the yeast starter into it. Aerate it thoroughly and cover it.

When the wort has drained to nearly the level of the hop filter bed, sparge the hops with 8 fluid ounces of boiling water for each ounce of hops, or until the extract content of the runoff drops below 5°Balling (SG 1020). Take care that no trub is rinsed free during the sparging. Do not attempt to collect the extract trapped in the hops by raking or pressing them.

Keep the wort covered while it is settling. The risk of contamination is minimized when the atmosphere is sanitary. At the very least, the area should be clean, dry, and free from drafts.

Measure the wort volume. If less than the prescribed volume is present, restore it with brewing water that has been boiled to sterilize it. Measure and record the wort pH and extract content. Determine extract efficiency using the table below.

TABLE 24

Extract Efficiency

1. Volume of wort, at 60°F (15.56°C:)   1._____
2. °Balling of wort, at 60°F: 2._____
3. Add 259 to line 2:   3._____
4. Multiply line 2 by line 3:   4._____
5. Divide line 4 by 3100:   5._____
6. Multiply line 1 by line 5:   6._____
   Line 6 is the pounds of extract in
   the wort.
7. Pounds of malt mashed-in: 2._____
8. Divide line 6 by line 7:   3._____

Line 8 is the extract efficiency of the mash. If the extract content of the wort is less than that which had been anticipated, then mash efficiency was poor. Correct in future brewings, or use this extract efficiency to determine the malt requirement of future brewings.

Pitching the Yeast

Most lagers require the pitching of .40 to .66 fluid ounces (8.5 to 14 grams) of thick, pasty yeast per gallon of wort to be pitched. Up to 1 fluid ounce (21 grams) of yeast is required to ferment a gallon of wort of less than $10°$Balling (SG 1040) or more than $16°$Balling (SG 1060).

TABLE 25

If the culture vessel is not graduated, the volume of the yeast culture, in fluid ounces, can be measured by the formula $\dfrac{(\pi r_2)h}{1.8046}$

1. Diameter of yeast-culture container $d = 1.$ _____
2. Divide line 1 by 2 ($r=d/2$): $r = 2.$ _____
3. Multiply line 2 by itself $r_2 = 3.$ _____
4. Multiply line 3 by 3.1416 $\pi r_2 = 4.$ _____
5. Multiply line 4 by the thickness (depth) of the yeast sediment: $(\pi r_2)h = 5.$ _____
6. Divide line 5 by 1.8046: $\dfrac{(\pi r_2)h}{1.8046} = 6.$ _____

Line 6 gives the fluid ounces of yeast sediment in the starter vessel.

Shake the starter vessel to mix the yeast sediment into a milky solution. Pitch only the amount of yeast necessary to ensure rapid initial fermentation. Any remainder may be frozen or covered with fresh wort, capped, and refrigerated, for use later in the brewing cycle or for subsequent brewings.

Kraeusening

When kraeusening, "new" beer equal to 10 percent of the primary fermenting volume at up to $5°F$ ($3°C$) above pitching temperature is used to introduce active yeast for fermentation. Kraeusen produces the strongest possible fermentation start.

Yeast Starter

A yeast starter is the equivalent of kraeusen beer but made up from a yeast culture roused into ten times its volume of wort. The 10:1 dilution is repeated at the point when strong fermentation becomes evident until the starter is at pitching strength (5 to 10 percent of the volume it will be pitched into). Yeast starters, like kraeusening, promote stronger and faster fermentation starts and blanket the ferment with CO_2 much sooner than does pitching yeast sediment.

Yeast starters should be made up from sterile bottled wort saved from previous brewings one to two days before they need to be pitched. The yeast culture should have been mixed with 2 to 5 percent of the primary fermenter volume of the wort to allow the culture to begin adapting to the wort while the remainder is being cooled and sedimented.

Decant all the chilled wort in excess of the amount needed for primary fermentation into sterile containers. Heat to boiling, cap and refrigerate until needed.

Rack the cooled wort off of its sediment into the primary fermenter, adding the yeast, by increments, as the wort runs into the fermenter. Allow the wort to splash into the fermenter and rouse the inoculated wort splashingly and thoroughly. Fill the fermenter and fit the airlock (blow-off) to it. The temperature at pitching should be 42 to 47°F (6–8°C).

Primary Fermentation: Five to Twelve Days

Temperatures quoted are for full-bodied, dextrin-rich lagers above 10°Balling (SG 1040) that are to be fully lagered. For maltose-rich wort to be fermented in less time, add 6 to 8°F (3–4°C) to the temperature. Do not, however, exceed 60°F (15°C) during primary fermentation and 45°F (7°C) during secondary fermentation.

TABLE 26

Primary Fermentation Temperature/Time Guideline

Temperature		Duration
50-55°F	10-13°C	5-8 days
48-50°F	9-10°C	6-9 days
41-48°F	5-9°C	6-12 days

Hold the inoculated wort, covered and fitted with a fermentation lock, at an ambient temperature of 45 to 50°F (7-10°C). Visually examine the ferment. A foam wreath forms at the sides of the fermenter as the lag phase ends. A light shone on the surface reveals active carbonic gas release.

Low Kraeusen

Twenty-four to thirty-six hours after pitching, the foam migrates to the center of the beer surface. If a closed-fermentation blow-off system is not being employed, malt and hop residues in the foam head must be skimmed off.

Check and record temperature, liquid pressure, and pH. The temperature should begin rising. Extract losses should daily approximate .5°Balling (SG 1002); the pH is noticeably dropping. The foam cover becomes tightly knit. A light shone on the beer reveals even more CO_2 release and a milky turbidity.

High Kraeusen

Three to four days after pitching, the foam rises up to form looser-knit, cream-colored "rocky heads." Daily check and record temperature, extract content, and pH. When the temperature of the ferment reaches 50 to 52°F (10-11°C), lower the ambient temperature so that the temperature of the ferment does not rise further. It should be brought down to 45°F (7°C) over the next several days. Do not reduce the

CARBOY WITH SIPHON

ferment temperature by more than 5°F (3°C) daily. The liquid pressure should fall by 1°Balling (SG 1004) daily. The pH should drop to about 4.5.

Post Kraeusen

Four to twelve days (six to ten days is usual) after pitching, the head formation slows as CO_2 production falls off. When disturbed, the foam head readily separates and reforms only very slowly.

Keep the ferment topped-up to its original volume to prevent the dessication of residues left stranded by evaporation on the sides or top of the fermenter. Scrape away the residue left by the receding foam head only if it can be accomplished without dislodging the scum back into the ferment.

If a diacetyl rest is being employed to foreshorten lagering, allow the temperature of the post-kraeusen ferment to reach 52°F (11°C). After two days, again lower the ambient temperature, bringing the beer down to 38 to 40°F (3–4°C) over three days' time.

Reduce the temperature of the primary fermenter to 38 to 40°F by manipulating the ambient temperature. Extract reduction should slow dramatically. The pH should not drop much below pH 4.5.

When the extract drop over a twenty-four-hour period slows to about 0.5°Balling (SG 1002), prepare to rack the beer into a secondary fermenter. Remove a sample glassful, agitate it, and examine it. The beer at this point should be clear, bright, and black. Distinctively visible yeast colonies in temporary suspension should settle out rapidly and firmly upon cooling. If the yeast does not settle out or if the beer is not clear, then it cannot be held for an extended period of aging and should probably be fined.

Make a hydrometer reading of the sample and record it. It should be roughly 25 to 35 percent of what the wort density (OG) was, or 1°Balling (SG 1004) above the expected final density (TG). Testing with "Dextrocheck" should show less than 5 percent reducing sugar.

Secondary Fermentation

Record the pH and temperature of the beer in the primary fermenter. Clean and sterilize the secondary fermenter, preferably rinsing with boiled water (or steam). Carefully rack the beer in the primary fermenter off of its settlement into the closed secondary fermenter. Take care not to carry along any of the sedimented yeast. Cease racking when the runoff becomes the least bit cloudy.

Run the beer into the secondary fermenter as quickly as possible, absolutely avoiding splashing. To reduce the surface area/head space and restore the volume, top up the fermenter with 5 percent kraeusen beer, sterile wort, or brewing water. Kraeusen beer should be added if yeast performance during primary fermentation was unsatisfactory.

Seed yeast for starters and culturing can be collected from the primary-fermenter yeast cake.

Fit the fermenter with a fermentation lock. Reduce the ambient temperature slowly from 38 to 40°F (3–4°C) down to 33 to 37°F (1–3°C). If the hydrometer reading at racking is one third the density of the cooled wort, ferment at 33 to 34°F (1–2°C) for seven to twenty-one days. If the reading is much less than one-third of the original hydrometer reading, the beer lacks slowly-fermenting dextrins and should be fermented for ten days at up to 37°F (3°C) before the temperature is reduced for lagering.

Beer that will not be lagered is usually held in the secondary fermenter for two to six weeks and is fermented down to the terminal extract value. Gelatin finings may be added when the hydrometer shows little or no extract reduction over the course of several days. The beer should be bottled ten days after fining. No reduction in the hydrometer reading should occur during the several days prior to bottling.

Lagering

The secondary fermenter should be very nearly full. Keep it topped up with sterile wort, or brewing water, as necessary. Fit the fermenter with a pressure valve only if it is a pressure vessel. *Do not lager under pressure in a glass carboy;* use a Cornelius keg or the like. Do not lager at above five pounds per square inch. Lager at 33 to 36°F (1–2°C) for seven to twelve days per each 2°Balling (SG 1008) of the original wort hydrometer reading. If the hydrometer reading at racking was much less than one-third the value of the wort reading (OG), the beer should not be lagered for more than one week for each 2°Balling of the wort reading. Lowering the temperature to 30 to 33°F (–1 to 1°C) reduces lagering times.

Keep the beer out of direct sunlight and avoid drafts and temperature fluctuations.

Fine the beer, if so desired, when the hydrometer reading is at or near the terminal extract value and no drop has been experienced in the last five days. Residual sugars should be less than 2 percent (Dextrocheck or other reducing-sugar analysis).

Prepare the finings by mixing one-eighth teaspoon of vegetable gelatin per gallon of beer with two to three teaspoons of cold beer, wort, or brewing water. Mix thoroughly, pressing the liquid into the gelatin to form a smooth paste. Allow fifteen to thirty minutes for the gelatin to become evenly moistened and the mix several tablespoons of beer or water into it. Mix it to a uniform consistency. Repeat, adding progressively larger volumes of liquid to the gelatin, until 8 fluid ounces of solution per gallon of beer is obtained.

Gently heat the solution to dissolve the gelatin. **Do not boil**. Thoroughly mix the warm solution into the aged beer by stirring or rocking the lager vessel for two to three minutes without aerating the beer. Allow the beer to resettle and rest undisturbed for ten to fourteen days before bottling.

The beer must be below 50°F (10°C) for the finings to have any effect. Use **only** pure gelatin to fine lager beer.

Add hop extract for a strong hop aroma with the finings.

Bottling

See the following table for the amount of kraeusen beer or priming sugar necessary to carbonate the beer. When the priming solution is actively fermenting, skim off its head and quietly run it into a sterilized close vessel with the aged beer. Cease racking the fermented beer as soon as its sediment is disturbed. Without splashing, rouse the beer for several minutes to induce carbon dioxide release from the beer.

Inspect the bottles. Reject any with chipped rims or residue deposits. Wash in warm water, using cleansing solution only if necessary. Thoroughly brush the inside surfaces. Sterilize bottles in live steam in .1 percent chlorine bath or in a 3 percent caustic soda bath at above 170°F (77°C). Rinse sterilant-treated bottles several times in pure, clean water. Invert to dry; alternatively stack wet bottles in an oven and heat to 200°F (93°C) to sterilize.

TABLE 27

For	Bottle Pressure* At:			Approximate: Oz. Dextrose Per Gal.:		Fl. Oz. Wort Kraeusen Per Gal.		
50°F	32°F	40°F	60°F			10°B	12°B	14°B
	Atmospheres							
2	1.2	1.5	2.5	1.2		13.5	11.2	9.6
2.5	1.5	1.9	3.2	1.5		17.	14.	12.
3	1.9	2.35	3.8	1.8		20.4	16.9	14.4
3.5	2.3	2.8	4.4	2.1		23.8	19.7	16.8

*AT SEA LEVEL. For elevations other than sea level, reduce bottle priming by approximately 3.3% for each 1,000' of elevation. 50°F is the standard temperature at which bottle pressure is gauged.

Carefully dispense the primed beer into clean, dry bottles, filling them to within three-fourths inch of the rim. Loosely cover the bottles for several minutes to allow carbonic-gas release to drive off oxygen in the head space before securing the caps and inverting the bottles to disclose leakage.

Hold at 45 to 50°F (7–10°C) for three to four days before beginning to reduce the temperature to 32 to 45°F (0–7°C). Store for at least ten to fourteen days. Highly carbonated beer should be conditioned down to near freezing. Do not subject the bottled beer to drafts or temperature fluctuations.

Draft Beer

Clean the keg as for bottles; if wooden, check pitch or paraffin surfacing for cracks or deterioration. Usually beer for draft is drawn into the keg with just less than 1 percent fermentable extract left in it to provide carbonation for cask conditioning. Otherwise, add kraeusen beer or priming solution in sufficient quantity to produce 2.75 atm. (40 lbs./ sq. in.) pressure. Rouse thoroughly to induce a mad condition.

Fill the keg to within two inches of the bung hole. After several minutes, drive in the bung with a rubber or wooden mallet. Condition ten to fourteen days before tapping.

Troubleshooting

Mash

Balled Starch in Mash: Poorly handled doughing-in of the crushed malt; malt too finely crushed. Correct with decoction mash.

Mash pH Too High: Brewing water overly alkaline; poor quality mash. Correct by adding organic acid or mineral salt.

Mash pH Too Low: Brewing water overly acidic; lactic-acid or acetic-acid bacteria-spoiled malt. Correct pH with alkaline mineral salts.

Mash Doesn't Saccharify: Lack of diastatic enzymes in mash, either destroyed at malting or by mash temperatures above 160°F (71°C); inappropriate pH. Add crushed pale malt and continue mashing; check pH. As a last resort, add diastatic enzyme preparation.

Set Mash: Poorly converted mash; malt poorly doughed-in; malt too finely crushed; mash poorly stirred up before filtering; too fast a runoff rate. In most cases, correct by thoroughly stirring up the mash and allowing it to resettle; cut the mash to within six inches of the bottom to reopen channels of extract flow in the mash. Press hot water up from under the false bottom. Reduce runoff/sparging rate.

Wort

Low Extract: Not enough malt used; poor filtering efficiency; unconverted starch due to insufficient crushing; balled starch from poorly handled doughing-in; wrong mash pH; insufficient mash enzyme activity. Check for unconverted starch by making an iodine test of a wort sample. Continue brewing the same volume at the lower density.

Poor Kettle Break: Flocks do not sediment; insufficient protein decomposition in mash; wort agitation insufficient; temperature too low; improper pH; too few hop tannins in the boil; poor quality malt. Increase heat and wort movement. Check pH and hop rate; correct if necessary. Or if the wort clears but throws very little sediment, then the mash protein-digestion is overdone.

Poor Cold Break: Wort cooled too slowly; improper pH; wort lacks tannins; excessive mash protein digestion. Cool to below 32°F to encourage sedimentation.

Wort Tastes Sour: Mash/wort pH too low; coliform, acetic, lactic- acid bacteria contamination. Check pH; heat wort to above 140°F (60°C) and re-cool; pitch quickly. Sourness may diminish with aging or be masked by adding burnt malt, finishing hops, or calcium carbonate.

Sour or Vinegar Taste/Smell: Acetic acid bacteria. As above.

Fermentation

Insufficient Lag Phase: Wort insufficiently aerated; too much trub carried into ferment; temperature too high. Ferment has strong solvent and fruity aroma.

Excessive Lag Phase: Too little yeast pitched; yeast weak, degenerated, poisoned, or shocked by temperature change; wort extract too low; inappropriate pH; wort too cold; excessive oxygenation of wort; poor starch conversion in the mash. Rouse in new yeast. Correct temperature to suit yeast strain.

Fruity or Vegetative Smell: From underoxygenation of the wort, excessive trub or degraded yeast culture; from coliform infection of the cooled wort. Irreversible. Avoid further contact with atmosphere.

Banana Odor: From underoxygenated wort, abnormal lag phase.

Celery Odor: H. protea, probably from tained yeast culture. Irreversible.

Disagreeable Smell/Taste; Turbidity, Acidity: Pediococcus or Bacillus contamination of the primary ferment. Irreversible.

Sour or Vinegar Taste/Smell: Acetic acid bacteria, commonly introduced during aeration, racking or bottling. Irreversible.

Sluggish Fermentation: Weak or inappropriate yeast strain; yeast degenerated, poisoned or shocked by temperature change; fermentation temperature too cold; iron, chlorine, or nitrates in the water supply; poor starch conversion in the mash; too low a wort extract; wort lacking in readily fermentable sugars or soluble nitrogen. Establish correct temperature and pH. Repitch.

Spotty Low-Kraeusen Head, Unable to Support Trub: Weak yeast; temperature too low; wort inadequately hopped; deteriorated hops. Raise fermentation temperature; rouse in new yeast.

Fermentation Ceases before High Kraeusen: Temperature

too cold; extract too low or from wort lacking readily-fermentable sugars or yeast nutrients. Establish correct temperature; repitch.

Yeast Break, Head Falls Prematurely: Temperature lowered prematurely; poor yeast strain; too fast a pH drop in the ferment (bacterial contamination); inadequate extract. Establish correct temperature, pH; repitch.

Poor Yeast Flocculation; Yeast Do Not Settle; Porous Sediment: Dusty yeast strain; wild yeast contamination; poor starch conversion in mash; inappropriate pH; temperature too high. Reduce temperatures. Fine the aged beer.

Haze in Beer after High Kraeusen: Insufficient protein reduction during mashing; inadequate boil; wild yeast contamination; dusty yeast pitched. Reduce temperature before racking and during lagering; fine; as last resort treat with papain or similar proteolytic-enzyme extract.

Yeast Floats to Surface after High Kraeusen: Fermentation contaminated by wild yeast; culture yeast degenerated; brewing water too soft; sudden temperature rise; pH too high. Skim and repitch. Degenerated yeast have an unpleasant smell; when yeast performance is poor or abnormal, sample the bouquet.

Bottled or Kegged Beer

Roughness: Excessive water hardness; insufficient boil; excess tannin; insufficient kettle evaporation; excessive oxygenation.

Fruity Taste: From higher alcohols and the products of their decomposition, the consequence of an abnormal lag phase, too high a fermentation temperature, or a deteriorated yeast strain. From coliform contamination of the yeast culture, splashing, or aeration during racking.

Sour Taste: From too low a pH; from acetic-acid bacterial contamination.

Bitter-Vegetable Taste: From deteriorated hops (oxidized B-acids).

Buttery (Diacetyl) Flavor: Where strong, from lactic-acid bacteria. Slight diacetyl flavor more often from too low a pitching rate, beer racked from its primary sediment too early or oxidized in the secondary, or may be characteristic of a poor yeast strain.

Cardboardy Taste: Oxidation of protein; from too much air in bottle headspace; trub carried into the ferment; warm storage, mishandling; insufficient boil, excessive aeration.

Sulfury Taste: Oxidation of protein; poor rinsing of sulfur-based sterilant; excessive extraction during sparging; too high a pH at sparging; from wild yeast, zymomonas or coliform bacteria. May be characteristic of yeast strain or from autolization of sedimented yeast.

Medicinal Taste: From autolization of yeast; wild yeast or bacteria; chlorine in the water supply.

Skunky Odor: Beer light-struck. Avoid direct sunlight during brewing.

Rotten Egg Odor: Hydrogen sulphide; fermentation by wild yeast; in bottled or kegged beer, may be from contamination by Zymomonas bacteria.

Thinness: Wort extract too low; excessive mash protein digestion; dextrin-poor extract.

Haze: Poor mash protein digestion; insufficient boil; wild yeast; bacteria; poor fermentation temperature control; poorly executed doughing-in.

Gelatinous Precipitate: Excessive sparging; poorly-degraded hemicellulose.

Lack of Head: Very poor protein degradation; lipids in ferment (excessive sparging); excessive protein digestion; overboiling; fining; insufficient or deteriorated hops.

Gushing: Temperature fluctuation; mishandling; old malt.

Problems encountered with bottled beer should be accentuated by holding a sample at 85°F (30°C) and visually monitoring it for several days. Precipitates or surface formations generally indicate microbial contamination. Culturing or flavor evaluation may pinpoint organism responsible.

BREWING LOG

BEER TYPE: °B: B.U.:
WATER SOURCE: pH: HARDNESS:
CLOSED FERMENTER CAPACITY:
COOLED WORT VOLUME:
EXTRACT SOURCE/
MODIFICATION: LBS:

MASH
Water for doughing in, volume:
Boiling water for mashing in, volume:
Acid rest, temperature: pH: duration:
Protein rest, temperature: pH: duration:
Saccharification rest, temp.:   pH: duration:
Iodine test results:
Water for temperature maintenance, volume:

Sparging water, volume: temperature:

Lauter mash, depth: ave. temperature:

1st runoff, density:
Last runoff, density: pH:
                            filtering duration:
Mashing/sparging observations:

Sweet wort volume: pH: density:
BOIL
Boiling period: volume to be evaporated:
Boiling hops, type: a.a.%   oz.:
Hot break assessment:
Aroma hops, type: oz.:
Finishing hops, type: oz.:

Cooled wort, volume:
temp.: pH: density:
Extract efficiency: cooling, duration:
Boiling/cooling observations:

FERMENT Pitching, date:
Yeast type: source: vol.:
Primary ferment, volume: temperature:
Low kraeusen, date:
temp.: pH: density:
High kraeusen, date:
temp.: pH: density:
Observations, primary fermentation:

Racking, date: temp.: pH: density:
Kraeusen/wort/water
added at racking, volume: density:
Fining, date:
Observations, secondary
fermentation/lagering:

BOTTLING
Kraeusen/priming solution, volume: density:
Bottling, date:
temp.: density: density:
Bottling volume: conditioning temperature:
Evaluation: date:

Evaluation: date:

Evaluation: date:

16. CLEANING AND STERILIZING

ALL BREWING EQUIPMENT MUST BE KEPT SCRUPU-lously clean. Wort-cooling, yeast-culturing, and fermenting equipment must also be made sterile. Equipment should be cleaned immediately after each use and all residues and particles washed off before it is sterilized. No abrasives should ever be used to scour brewing equipment with the exception of copper or stainless steel kettles.

Actually cleaners should be used sparingly and then only on equipment that has been badly neglected and is too soiled to be cleaned by being soaked in water and then rigorously scrubbed. Where deposits have formed, only the deposits themselves should be treated for removal, and then preferably by nothing more than a thick paste of fresh yeast.

Sterilizing with boiling water or steam is preferable to using chemical sterilants. Heating equipment to above 140°F (60°C) for twenty minutes eliminates most microbes, while heating to above 170°F (77°C), boiling or steaming sterilizes any equipment that does not have impenetrable deposits. Sterilizing wet bottles and small pieces of equipment in an

211

oven at 200°F (93°C) or in a dishwasher with a heat-drying cycle is oftentimes the most practical method.

Sterilizing solutions should only be applied where equipment size, shape, or manufacture—or severe contamination—makes heat sterilization impractical. The cleansers and sterilants specified below should not be misconstrued as being substitutes for prompt and thorough cleaning and sterilizing with pure, clear 180°F (82°C) plus water. All cleaning and antiseptic solutions should be freshly made up as needed, as most lose their potency during storage.

A thorough rinsing after using a cleanser or sterilant is very important for protecting the taste of the beer. Scrub or swab all surfaces with rinse water. Grossly inefficient rinsing can be identified by monitoring the pH of the rinse water for change.

The usual cleaning cycle includes a cold-water soaking, either a hot or cold cleaning as appropriate, and a cold rinse. For fermenting equipment, heat sterilization or the application of a sterilant (usually in cold water followed by a hot rinse) is also necessary. See the appendix on "Useful Information" for the preparation of percentage solutions.

Following is a detailed look at how to clean various materials with different solutions:

Construction

Stainless Steel: Clean with 2 to 3 percent hot caustic-soda solution and mild detergent at 170°F (77°C), followed with one or more rinses with water over 140°F (60°C). Periodic application of acid cleansers removes *beerstone,* or deposits of oxalic lime and organic matter. Use 5 percent sodium or potassium metabisulfite, calcium sulfite, sulfuric or sulfurous acid as a sterilant.

Copper: Only noncorrosive cleansers should be used. Caustic soda especially must be avoided. As copper is commonly used only for kettle fabrication, it should only need to be scoured with sand or other silica abrasive.

Glass, Glazed Porcelain: Most cleansers and sterilants are suitable for use on glass or glazed porcelain; only phosphoric acid should not be used. A 2 to 3 percent caustic-soda solution is the preferred cleanser. Trisodium phosphate or mild detergents may be substituted. Microorganic contamination may be countered by application of chlorinated trisodium phosphate or more commonly by household bleach in .5 percent aqueous solution. After acid cleansing, any of the acid sterilants should be used.

Plastics, Enamelware: A 2 to 3 percent caustic soda solution will not harm these surfaces, but mild detergents are more commonly used. Either fabricant requires application of a cleanser more frequently than glass or metal surfaces. Sterilants may be .5 percent chlorine bleach, 5 percent chlorinated trisodium phosphate solution (alkaline), or sodium or potassium metabisulfite (acid).

Aluminum: Only mild detergent with an acid cleanser (5 percent nitric or up to 10 percent phosphoric acid) should be used. Compatible sterilizing agents include sodium and potassium metabisulfite and sulfurous acid.

Wood: Rinse and brush wooden articles and then immerse them in boiling water immediately after use. Because of wood's natural porosity, use of cleansers should be avoided. Where absolutely necessary, a hot 2 to 3 percent solution of caustic soda or 5 percent sodium carbonate or bicarbonate can be applied, but it must be rinsed away by several long baths, from hot to cold. A 5 percent metabisulfite sterilizing followed by several clear-water rinses may be employed, but boiling or steaming is preferred. Any solution applied to wood is likely to leach into it and is very difficult to coax back out of it.

Do not let wood implements sit damp between brewings. They must be dried thoroughly after cleansing.

Equipment
Malt Mills and Screen: These need only be cleaned with a

stiff brush after every use. The cleaning, however, must be thorough.

Mash and Lauter Tubs: These should be kept wet after use and then scrubbed clean, rinsed, and dried. A *false bottom or grain bag* in the tubs must at least occasionally be boiled in a 2 to 3 percent caustic soda solution or be scrubbed with an appropriate cleanser.

Brew Kettles of Copper, Stainless Steel or Aluminum: Articles of this construction are the only ones used in brewing upon which an abrasive should be used. In fact, they benefit by its employment. The abrasives not only scour away calcified deposits but pitting and etching of the kettle surface improves heat transfer and protein coagulation during wort boiling. A thick paste of fresh yeast should be brushed onto any stubborn deposits and kept moist before scrubbing. The yeast is finally rinsed away with clean, cold water.

Immersible Heating Elements: These must periodically be soaked in 10 percent trisodium phosphate solution and then scrubbed to remove scale.

Fermentation Locks: The locks should always be soaked in caustic soda solution and then flushed clean after every use. Use of an antiseptic solution in the fermentation lock is not necessary, but a lock should be changed as soon as it becomes dirty.

Fermenters: Insofar as possible, fermenters should only be cleaned by a thorough brushing in cold water after use and then be heat-sterilized before their next use. Any beerstone deposits that do not come free should be covered with yeast paste. A mild detergent or cleanser (3 percent caustic soda, 5 percent trisodium phosphate, or 2 percent nitric acid) may be added. The paste should be kept moist for a day and then the deposit scrubbed away. Where a cleanser is necessary, use caustic soda. Where a sterilant is necessary, use household bleach.

Plastic Tubing: Used for wort cooling or siphoning, plastic tubes should be boiled in caustic soda and thoroughly flushed. Hydrogen peroxide can also be used to clean and sterilize tubing.

Bottles: Clean-looking bottles can be washed in 170°F (77°C) water, boiled, or steamed. Dirty bottles should be soaked and then scoured with 2 to 3 percent caustic soda, 5 percent trisodium phosphate or a mild detergent solution, followed by several rinses with water over 140°F (60°C).

Alkaline Cleansers

Sodium Hydroxide: This is caustic soda, NaOH. It is effective only when it is used hot. A most effective solvent, it hydrolizes most malt and wort residues. It may, however, leave calcium salt residues, except when it is applied with a detergent or the sequestering agent E.D.T.A. ($C_{10}H_{12}N_2Na_4O_8$). It is highly corrosive and should not be used on copper surfaces. It is the principal component of commercial dishwashing detergent.

Sodium Carbonate: This compound is washing soda, $Na_2CO_3 \cdot 10H_2O$. It is applied hot but is far less effective than other cleansers mentioned.

Sodium Bicarbonate: Commonly called baking soda, $NaHCO_3$, this is similar to sodium carbonate in effect.

Trisodium Phosphate: A common household cleanser, TSP, $Na_3PO_4 \cdot 12H_2O$, is a very effective solvent, especially for calcified deposits such as boiler scale. Chlorinated trisodium phosphate adds some bacteriacidal capability to its cleansing.

Acid Cleansers

Nitric Acid: Called aqua fortis, HNO_3, this substance is caustic but does not corrode aluminum. It is corrosive to other metals. It can also be used as a sterilant.

Phosphoric Acid: Phosphoric acid, H_3PO_4, is a substitute for nitric acid when cleaning aluminum. Do not use on porcelain.

Alkaline Sterilants

Sodium Hypochlorite: This is common household chlorine bleach, Clorox, or chlorinated soda, $NAClO \cdot 5H_2O$. It is a very effective sterilant. It is usually used in strengths less than 1 percent in aqueous solution, but it is effective in distilled water at less than .05 percent (.3 fl. oz. in five gal.) with reasonable contact time. At this concentration, the sterilant may not need to be rinsed so long as objects are well drained.

Caution: This cleanser produces poisonous chlorine gas in contact with acid compounds. This reaction also strongly corrodes stainless steel.

Acid Sterilants

Hydrogen Peroxide: H_2O_2 is used primarily as a sterilant, but it is also a very effective solvent for cleaning flexible tubing.

Sodium Metabisulfite: $Na_2S_2O_5$ is an antifermentive. **Caution**: In the presence of acids, it produces noxious sulfur dioxide (burnt-match) odor.

Potassium Metabisulfite: $K_2S_2O_5$ is similar to the sodium salt.

Calcium Sulfite: $CaSO_4 \cdot 2H_2O$ is commonly used by commercial breweries. In contact with the atmosphere, it oxidizes to $CaSO_4$.

Sulfuric Acid: Sulfuric acid, H_2SO_4, is a caustic acid, corrosive to most metals. As *sulfurous acid,* SO_2, it is commonly used in commercial breweries in 6 percent aqueous solution.

Alcohol, Ethyl or Isopropyl: This is useful only for sterilizing small articles. It is effective only with reasonable contact time.

17. EQUIPMENT

OLLOWING IS A LIST OF EQUIPMENT USEFUL for brewing. Of course, each brewer has his equipment preferences. This list, however, gives brewers a start.

pH Papers: These are wide range, pH 2 to 10, and narrow range, pH 4.2–6.2 (5.2–6.8, 5.2–7.4). Accurate, easy-to-read pH meters, such as reasonably priced units marketed for home swimming pool use, can also be used.

Water Test Kits: These kits test for chlorine, nitrite, nitrate, ammonia, and pH. All are inexpensively available at aquarium-supply shops. Also, these kits and iron, calcium, and other mineral-ion tests are available through laboratory-supply houses. Test kits, especially for water hardness, are more valuable to the homebrewer—and more versatile—than municipal water-supply analyses, the moreso when the two are used in conjunction.

Kettle for Water Treatment: This is for boiling or mineral-salt treatment of brewing water. The brewing kettle is generally used.

Gram Scale: A gram scale is necessary for accurately dispensing mineral salts. These are usually quite inexpensive,

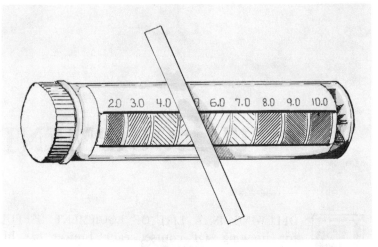

pH PAPERS

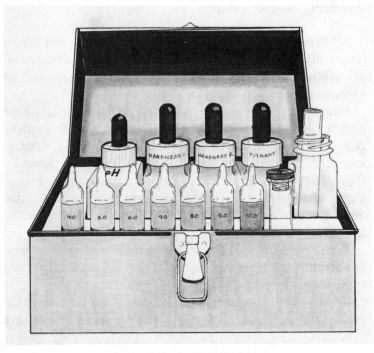

pH AND HARDNESS TEST KIT

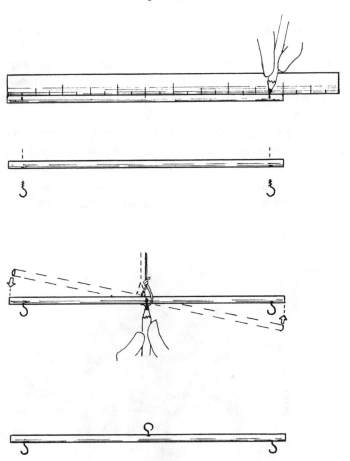

CONSTRUCTING A BALANCE SCALE

but because the accuracy of a cheap scale is likely suspect, it should be calibrated using a substance of known weight to correct any inaccuracy.

Construction of a simple balance scale can eliminate the need to purchase this or any scale. To use the balance scale, suspend a substance known to be of the weight desired from one side, and add the substance being measured to the other side until the loads level.

Covered Water-Storage Vessel: This is for treated water. Any idle fermenter should serve the purpose.

Graduated One-Quart Measuring Cup: A Pyrex cup is more serviceable than either glass or plastic. Use it to measure and dispense water, malt, and mash. It is indispensable as a dipper and for mixing during mashing and wort boiling.

Malt Scale: Some brewers use malt scales in the one-to-ten-pound range; however, malt may be accurately measured by volume to eliminate the need for this piece of equipment.

Malt Mill: Unless crushed malt is purchased, some sort of a mill is necessary. Counter-top grain ("maize") mills such

MILL

as that pictured yield the most satisfactory grist of any of the home mills. Coffee mills and others equipped with cutting blades are wholly unsatisfactory.

Screens: Screens are used to gauge the degree of crushing. A kitchen colander, sieve, flour sifter, or various sizes of screening can be used to separate several proportions of malt particle sizes. A rough comparison can then be made against separation by standard screens of a well-crushed malt.

Lactic-Acid Mash Tub: This is necessary where a lactic-acid mash is being made to reduce pH at doughing-in. It is of roughly 5 percent mash tub capacity. A well-insulated thermos or jug serves best, as temperature maintenance is imperative during the long rest.

Mash Tub: This may be a food-safe plastic bucket, glazed stoneware crock, insulated plastic ice chest, or beverage cooler. Capacity should be roughly equal to fermenter capacity.

If it is to double as a lauter tub, it needs to be cylindrical and equipped with a spigot, false bottom, or filter bag, and the means to flush the space between. On the whole, however, it is far easier to manage mashing and filtering in separate containers; this leaves the mash tub fitted with a spigot from which to dispense the sparge water.

Aside from their fragility and cumbersome weight, well-glazed stoneware crocks offer a good choice for a mash tub, primarily because they hold heat relatively well and are able to be readily and thoroughly cleaned. These are the two most important criteria in the selection of a mash tub. The only shortcoming is that most crocks do not come fitted with a spigot and thus cannot be used to hold sparge water.

Food-safe, insulated, hard-plastic picnic chests hold mash temperature exceedingly well, but care must be taken during cleaning so that the surfaces are not abraded. High temperatures may also distort the surfaces [high-density polyethylene at $170°F$ ($77°C$)].

Large stainless steel pails or kettles are easy to clean, rugged, and lightweight, but they cannot maintain rest temperatures unless they are insulated. A jacket cut from styrofoam or a wrapping for the tub from any of the myriad of insulating materials will improve its performance. It should be used to stabilize the temperature of a stovetop mashing.

A heating element, whether it is integral or a hand-held immersible unit, is somewhat effective, but even temperature dispersal can be achieved only by demonic stirring. Some overheating and caramelization of the mash is inevitable and clean-up may be tedious.

Rigid plastic pails and buckets hold heat somewhat better than do those of stainless steel but not as well as is required. They are very inexpensive and can be fitted with a hardware-store spigot with relative ease. Use only food-safe heat-resistant plastic.

Enameled steel kettles should be avoided as they chip easily and expose the mash to certain iron contamination.

Large Stainless Steel Spoon: This is preferably of one-piece construction. It is used throughout the brewing.

Paddle: This is used to stir the mash and boiling wort; it is easier to use and more effective than a spoon. It may be cut from a hardwood board.

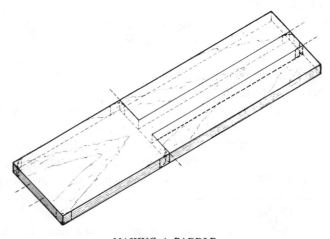

MAKING A PADDLE

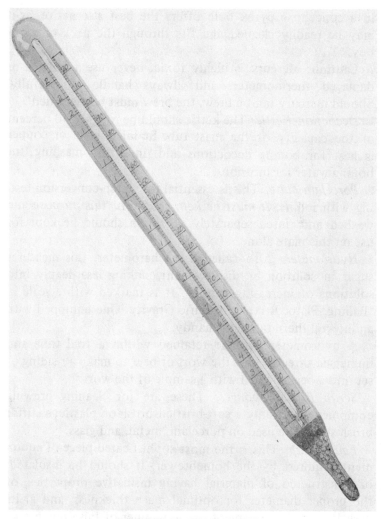

IMMERSIBLE THERMOMETER

A good combination is using the one-quart measuring cup to mix the mash and the long-handled spoon for keeping extract from caramelizing on the kettle's bottom.

Immersible Thermometer: In the 32 to 212°F (0–100°C) range, this is indispensable. The floating type that is sealed in a concentric pyrex bulb offers the best alternative, as it may be readily cleaned and fits through the neck of a carboy.

Caution: Mercury is highly toxic; **never** use a cracked or damaged thermometer, and always handle it carefully. Should mercury taint a brew, the brew **must be discarded!**

Decoction Kettle: The kettle should be roughly 50 percent of the capacity of the mast tub. Stainless steel or copper is best for boiling decoctions and, in British mashing, for boiling water for infusions.

Porcelain Plate: This is essential for starch-conversion testing with iodine. *It must be kept solely for this purpose* and washed and rinsed separately. A spoon should be kept for use on this plate alone.

Hydrometer: Also called a saccharometer, this measures sugar in solution by displacement, sinking less deeply into solutions of increasing density. It is marked with a scale in °Balling, Plato, Brix, or Specific Gravity. One equipped with an integral thermometer is handy.

A hydrometer may be retained within a trial tube and immersed directly into the wort or beer to make a reading or set into a beaker filled with a sample of the wort.

Scrub Brush, Sponges: These are for cleaning brewing equipment. Use only a soft-bristled brush on plastic; a stiffer brush should be used on porcelain, metal, and glass.

Lauter Tub: This is the most sophisticated piece of equipment required by the homebrewer. It should be insulated, or constructed of material having insulative properties, of the proper diameter for optimal mash thickness, and at its base it must have a spigot, some manner of false bottom or filter-bag set above it, and the means to flush the space between them.

A fine-mesh bag, or one fashioned of canvas sides and a mesh bottom, is commonly used for holding the mash but presents several disadvantages. These literally "bag" at their bottoms, even when resting on a slotted base such as is used

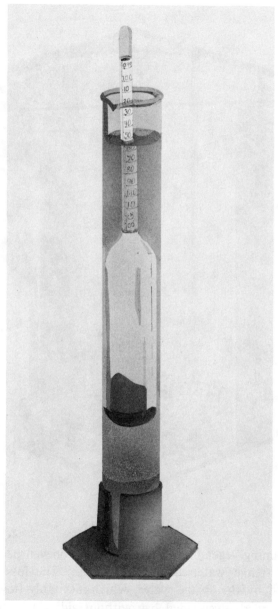

HYDROMETER

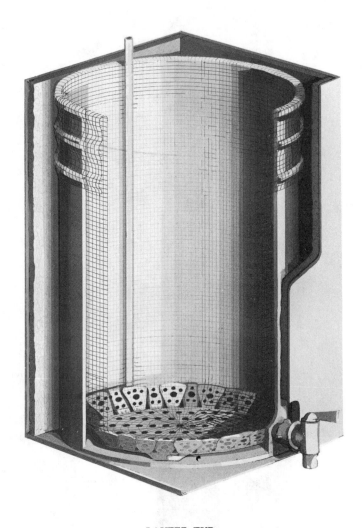

LAUTER TUB

for steaming vegetables. This encourages uneven percolation of the sparge water through the mash. The loss is compounded by the sparge water, which inevitably flows down outside of a canvas-sided bag without aiding whatsoever in the dilution of the extract in the grain bed.

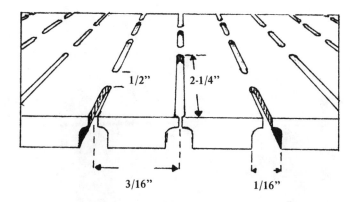

1/2" end bar, 2-1/4" long, 3/16" on centers
Slot Widths: .020" decoction, 1/32" infusion

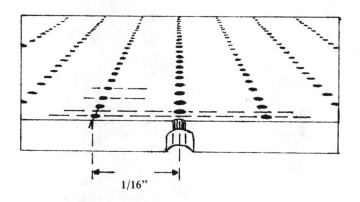

1/32" dia. side-staggered perforations on 1/16" centers

FALSE BOTTOM CROSS SECTIONS

False bottoms fitted tightly to the inside of the lauter tub and one-eighth to two inches above its base are employed by commercial brewers. Until a similar design becomes available to homebrewers, either the mesh bag or some other arrangement must be used.

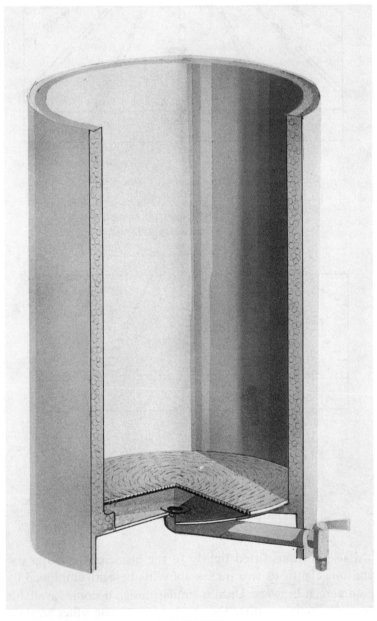

LAUTER TUB

The lauter tub should be of roughly the same capacity as the mash tub and must be selected with consideration for the effect of its diameter upon mash depth. Mashing ten pounds of malt, a grain depth of six inches requires a diameter of fourteen inches, for a twelve-inch-deep filterbed, a diameter of ten inches is needed, and for eighteen inches, a diameter of eight inches. For twenty pounds of malt, these figures become twenty inches, fourteen inches, and twelve inches.

Some manner of spigot is also a prerequisite of any lauter tub.

Flushing the space between the false bottom and the base of the lauter tub may be accomplished by forcing sparge

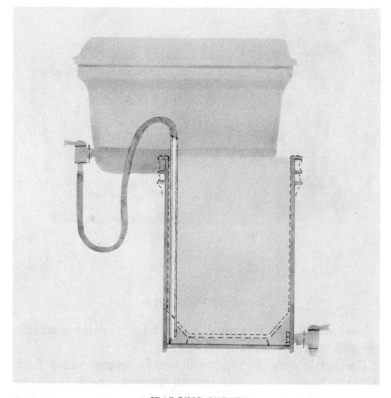

SPARGING SYSTEM

water through an inlet set opposite the spigot or through a tube thrust down through the mash to the false bottom. This may also be used for underletting a set mash.

Sparger: A sparger is used to introduce a finely-dispersed, regulated flow of 170 to 176°F (77–80°C) water to the lauter tub. A perforated stainless steel, copper, or plastic tube or sprinkling head attached by a length of flexible tubing to the mash tub, a pail, kettle, water tote, or "beer sphere" having a spigot may be used.

An insulated mash tub, filled with the hot sparge water while the mash is setting in the lauter tub, makes the most economical and easily-managed arrangement. This fact should greatly influence the selection of the mash tub.

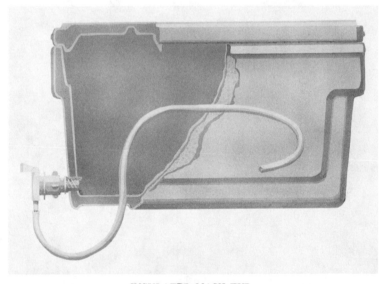

INSULATED MASH TUB

Wort Kettle: This is usually of 40 to 50 percent greater capacity than the closed fermenters.

The kettle may be equipped with a spigot—and a false bottom, hopsack, or cheesecloth pressed down over the kettle's outlet—to filter hop and break residues from the wort. If the kettle has no spigot, filtering may be accomplished by ladling the hops into a cotton or flannel trub filter-bag, a colander, or the lauter tub, and siphoning the wort through flexible tubing to run it over the hop filterbed. Where hop pellets are used, the wort can be siphoned directly off its trub.

In terms of heat-transfer efficiency, a kettle is best fabricated from copper, but stainless steel is far easier to obtain, clean, and maintain. The exception here is the not-uncommon copper jam boiler, which makes an excellent asymmetrically-heated kettle for five-gallon brewing. At this volume any metal kettle may be set directly on a range top to heat (although electric heating elements may not be able to heat five or six gallons of wort to boiling). Nontoxic plastic boilers (polypropylene or teflon) equipped with integral heating elements also perform satisfactorily, although they are more difficult to maintain.

COPPER JAM BOILER

The brew kettle is commonly used to boil the brewing water where carbonate salts need to be precipitated.

Mark any kettle with volume gradations by etching them into the surface or painting them on with nontoxic enamel.

Wine Theif. This is for taking samples from the kettle or the ferment. It should be Pyrex or glass.

Hop Scale: Used to dispense hops by weight, an inexpen-

HOP SCALE

sive, plastic "calorie-counter" scale suffices. Calibrate it with an object or substance of known weight.

Hop Sparger: This may be the same arrangement as used for sparging the mash, so long as boiling water doesn't distort or crack it. Otherwise, sprinkle the water from a ladle.

Wort Cooler: The usual practice of cooling the wort by setting the kettle into a tub of ice or cold running water is woefully ineffective. Slow cooling doesn't precipitate the cold break well and prolongs the time the wort must spend at temperatures conducive to bacterial growth.

Running the wort through fifteen to twenty feet of one-quarter-inch outside diameter copper tubing coiled into chipped ice will reduce wort temperature from boiling down to at least 90°F (32°C). A concentric-tubing cooler can be made by jacketing such tubing with one-half-inch inside diameter tubing or garden hose, using a "running tee" for the connection where the inner tubing emerges, and filling the space between with pressurized tap water running in counterflow to the bitter wort. Wort run through a concentric tubing cooler can be cooled below 60°F (15°C).

The arrangement is more simply constructed than might be expected. Its drawback is that it is difficult to rinse free of extract deposits and impossible to know whether or not one has. The copper tubing must be thoroughly flushed with water immediately after use, followed by rinsing with chlorine bleach and hot water.

A wort cooler made up of fifteen to thirty feet of copper tubing coiled so that it can be set directly into the wort kettle is easier to sanitize. It allows the cold break to be precipitated in the kettle, eliminating the need for running the wort into a separate cooling and settling tank. It is, however, a little less efficient than running the wort itself through copper.

Wort-Storage Jars: For a five-gallon brewing, vacuum seal canning jars of half pint, pint, and quart capacities should be used. Several quart jars are needed to hold wort for kraeusen-

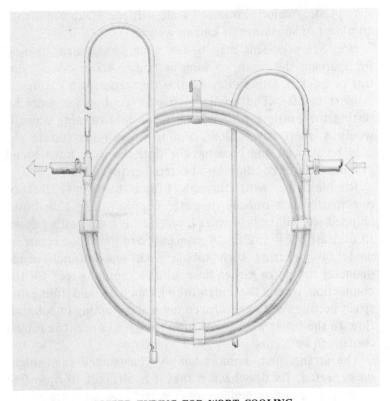

COPPER TUBING FOR WORT COOLING

ing or topping-up. Otherwise, ordinary beer bottles may be used.

Yeast-Pitching Equipment: This equipment is needed to culture yeast to pitching strength, by repeatedly doubling volumes with sterile wort. Unless the yeast strain is very strong, for a five-gallon batch, half pint, pint, quart, and gallon glass containers are needed. Preferably, these should be constricted-neck bottles and should be fitted with a stopper and fermentation lock.

Yeast-Culturing Equipment: Culturing from a single cell requires a 600X to 1200X microscope fitted with a precision graduated stage, as well as slides and cover glasses, petri

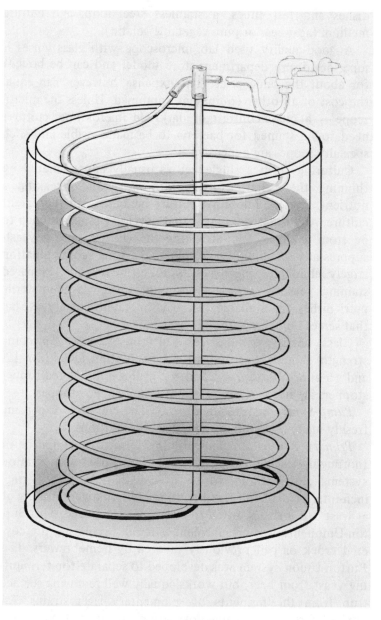

WORT COOLER

dishes and test tubes, a stainless steel loop, and culture medium (agar-agar or pure vegetable gelatin).

A good-quality used lab microscope with glass lenses is superior to any department-store model and can be bought for about the same price. The expense, however, can equal the cost of all other equipment combined. Unless the microscope is a phase-contrast or darkfield microscope, cultures need to be stained for bacteria to be made visible and such specialty scopes are expensive.

Culturing from a single cell is usually approximated by thinning the parent culture with wort and streaking a nutrient, bacteria-inhibiting culture medium with the parent culture. Any isolated colonies that develop can be assumed to be from a single cell. Streaking the culture onto a yeast-suppressant medium to disclose bacterial contamination largely eliminates the necessity for a microscope. Prepared staining, yeast-or-bacteria suppressant nutrient agar in sterile petri dishes are available through the catalog of a yeast lab that serves homebrewers.

Glass bottles or jugs for culturing yeast to pitching strength should be fitted with fermentation locks; for 12- and 16-ounce bottles, #1 and #2 drilled-and-tapered rubber stoppers are needed; for quart bottles, use a #3 stopper.

Pump-Spray or Squeeze Bottles: These are for dispensing freshly made-up cleaning and antiseptic solutions.

Primary Fermenter: The primary fermenter should be of thoroughly cleanable construction. For closed-fermentation systems, a five-gallon carboy fitted with three feet of one-inch-interior diameter flexible tubing (alternatively, tubing of at least 3/8 inch i.d. fitted to a carboy cap) is used. This Burton-Union inspired arrangement is rapidly replacing the covered crock or pail previously favored by homebrewers. The Burton-Union system was developed to separate top-fermenting yeast from beer, but works equally well removing surface trub from the ferments of sedimentary lager strains. An "open" fermenter should not have a constricted neck, but must be of up to 25 percent greater capacity than the closed secondary fermenter and be covered by a close-fitting lid equipped with a fermentation lock. Commonly-used food-safe plastic pails are very inexpensive but are a nuisance to clean and sterilize after a bit of use. They must be replaced or relegated to use as a mash tub or the like as their surfaces become badly abraded. Glazed stoneware crocks offer a reasonable choice for an open primary fermenter. Stainless steel is almost as readily cleaned and is lighter and less fragile, but an affordable vessel, even used, may be hard to come by.

A fermentation lock must be fitted through the cover of the primary fermenter, so that all exchange between the fermenter and the atmosphere takes place through the air-lock. It should be of adequate size to allow the release of copious amounts of carbon dioxide produced during the primary fermentation without splashing the liquid within the lock. The concentric type serves best. The traditional chemist's airlock is more appropriate for use during the less volatile secondary fermentation and for yeast culturing.

Refrigeration: Unless the heat produced during primary fermentation is attempered by enclosure within a refrigerator, the fermenter must be jacketed with ice or cold water. A used refrigerator, however, is almost always the simplest, most reasonably affordable solution for controlling fermentation temperatures. Serviceable but cosmetically second-class commercial coolers, refrigerated display cases, or freezers may be found at reasonable prices.

For economy, a refrigerator, ice chest, or any other cooling arrangement should be placed in the coolest possible location out of direct sunlight.

Flat, Slotted Spoon: This is needed to skim debris from the kraeusen head. A stainless-steel kitchen spatula works well.

Long-Handled Spoon: For the collection of yeast from the bottom of the primary fermenter, a thin spoon works better than a thick one.

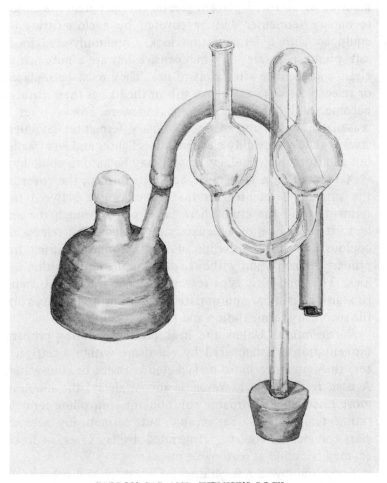

CARBOY CAP AND CHEMIST'S LOCK

Siphon Tubing: To rack wort or beer off its sediment, a four-foot length of flexible tubing is affixed to pyrex or rigid-plastic tubing with an opening drilled in its side and its end capped, crimped, or plugged. Plastic tubing should be replaced as it becomes discolored, cracked or stiff with use.

Secondary/Lager Fermenter: This should have a constricted neck to reduce airspace above the ferment. Glass presents the most readily cleaned surface. For five-gallon brewings, the traditional glass carboy is the uncontested choice (and presents a compelling reason for brewing in five-gallon batches). Use a carboy cap or #6-1/2 or #7 tapered neoprene or rubber stopper to seal the carboy and hold the fermentation lock.

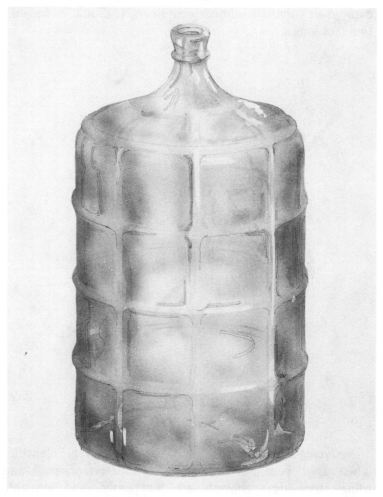

FIVE-GALLON GLASS CARBOY

Where refrigerated-space is limited, lager in one-gallon glass jugs fitted with #6 or #6-1/2 stoppers. For lagering under pressure, use a Cornelius keg.

When selecting any closed fermenter, bear in mind that its capacity determines the relative sizes of all other brewing vessels.

Long-Handled Bottle Brush: Use this to scour the inside of carboys or other closed-neck containers. It should be roughly two feet long.

LONG-HANDLED BOTTLE BRUSH

Reducing-Sugar Analysis Kit: This positively identifies when aged beer has fermented out. "Dextrocheck" and other urine-sugar reagents are inexpensive and available at any pharmacy.

Priming Tub: This is for rousing priming solution into aged beer in preparation to bottle. A clean carboy or fermenter is usually employed.

Keg: For draft beer, a five-gallon pre-mix syrup tank (Cornelius keg) used by the soft drink industry is the first choice of homebrewers.

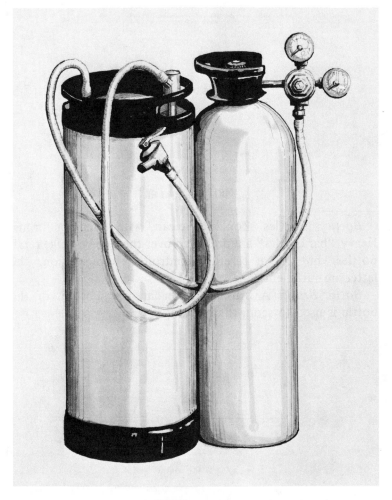

CORNELIUS KEG

Bottle Filler: When the priming tub has no spigot, the beer should be siphoned into bottles. The siphon tubing mentioned above is generally used. A shut-off valve caps the end of 3/8-inch outside diameter tubing and opens only when it is pressed against the bottom of a bottle. This reduces oxygen uptake by the beer and makes bottling less messy.

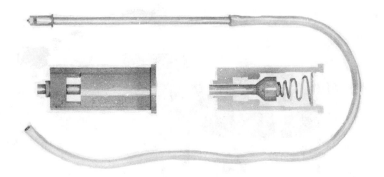

BOTTLE FILLER

Bottles: Bottles should be clean, with unchipped rims. Heavy "bar bottles" are preferred over the lighter gauge retail bottles, but in a carefully-controlled fermentation, the latter are sufficient.

Bottle Brush: A brush that reaches the bottom of the bottle is used to scour them during cleaning. A bottle-washer

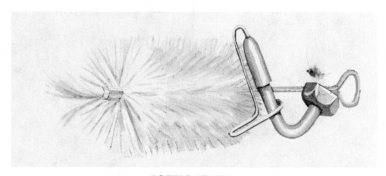

BOTTLE BRUSH

faucet attachment or a multiple-bottle washer made from copper tubing may also be found to be handy.

Bottle Rack: A bottle rack holds inverted empties after the work of emptying them is done. A Christmas-tree type rack conserves counter space.

Caps (or other suitable stoppers): Crown-type caps are most common, although corks can be used (#7 straight or #8 tapered for 12- and 16-oz. bottles; #8 straight or #9 tapered for quart bottles, and #10 straight or #14 tapered for gallon jugs).

Capper: This secures crown-type caps. It should be chosen for its ability to evenly seal bottles without chipping their rims or cracking the bottle necks. The best arrangement is the bench-type. Other cappers may not be so expensive, but neither do they work so well.

APPENDIX A

Basic Homebrewing from Malt-Extract Syrup

For Five Gallons:

Prepare a yeast starter one or two days in advance. Pitch 14 grams of lager yeast that has been dissolved in warm water into one quart of wort (saved from a previous brewing). Fit with a fermentation lock. Hold at 46 to 52°F (8–11°C). It should be actively fermenting when pitched.

Dissolve the malt extract syrup (a liquid concentrate of boiled wort) into 5-1/2 gallons of brewing water in a kettle of at least 7-gallon capacity. For cooled wort of 9°B, use 6.6 pounds of extract; for 11°B, use 8.35 pounds; for 13°B, use 9.9 pounds. Check the pH. It should be 5.5 to 5.8. Correct the acidity with mineral salts only if the pH is inappropriate. Heat to boiling.

Add hop pellets to the kettle. Stir to mix and prevent burning the extract on the heated surface. Boil vigorously. If foam begins to build on the surface of the boil, reduce the heat to prevent boilover. Add water as necessary. Periodically examine sample glassfuls, first hot and then after force cooling, to assess the formation of the hot and cold break. After

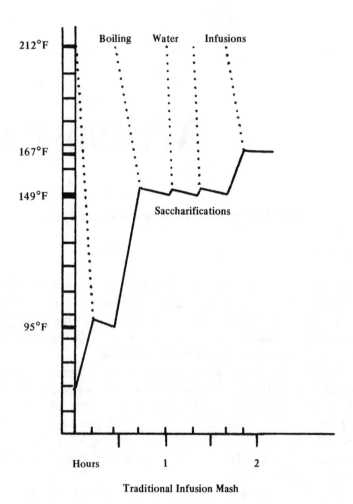

Traditional Infusion Mash

the cold break has been induced in a sample, add finishing hops and boil 10 to 15 minutes more. The boiling period should be 1-1/2 to 2 hours. After boiling, 5-2/3 gallons of wort at pH 5.3 to 5.5 and the desired liquid pressure, hydrometer reading corrected to 60°F (15.56°C), should be present.

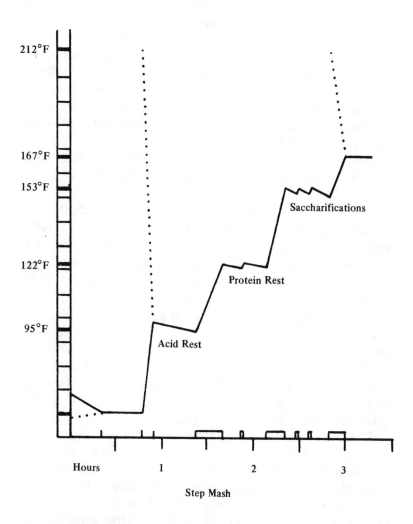

Step Mash

Cover the wort, remove it from the heat, and allow it to settle. Place an immersible wort chiller in the kettle or run it through a counterflow cooler. Force cool the wort to below 50°F (10°C). Remove, bottle, and refrigerate one quart of it.

Allow the wort to settle, then siphon it off of its hop and

trub sediment, splashing it into a 5-gallon carboy with one quart of yeast starter. The starter should be very actively fermenting; shake the sediment into suspension before pitching. Further rouse the inoculated wort by rocking the carboy. Top-up the carboy with sterile (boiled) water to just below the neck. Fit with a "blow-off" tube. Place the free end of the blow-off tube into a half-gallon jug, covered by an ounce of chlorine bleach in one quart of water. Hold at 46 to 48°F (8–9°C) until fermentation starts.

Only uncover the ferment as necessary, and then only briefly. Follow sanitary procedures. Samples are most safely taken with a sterilized wine theif.

Top-up the carboy with deoxygenated (boiled) sterile wort or water as beer is expelled through the blow-off tube; change the sterilant solution in the airlock daily. The temperature of the ferment will rise. Manipulate the ambient temperature so that it does not rise above 55°F (13°C) [by lowering the ambient temperature to 40 to 50°F (4–10°C)].

The end of primary fermentation is signaled by the disappearance of the foam cover from the surface of the ferment and the falling-off of CO_2 release. Take a sample from the carboy; testing with Dextrocheck should show less than 5 percent reducing sugar left in the post-kraeusen beer [usually this is 25 to 35 percent of the original wort gravity, or 1°B (SG 1004) above the expected final density].

Siphon the beer off of its sediment into a second sterilized carboy. Avoid splashing. Top-up the carboy with sterile wort or water; fill it right up to the neck. Fit with a fermentation lock. After three days, reduce the temperature of the ferment to 34 to 37°F (2–3°C). Periodically check the extract content, temperature, and pH of the beer. After three to five weeks, the hydrometer reading should show no further drop and be very nearly at the expected final reading. The pH should be below 4.5. Add gelatin finings to clear the beer ten days before bottling.

Prepare the priming solution one or two days before bottling. Mix 8 ounces (avoir.) of dextrose into one quart of brewing water. Pitch with .1 to .2 fluid ounces (2 to 4 grams) of sedimentary lager yeast.

Bottle when no drop in the hydrometer reading has been experienced for several days and the priming solution is actively fermenting. The sugar analysis of the aged beer should show less than 2 percent.

Inspect, wash, sterilize, rinse, and dry 21 one-quart bottles. Rouse the priming solution. Quietly siphon or decant the fermented beer into a carboy with the frothy priming solution, very gently rocking the carboy to mix the yeast into the beer without aerating it. Cover the beer and siphon it into the bottles, filling them to within 3/4 inch of the rim. Loosely cover the bottles and leave them for several minutes before securing the caps. Invert the bottles to disclose leakage. Hold at 45 to 50°F (7–10°C) for several days, and then store at 32 to 45°F (0–7°C) for from ten days to six weeks before serving.

APPENDIX B

The Infusion Mash

An infusion mash is employed for the extraction of well-modified malts. Duration is usually 1-1/2 to 3 hours.

Dough-in the crushed malt by sprinkling it with boiling water and kneading the grist until it is evenly moistened. Continue working boiling water into the mash until the 149°F (65°C) strike temperature is reached. Usual dilution is 40 to 48 fluid ounces of water per pound of grist. For light, dry beer, 145 to 149°F (63–65°C) may be the strike temperature; for sweet or full-bodied beer, a tight mash at 152 to 154°F (67–68°C) is required.

The mash pH should be 5.2 to 5.3. Maintain the strike temperature by applying heat to the mash kettle, by decoction of part of the mash, or by boiling water infusion. The latter method may favor maltose formation and is sometimes avoided, although conservative thinning is rarely detrimental to the usual thick mash. Monitor saccharification. If in one hour the iodine reaction is neither negative nor faintly-red (traditionally-sweet British beer styles need not be wholly saccharified), the mash temperature may have to be lowered. In any case, after two hours the saccharification rest should be ended, as a longer mash is not likely to convert any more starch.

The saccharification rest is terminated by increasing the mash temperature to 170 to 176°F (77–80°C) with a boiling water infusion. The temperature should be held at above 170°F (77°C) and the mash roused into suspension over a 10-to-15 minute period.

APPENDIX C

The Step Mash (Modified Infusion Mash)

In 2-1/2 to 5 hours:

The modified-infusion method (step mash, temperature-programmed mash) mimics the traditional decoction-mash sequence, but with less satisfactory results (primarily because no part of the mash is ever boiled). It is, however, far more effective in dealing with undermodified malt than an infusion mash, and a great deal simpler and less time-consuming than a decoction mash. It has displaced both Continental and British tradition in most commercial breweries.

Heat is applied directly to the mash tub to raise the temperature and to restore temperatures as they fall off during the mash rests. Consequently a very thick mash can be formed. Caution should be used when applying heat as strike-temperatures can be unwittingly exceeded if not carefully monitored, and if the mash is not constantly and thoroughly mixed.

Crush the malt, dough-in, and bring it to rest at 95°F (35°C), as for decoction mashing. The pH should be near 5.5. After 30 minutes, apply heat to the mash tub to raise the temperature to an even 122°F (50°C) in 15 minutes; hold it for 30 minutes. The pH should have dropped to 5.3. Heat to saccharification temperature, following the decoction-mash time sequence. After 15 minutes begin testing for starch conversion. When no iodine reaction is observed, infuse the mash with boiling water to raise its temperature to 167 to 170°F (75–77°C). Hold the temperature and thoroughly mix the mash for 10 to 15 minutes before transferring it to the lauter tub for sparging.

APPENDIX D

Weights and Measures

Abbreviations

U.S. Liquid Measure		Liquid Measure	
dram	dr.	liter	l
fluid ounce	fl. oz.	milliliter	ml.
pint	pt.	deciliter	dl.
quart	qt.	dekaliter	dkl.
gallon	gal.		
barrel	bbl.		

Metric System			Metric System Units	
micro	μ	.0001	gram	g
milli	m	.001	meter	m
centi	c	.01	square meter	m_2
deci	d	.1	cubic meter	m_3
deka	dk	10.		
hecto	h	100		
kilo	k	1000		

Capacity

To express any volume in another unit of measure, convert the measure in the left hand column to any unit in the right hand column by multiplying by the factor shown.

microliter = .000 000 1 l

milliliter = $1cm_3$ = .2705 fl. dr. = .0338 fl. oz. = .001 l = 0.06102 cu. in.

fluid dram = 3.697 ml. = .125 fl. oz.

centiliter = 10 ml. = .3382 fl. oz. =.01 l

tablespoon = 14.7865 ml. = .5 fl. oz.

Imperial fluid ounce = 28.4125 ml. = 1.0409 fl. oz. (U.S.)

deciliter =100 ml. = 3.3815 fl. oz. = 1.l.

fluid ounce = 29.5729 ml. = 2 tblspn. = 1.8046 cu. in.

cup = 228.6 ml. = 8 fl. oz. = .2286 l

pint = 473.166 ml. = 16 fl. oz. = 2 cups = .8327 Imp. pt. = .4732 l = 28.875 cu. in.

Imperial pint = 568.25 ml. = 20 Imp. fl. oz. = 19.2152 fl. oz. (U.S.) = 1.2009 pt. (U.S.) = .56825 l

quart = 946.332 ml. = 31 fl. oz. = 4 cups = .8327 Imp. qt. = .94631 l = 57.75 cu. in.

liter = 1000 ml. = 33.8148 fl. oz. = 2.1134 pt.= 1.0567 qt. = .2642 gal. = 1 kg. of water at $4°c$ = 61.0234 cu. in.

Imperial quart	= 1136.5 ml. = 40 Imp. fl. oz. = 38.4303 fl. oz. (U.S.) = 1.2009 qt. (U.S.) = 1.1365 l
gallon	= 3785.334 ml. = 128 fl. oz. = 16 cups = 8 pt. = 4 qt. = 3.7853 l = 8327 Imp. gal. = 231 cu. in.
Imperial gallon	= 4546 ml. = 160 Imp. fl. oz. = 153.7234 fl. oz. (U.S.) = 4.5460 l = 1.2009 gal.
dekaliter	= 10 l = 2.6418 gal.
1/8 barrel	= 3.875 gal.
1/4 barrel	= 7.75 gal.
1/2 barrel	= 15.5 gal.
barrel	= 31 gal. = 1.1734 hl. = .729 Imp. bbl. = 7056 cu. in.
Imperial barrel	= 43.4 gal. (U.S.) = 36 Imp. gal. = 1.6365 hl. = 1.4 bbl. (U.S.)
hectoliter	= 100 l = 26.4178 gal.

Submultiples of Capacity (U.S. Liquid Measure)

Gallons	Fl. Oz.	Fl. Pt.	Fl. Qt.
.0078	1		
.0156	2		
.0313	4	1/4	
.0469	6		
.0625	8	1/2	1/4
.0938	12	3/4	
.125	16	1	1/2
.1563	20	1 1/4	
.1875	24	1 1/2	3/4
.2188	28	1 3/4	
.25	32	2	1

.375	48	3	1 1/2
.50	64	4	2
.75	96	6	3
1.00	128	8	4

Weights and Measures, U.S. and Metric Systems

Cubic Measure (Volume)

cubic centimeter = 1 ml. = .06102 cu. in.

cubic inch = 16.3872 cm_3

cubic decimeter = 61.0234 cu. in. = 1 l

cubic foot = 1728 cu. in. = 28.316 dm_3 = 28.316 l = .0283 m_3

Dry Measure

dry pint = 33.6003 cu. in. = .5506 l

dry quart = 67.2006 cu. in. = 2 pt. = 1.1012 l

liter = 61.0234 cu. in. = .9081 qt.

peck = 537.605 cu. in. = 8 qt. = 8.8096 l

bushel = 2150.42 cu. in. = 32 qt. = 4 pecks = 35.2383 l = .3524 hl.

barrel = 7056 cu. in. = 105 qt.

hectoliter = 6102 cu. in. = 110. 12 qt. = 100 l = 2.8375 bu.

Weight

microgram = .000 000 1 g.

milligram = .015432 grains = .001 g.

centigram = .1543 grains = .01 g.

grain = 64.7989 mg. = .0648 g.

gram = 1000 mg. = 15.432 grains = .03527 oz. (avoir.) = .00220462 lb.

ounce (avoirdupois) = 437.5 grains = 28.3495 g.

pound = 7000 grains = 453.5924 g. = 16 oz. = .4536 kg.

kilogram = 1000 g. = 35.274 oz. (avoir.) = 2.2046 lb.

Linear Measure

millimeter = .03937 in. = .001 m.

centimeter = .3937 in. = .01 m.

inch = 25.4 mm. = 2.54 cm.

decimeter = 3.937 in. = .1 m.

foot = 30.48 cm. = 12 in. = .3048 m.

yard = 91.44 cm. = 36 in. = 3 ft. = .9144 m.

meter = 39. 37 in. = 3.2808 ft. = 1.09361 yd.

Square Measure

square cen-timeter = .1550 sq. in.

square inch = 6.4516 cm_2

square decimeter = .1076 sq. ft.

square foot = 929. 0341 cm_2 = 144 sq. in. = .0929 m_2

Temperature

°Fahrenheit	°Centigrade	°Reaumur
30	-1.11	
32	0	0
35	1.67	
40	4.44	
41	5	4
45	7.22	
50	10	8
55	12.78	
59	15	12
60	15.56	
65	18.33	
68	20	16
70	21.11	
77	25	20
80	26.67	
86	30	24
90	32.22	
95	35	28
100	37.78	
104	40	32
110	43.33	
113	45	36
122	50	40
131	55	44
140	60	48
145	62.78	
149	65	52
155	68.33	
158	70	56
160	71.11	
167	75	60
170	76.67	

176	80	64
180	82.22	
185	85	68
194	90	72
200	93.33	
203	95	76
212	100	80
221	105	84
230	110	88

Conversion

$$^\circ C \text{ to } ^\circ F = \frac{(^\circ C)\,9}{5} + 32$$

$$^\circ R \text{ to } ^\circ F = \frac{(^\circ R)\,9}{4} + 32$$

$$^\circ F \text{ to } ^\circ C = \frac{(^\circ F - 32)\,5}{9}$$

$$^\circ R \text{ to } ^\circ C = \frac{(^\circ R)\,5}{4}$$

$$^\circ F \text{ to } ^\circ R = \frac{(^\circ F - 32)\,4}{9}$$

$$^\circ C \text{ to } ^\circ R = \frac{(^\circ C)\,4}{5}$$

Density

°Balling	°Specific Gravity	Lbs. Extract/Gal.
0	1000	0
.5	1002	.042
1.0	1004	.084
2.5	1010	.210
3.0	1012	.253

°Balling	°Spec. Gravity	Lbs. Extract/Gal.
4.0	1016	.339
5.0	1020	.425
6.0	1024	.512
6.25	1025	.534
7.0	1028	.6
8.0	1032	.688
8.75	1035	.755
9.0	1036	.788
10.0	1040	.867
11.0	1044.5	.958
12.0	1049	1.049
12.5	1050	1.095
13.0	1053	1.141
14.0	1057	1.234
14.7	1060	1.3
15.0	1061	1.328
15.88	1065	1.41
18.0	1074	1.613
20.0	1080	1.806
24.0	1098	2.204

Balling (Plato) is a brewer's measure expressing the weight of any substance in solution as a percentage of the weight of that solution, based upon corn sugar (glucose) dissolved in pure water (1 lb. of sugar in 100 lbs. of water = 1%, or 1° Balling or Plato). Plato's table is more accurate than Balling's, but it is not commonly used by homebrewers.

Specific gravity is the metric system expression of density; in brewer's usage, s.g. 1.010 is written as 1012 and etc., or abbreviated to s.g. 12, and etc.

Conversion

$SG = (B°).004 + 1;$ $\quad (12).004 + 1 = $ s.g. 1048

$°B = \dfrac{s.g.-1;}{.004}$ $\quad (1.048 - 1) \div .004 = 12°B$

Expected Alcohol Percentage

°Balling Apparent Attenuation	% Alcohol By Volume	% Alcohol By Weight
4	2.10	1.65
5	2.60	2.05
6	3.15	2.45
7	3.70	2.90
8	4.20	3.30
9	4.75	3.70
10	5.25	4.15
11	5.75	4.50
12	6.30	4.95
13	6.85	5.35
14	7.35	5.75

Multiply apparent attenuation °B by .516 or SG by .129 = % alcohol v/v (approx.). W/w = v/v times .785.

Hydrometer Correction
For Temperatures Other Than 60°F (15.56°C)

If Temperature Is:		Add to Hydrometer Reading:	
°F	°C	°B	°S.G.
32	0	−.2	−.0008
35	1.67	−.22	−.0009
40	4.44	−.23	−.0009
50	10	−.17	−.0007
70	21.11	.25	.001
80	26.67	.5	.002
90	32.22	1.0	.004
100	37.78	1.5	.006
110	43.33	2.0	.008
120	48.89	2.5	.010
130	54.44	3.2	.013

°F	°C	°B	°S.G.
140	60.0	4.0	.016
150	65.55	4.5	.018
160	71.11	5.5	.022
170	76.67	6.25	.025
190	87.78	8.0	.033
212	100.0	10.0	.040

Examples

°Balling: Temperature is 170°F. Hydrometer reading is 7°B. Factor for 170°F is 6.25°B. 7 + 6.25 = True Density is 13.25°B.

Specific Gravity: Temperature is 21°C. Hydrometer reading is s.g. 1.049. Factor for 21°C is s.g. .001. s.g. 1.049 + .001 = Correct Specific Gravity is 1.050 (1050).

Pressure at 50°F, at Sea Level

1 lb./sq. in. = 750 kg./m$_2$ = 27.7 in. water = .06895 atm.

1 atmosphere = 10$_5$Nm^{-z} = 750/mmHg = 1102 kg./m$_2$ =
407.2 in. water = 1.101325 bar
= 14.696 lb./sq. in. = 1.03 kg./cm$_2$ =

Water at 212°F at sea level = 14.7 lb./sq. in.

Atmospheres of Pressure	Boiling Point	
	°F	°C
1	212	100
1.5	234	112.2
2	249	120.6
3	273	134
4	291	144
10	356	180
17	401	205

Pressure, at Temperatures Other Than 50°F

Atm.				Temperature		
	At 50°F		40°F	59°F	68°F	77°F
1.0	Lbs.	14.7	10	20	22	24
2.0	per	29.4	20	34	40	43
2.5	sq.	36.8	25	43	50	53
3.0	in.	44.1	30	52	63	65
4.0		58.8	40	70	79	88

Water Hardness

Part per million (in metric usage, milligram/liter)	= 1 part $CaCO_3$ per 1,000,000 parts (water = 1mg/l = .1 part per 100,000 = .07 Clark° = .0583 gpg (U.S.) = .056 German°
Grain per Gallon (U.S.)	= 1 part $CaCO_3$ per 58,310 parts water = 17.1497 ppm = 1.2 Clark°
Clark Degree (grain per gallon, U.K.)	= 1 part $CaCO_3$ per 70,000 parts water = 14.25 ppm = .833 gpg (U.S.) = .8 German° = .7 millival
German Degree	= 1 mg Ca per 1000 1. = 1 part CaO per 100,000 parts water = 17.9 ppm as $CaCO_3$ = 1.4285 Clark°
French Degree	= 1 mg $CaCO_3$ per 1000 1.
Millival	= .001⁻ ion concentration = 20.357 ppm

Water

At sea level, pure water (H_2O; 11.188% hydrogen, 88.812% oxygen by weight) freezes at 32°F (0°C), boils at 212°F (100°C). It is most dense at 39.2°F (4°C). One gallon at 60°F (15.56°C) weighs 58,310 grains. At 68°F, one cubic foot weighs 64.3 lbs., one ounce (avoir.) equals .96 fl. oz., one lb. equals .12 gal. and one cu. in. equals 16.36 g. At 32°F (0°C), water weighs .9987 g/ml, but as ice weighs .917 g/ml.

Density of Water

Temperature				Weight/Volume	
°F	°C	g/cm$_3$	oz/fl. oz.	lb./gal.	lb./gal. (U.K.)
32	0	.99987	1.0430	8.3347	10.008
39.2	4.0	1.00000	1.0432	8.3362	10.01
60.0	15.56	.99905	1.0422	8.3283	10.0
68	20	.99823	1.0413	8.3217	9.99
77	25	.99707	1.0390	8.3122	9.98
212	100	.95838	.9998	7.9894	9.6

Boiling Point, at Various Elevations

Boiling Point drops approx. 1°F(.56°C) for each 550' (170m.) increase in altitude

Elevation	Boiling Point
–1000'	213.8°F(101°C)
sea level	212°F(100°C)
1000'	210.2°F(99°C)
2000'	208.4°F(98°C)
3000'	206.5°F(97°C)
4000'	204.7°F(96°C)
5000'	202.9°F(95°C)

Useful Information

Decimal Equivalents

1/64	.015	9/32	.281
1/32	.031	5/16	.312
3/64	.046	11/32	.343
1/16	.062	3/8	.375
5/64	.078	13/32	.406
3/32	.093	7/16	.437
7/64	.109	15/32	.468
1/8	.125	1/2	.500
9/64	.140	9/16	.562
5/32	.156	5/8	.625
11/64	.171	11/16	.687
3/16	.187	3/4	.750
13/64	.203	13/16	.812
7/32	.218	7/8	.875
15/64	.234	15/16	.937
1/4	.250	1	1.000

One bushel of barley weighs 48 lbs.
One bushel of malt weighs 34 lbs.
One barrel of water at 60°F(15.56°C) weighs 258 lbs.

Ethyl alcohol boils at 173°F(78.5°C)

No amount of heat applied to a vessel will increase its temperature once a liquid has reached its boiling point. Only pressure can increase temperature, by raising the boiling point.

To test a thermometer, insert it in chipped ice, and into the steam just above the surface of boiling water; adjust the second reading to account for elevation above sea level.

Percentage/Decimal Equivalents

%	Decimal	%	Decimal
.01	.0001	5	.05
.5	.005	10	.1
1.0	.01	12.5	.125

Percentage Solutions

%	Oz. (Avoir)	Grams	W/V	W/W-Dissolved In: (to make up 1 qt.)
1	.33	9.4	in enough	31.66 fl.oz.
2	.67	18.9	water to	31.36
3	1	28.4	make up	31.04
4	1.33	37.8	1 quart	30.72
5	1.67	47.3	of solution	30.4
10	3.33	94.5		28.8

For water, weight/volume (w/v) and weight/weight (w/w) solutions are identical. Otherwise, a w/w% solution at 10% will be 1% stronger than a w/v% solution at 10%.

% solutions:	in 10 ml.,	100 ml.,	1 l. water
5%	.5g	5 g	50 g
10%	1.0g	10 g	100 g
25%	2.5g	25 g	250 g

Useful Formulas

Diameter of a circle = circumference $\times$ .31831
Circumference of a circle = diameter $\times$ 3.1416

Area of a circle = diameter × .7854
$$= \text{radius} \times 3.1416$$
Volume of a cylinder $= (\pi r_2)h = $ cu. in.
$$= \frac{(\pi r_2)h}{1.8046} = \text{fl. oz.}$$
Doubling the diameter of a cylinder increases its volume 4X.

Conversions

Gallons (U.S.) to Lbs. (Avoir.) = (8.33 × s.g.) gals.

Lbs. (Avoir.) to Gallons (U.S.) $= \dfrac{\text{lbs.}}{8.33 \text{ (s.g.)}}$

Milliliter to Grams = ml. (s.g.)

Grams to Milliliters $= \dfrac{\text{g}}{\text{s.g.}}$

Milliliters to Ounces (Avoir.) $= \dfrac{\text{ml. (s.g.)}}{28.35}$

Ounces (Avoir.) to Milliliters $= \dfrac{\text{oz. (28.35)}}{\text{s.g.}}$

BREWER'S GLOSSARY

Achroodextrins. Simple "border" dextrins, from the reduction of starch (amylopectin) by alpha amylase; negative reaction with iodine.

Acrospire. The germinal plant-growth of the barley kernel.

Adjuncts. Fermentable extract other than malted barley. Principally corn, rice, wheat, unmalted barley, and dextrose.

Aerate. To saturate with atmospheric air; to force oxygen into solution.

Aerobic. An organism requiring oxygen for metabolism.

Agar. Agar-agar. A non-nitrogenous, gelatinous solidifying agent, more heat-stable than gelatin. Culture medium for microbial analysis.

Agglutination. The grouping of cells by adhesion.

Albumin. Intermediate soluble protein subject to coagulation upon heating. Hydrolized to peptides and amino acids by proteolytic enzymes.

Aldehydes. An organic compound that is a precursor to ethanol in a normal beer fermentation via the EMP pathway. In the presence of excess air, this reaction can be reversed with alcohols being oxidized to aldehydes. This typically generates papery/woody flavor notes.

271

Aleurone layer. The enzyme and pentosan-bearing layer enveloping and inseparable from the malt endosperm.

Alpha-acid. a-acid. The principle bittering agent of the hop, more soluble when isomerized by boiling. From the alpha-resin of the hop.

Ambient temperature. The surrounding temperature.

Amino acids. The smallest product of protein cleavage; simple nitrogenous matter.

Amylodextrin. From the diastatic reduction of starch; the most complex dextrin from hydrolysis of starch with diastase. Purple reaction with iodine.

Amylopectin. Branched starch chain; shell and paste-forming starch.

Amylolysis. The enzymatic reduction of starch to soluble fractions.

Amylose. Straight chain of native starch; a-D-glucose (glucose dehydrate) molecules joined by a-(1-4) links.

Anaerobic. Conditions in which there is not enough oxygen for metabolic function. Anaerobic microorganisms are those which can function without the presence of oxygen.

Anion. An electro-negative ion.

Aqueous. Of water.

Attempter. To regulate or moderate fermentation temperature, as by maintaining ambient temperature cooler than the fermentation temperature.

Attenuate. Fermentation, reduction of the extract/density by yeast metabolism.

Autolysis. Self-digestion by yeast cells in nutrient-depleted solutions.

Bacteriostatic. Bacteria inhibiting.

Balling, degrees. A standard for the measurement of the density of solutions, calibrated on the weight of cane sugar in solution, expressed as a percentage of the weight of the solution (grams per 100 grams of solution).

Beerstone. Brownish-gray deposits left on fermentation equipment. Composed of calcium oxalate and organic residues.

Buffer. A substance capable of resisting changes in the pH of a solution.

Carbonates. Alkaline salts whose anions are derived from carbonic acid.

Cation. Electro-positive ion.

Chill-proof. Cold fermentation to precipitate chill-haze.

Closed fermentation. Fermentation under anaerobic conditions, to minimize risk of contamination and oxidation.

Coliform. Water-borne bacteria, often associated with pollution.

Colloid. A gelatinous substance-in-solution.

Decoction. Boiling, the part of the mash that is boiled.

Density. The measurement of the weight of a solution, as compared with the weight of an equal volume of pure water.

Dextrin. Soluble, gummy polysaccharide fraction, from hydrolysis of starch by heat, acid or enzyme.

Diastase. Starch-reducing enzymes; usually alpha and beta amylase, but also limit dextrinase and a-glucosidase (maltase).

Diketone. Aromatic, volatile, compound perceivable in minute concentration, from yeast or pediococcus metabolism. Most significantly the butter flavor of diacetyl, a vicinal diketone (VDK). The other significant compound (of relevance to brewing) is 2,3-pentanedione.

Disaccharides. Sugar group; two monosaccharide molecules joined by the removal of a water molecule.

Enzymes. Protein-based organic catalysts that effect changes in the compositions of the substances they act upon.

Erythrodextrin. Tasteless intermediate dextrin. Violet to red reaction with iodine.

Essential oil. The aromatic volatile liquid from the hop.

Esters. "Etherial salts" such as ethyl acetate; aromatic compounds from fermentation composed of an acid and an alcohol, principally the "banana" ester. Associated with wild-yeast fermentation, although esters also arise in high-gravity brewing even with pure cultures. Some top-fermenting yeast strains are prized for their ability to create esters.

Extract. Soluble constituents from the malt.

Extraction. Drawing out the soluble essence of the malt or hops.

Faecal bacteria. Coliform bacteria associated with sewage.

Fining. Clarifying beer, in British practice with isinglass, with lagers, gelatin.

Flocculation. The coagulation of phenols and proteins by boiling; the hot break during the boil, and the cold break upon cooling.

Germination. Sprouting of the barley kernel, to initiate enzyme development and conversion of the malt.

Glucophilic. An organism that thrives on glucose.

Gravity. Specific gravity. Density of a solution as compared to water; expressed in grams per milliliter (water, 1 ml weighs 1 g, hence s.g. 1.000.)

Hexose. Sugar molecules of six carbon atoms. Glucose, fructose, lactose, mannose, galactose.

Homofermentive. Organisms that metabolize only one specific carbon source.

Hydrolysis. Decomposition of matter into soluble fractions by either acids or enzymes in water.

Hydroxide. A compound, usually alkaline, containing the OH (hydroxyl) group.

Inoculate. The introduction of a microbe into surroundings capable of supporting its growth.

Isomer. Iso-. Organic compounds of identical composition and molecular weight, but having a different molecular structure.

Kraeusen. The period of fermentation characterized by a rich foam head. Kraeusening describes the use of beer covered by a "cauliflower" head to induce fermentation in a larger volume of wort or extract-depleted beer.

Lactophilic. An organism that metabolizes lactate more readily than glucose.

Lager. "To store." A long, cold period of subdued fermentation and sedimentation to active (primary) fermentation.

Lauter. The thin mash after saccharification; its clear liquid.

Lipids. Fatlike substances, especially triacylglycerols and fatty acids. Affect ability of beer to form a foam head. Upon decomposition contribute stale flavors.

Maltodextrin. Isomaltose; also amylodextrin, or an impure mixture of glucose with the compounds formed of it.

Maltose. A disaccharide of two glucose molecules, and the primary sugar obtained by diastatic hydrolysis of starch. One-third the sweetness of sucrose.

Mash, mashing. The process of enzymatically extracting and converting malt solubles to wort, in an aciduric aqueous solution.

Microaerophile. An organism that is inhibited in an oxygenated environment, and yet requires some oxygen for its metabolic functions.

Modification. The degree to which malt is converted, manifested by the extent of acrospire growth.

Mole. Gram-molecular weight. The sum of the atomic weights of all the atoms of any molecule, in grams.

Monosaccharides. Single-molecule sugars.

Oligosaccharides. Sugars of more than three molecules, less complex than dextrins.

Oxidation. The combination of oxygen with other molecules, oftentimes causing off-flavors.

PPM. Parts per million (g/ml). The measurement of particles of matter in solution.

Pectin. Vegetable substance, a chain of galacturonic acid that becomes gelatinous in the presence of sugars and acids.

Pentosan. Pentose-based complex carbohydrates, especially gums.

Pentose. Sugar molecules of five carbon atoms. Monosaccharides from the decomposition of pentosans, unfermentable by yeast. Xylose, arabinose.

Peptonizing. The action of proteolytic enzymes upon protein, yielding albumin/proteoses, peptides and amino acids.

Phenols. Aromatic hydroxyl precursors of tannins (polyphenols). Phenolic describes medicinal flavors in beer, from tannins, bacterial growth, or inferior top yeast.

Phosphate. A salt or ester of phosphoric acid.

Pitching. Inoculating sterile wort with a vigorous yeast culture.

Plasma. Protoplasm. The substance of cell bodies, excluding the nucleus (cytoplasm), in which most cell metabolism occurs.

Plato, degrees. Like degrees Balling, but Plato's computations are more exact.

Polymer. A substance having identical elements in the same proportion as another, but of higher molecular weight. Polyphenols from phenols, polypeptides from peptides.

Polysaccharides. Carbohydrate complexes able to be reduced to monosaccharides by hydrolysis.

Precipitation. Separation of suspended matter by sedimentation.

Precursor. Matter subject to polymerization.

Priming solution. A solution of sugar in water added with yeast to the aged beer at bottling to induce fermentation (bottle conditioning).

Protein. Generally amorphous and colloidal complexed amino acid, containing about 16 percent nitrogen with carbon, hydrogen, oxygen and possibly sulfur, phosphorous, and iron. True protein has a molecular weight of 17,000 to 150,000; in beer protein will have been largely decomposed to mol. wt. 5,000 to 12,000 (albumin or proteoses), peptides (400–1,500) or amino acids. Protein as a haze fraction ranges between mol. wt. 10,000 to 100,000 (average 30,000), as the stabilizing component of foam 12,000 to 20,000.

Proteolysis. The reduction of protein by proteolytic enzymes to fractions.

Racking. The transfer of wort or beer from one vessel to another.

Reagent. A substance involved in a reaction that identifies the strength of the substance being measured.

Resin. Noncrystalline (amorphous) plant excretions.

Rest. Mash rest. Holding the mash at a specific temperature to induce certain enzymatic changes.

Ropy fermentation. Viscous, gelatinous blobs, or "rope," from bacterial contamination.

Rousing. Creating turbulence by agitation; mixing.

Ruh beer. The nearly fermented beer, ready for lagering. Cold secondary fermentation.

Solubilization. Dissolval of matter into solution.

Sparge. The even distribution or spray of water over the saccharified mash, to rinse free the extract from the grist.

Specific gravity. Density of a solution, in grams per milliliter.

Sporulation. Ascospore formation, reproduction by division of the cell contents.

Strike temperature. The target temperature of a mash rest, the temperature at which a desired reaction occurs.

Substratum. The substance in or on which an organism grows.

Tannin. Astringent polyphenolic compounds, capable of colloiding with proteins and either precipitation or forming haze fractions.

Terminal extract. The density of the fully fermented beer.

Thermophilic. "Heat loving"; bacteria operating at unusually high temperatures.

Titration. Measurement of a substance in solution by addition of a standard disclosing solution to initiate an indicative color change.

Trisaccharide. A sugar composed of three monosaccharides joined by the removal of water molecules.

Trub. Precipitated flocks of haze-forming protein and polyphenols.

Turbidity. Sediment in suspension; hazy, murky water.

Valence. The degree to which an ion or radical is able to combine directly with others.

Viscosity. Of glutinous consistency; the resistance of a fluid to flow. The degree of "mouth-feel" of a beer.

Volatile. Readily vaporized, especially essential oils and higher alcohols.

Wort. Mash extract (sweet wort); the hopped sugar-solution· before pitching (bitter wort).

Wort gelatin. Culture medium made up from wort as a nutrient source and gelatin to solidify it, for surface-culturing yeast.

BIBLIOGRAPHY

Abel, Bob. *The Book of Beer.* Chicago, 1976.

American Public Health Association. *Standard Methods for the Examination of Water and Wastewater.* Washington, 1971.

American Society of Brewing Chemists. *Methods of Analysis.* St. Paul, Minnesota, 1976.

Anderson, S. F. *The Art of Making Beer,* New York, 1971.

Bailar, J. C., Kleinberg, J., Moeller, T. *University Chemistry.* Boston, 1965.

Baker, Pat. *The New Brewers Handbook.*

Baron, Stanley Wade. *Brewed in America.* Boston, 1962.

Berry, C. J. J. *Home Brewed Beers and Stouts.* Andover, England, 1963.

Briggs, D. E., Hough, J. S., Stevens, R. and Young, T. W. *Malting and Brewing Science.* 2 vols. London, 1971.

Burch, Byron. *Quality Brewing.* San Rafael, California, 1974.

Chapman, A. C. *Brewing.* Cambridge, 1912.

Conner, Jay and Tobey, Alan. "Hop Pellets vs. Whole Hops." Proceedings, A.H.A. Conference, Boulder, Colorado, 1984.

Despain, R. O. *The Malt-Ease Flagon.* Berkeley, 1978.

Eckhard, Fred. *Mashing for the North American Home Brewer.* Portland, Oregon, 1974.

_____. *A Treatise on Lager Beers.* Portland, Oregon, 1970.

_____. "The Use of Hops in Your Beer." *Amateur Brewer #4.* Portland, Oregon 1977.

Ferguson, W. B. "The Chemistry of a Brewer's Vat," *Science for All.* London, 1978.

Findlay, W. P. K., ed. *Modern Brewing Technology.* Cleveland, 1971.

Foster, Terence. "Yeast Culture and Propagation." Proceedings, A.H.A. Conference, Boulder, Colorado, 1983.

_____. "Yeast, An Essential Ingredient." *Zymurgy,* vol. 7, #1. Spring 1984.

_____. "In the Beginning—There Was Malt." *Zymurgy,* vol. 7, #4. Winter 1984.

Garret, A. B., Richardson, J. S., Montague, E. J. *Chemistry.* Boston, 1976.

Geraghty, James J. *Water Atlas of the United States.* Port Washington, New York, 1973.

Hahn, Peter C. *Chemicals from Fermentation.* New York, 1968.

Henius, Max. *Danish Beer and Continental Beer Gardens.* New York, 1914.

Hopkins, R. H. and Krause, B. *Biochemistry Applied to Malting and Brewing.* New York, 1937.

Hopkins, R. H. "Brewing; Alcohol; Wine and Spirits," *What Industry Owes to Chemical Science.* Brooklyn, 1946.

Hunt, Brian. "Spoilage and Sanitation in Homebrewing." *Zymurgy,* vol. 7, #2. Summer 1984.

Jackson, Michael. *The World Guide to Beer.* London, 1977.

Kenny, Stephen T. "Hop Varieties." *Zymurgy,* vol. 8, #1. Spring 1985.

Kieninger, H. "The Influence of Raw Materials and Yeast on the Various Beer Types." Proceedings, A.H.A. Conference, Boulder, Colorado, 1984.

Lewis, Michael. "Microbiological Controls in Your Brewery." Proceedings, A.H.A. Conference, Boulder, Colorado, 1983.

Line, Dave. *The Big Book of Brewing*. Andover, England, 1974.

———. *Brewing Beers Like Those You Buy*. Andover, England, 1981.

Matson, Tim and Lee Ann. *Mountain Brew*. Thetford Center, Vermont, 1975.

Miller, David. *Homebrewing for Americans*. Andover, England, 1981.

Moore, William. *Home Beermaking*. Oakland, 1980.

Morgan, Scotty. *Brew Your Own*. San Leandro, California, 1979.

Muldoon, H. C. and Blake, M. I. *Systematic Organic Chemistry*. New York, 1957.

Nowak, Carl A. *Modern Brewing*. St. Louis, 1934.

Papazian, Charlie. *The Joy of Brewing*. Boulder, Colorado, 1980.

Peppler, H. J., ed. *Microbial Technology*. New York, 1967.

Porter, John H. *All About Beer*. Garden City, New Jersey, 1975.

Robertson, James D. *The Great American Beer Book*. New York, 1978.

Ross-MacKenzie, John A. *A Standard Manual of Brewing*. London, 1927.

Shales, Ken. *Advanced Home Brewing*. Andover, England, 1972.

Siebel, Ron. "The Origins of Beer Flavor in the Brewery." Proceedings, A.H.A. Conference, Boulder, Colorado, 1983.

Stecher, P. G., ed. *The Merck Index of Chemicals and Drugs*. Rahway, New Jersey, 1960.

Taylor, E. W. *The Examination of Waters and Water Supplies*. London, 1949.

Thresh, John C. *Water and Water Supplies*. Philadelphia, 1900.

United States Department of Agriculture. *Hop Production.* Washington, D.C., 1961.

Vogel, E. H., Leonhardt, H. G., Merten, J. A., Schwaiger, F. H. *The Practical Brewer.* St. Louis, 1947.

Vrest, Orton. *Home Beer Book.* 1973.

Wahl, Robert and Henrius, Max. *The American Handy Book of the Brewing, Malting and Auxiliary Trades.* 2 vols. Chicago, 1908.

Weast, Robert C., ed. *Handbook of Chemistry and Physics.* West Palm Beach, Florida, 1978.

Weiner, Michael A. *The Taster's Guide to Beer.* New York, 1977.

INDEX

Acetaldehyde 84, 148, 151, 152, 164
Acetyl Co A 147, 148, 151
Acid 36, 38, 42
  acetic 147
  acetohydroxy 151–153, 155, 157
  amino 21, 22, 69, 73, 74, 88, 103, 113, 128, 132, 143, 147, 151, 167, 163, 272
  boric 45
  butyric 82
  carbonic 33, 45, 54
  citric 56, 187
  ethylacetic 82
  fatty 22–23, 147, 151, 157
  galacturonic 275
  gluconic 82
  hydrochloric 45
  lactic 56, 80–81, 108, 187
  linoleic 23
  nitric 45, 214, 215
  oleic 23
  organic 28, 42, 56, 87, 154
  palmitic 23
  phosphoric 45, 213, 215
  phytic 23, 88, 107, 113
  pyruvic 146–149, 151–152
  sulfuric 28, 45, 47
  tannic 164

Acyl Co A 147
Adjuncts 180, 271
ADP 146, 151, 152
Agar 76, 236, 271
  nutrient 76, 236
Aging See Lagering, bottle conditioning
Albumin 21, 22, 60, 92, 110, 118, 128, 132, 154, 271
  coaguable 113
Albuminoids 113
Alcohol 1, 23, 69, 70, 89, 135, 147
  ethyl 87, 151, 152, 164, 216, 267
  expected 263
  fusel 87, 143, 144, 147–148, 151, 154, 157, 163, 207, 277
  isopropyl 216
Aldehydes 23, 87, 143, 147–148, 151, 157, 163, 271
Aliphatic hydrocarbons 23
Alkaline 36–38
Aluminum 29, 32
Amine 88
Amino acids See Acid, amino
Ammonia 51
Ammonium persulfate, acidified 78, 159
Amylopectin 18, 19, 88–89, 113, 272

Amylose 18, 19, 88–89, 117, 272
Anion 38, 45–46, 47, 52–53, 272
   acid 45–46
Aqua fortis See Acid, nitric
Arabinose 20
Atom 37
   stable 37
   unstable 37–38, 40
ATP 146, 151, 152
Attenuation 69, 73
Aufkraeusening 142, 163–164
Autoclaving 76

Bacteria 29, 60, 77, 79–85, 106,
   140, 158–159, 161–162
   Acetobacter 82
   acetic acid 82, 83–85, 108, 162,
     205, 206
   Acetomonas 82
   Achromobacter 82
   Achromobacter anaerobium 83
   Achromobacteraceae 82
   Aerobacter 83
   aerobic 81–82, 108
   airborne 161
   anaerobic 80, 82, 108
   Bacillus 108
   butyric acid 82, 84, 108
   Clostridium butyricum 82–82,
     108–109
   cocci 80
   coliform 53, 82, 84, 205, 206,
     208, 272
   contamination 114
   culturing 84
   Enterobacteriaceae Hafnia 83
   Enterobacteriaceae Klebgiella 83
   faecal 82, 84, 272
   Gluconobacter 82
   glucophilic 82, 274
   Gram-negative 81–84
   Gram-positive 80–81
   Gram stain 80
   Hafnia protea 83, 85, 206
   heterofermentive 80, 81
   homofermentive 80
   lactic acid 80–81, 83–85, 106,
     112, 145, 162, 205, 280
   Lactobacillaceae 80
   Lactobacillus 80–81
   Lactobacillus brevis 108
   Lactobacillus bulgaris 108

Lactobacillus delbrucki 56, 80–81,
   108
lactophilic 82, 274
microaerophilic 80, 275
mutation 80
Obesumbacterium 83
Obesum proteus 83
Pediococcus 80–81
Pediococcus cerevisiae 81
Peptococcaceae 80
Pseudomonaceae 82
Pseudomonaceae Aeromonas 83
Pseudomonaceae Zymomonas
   83
Pseudomonas 82
sarcina 80, 117
termo 82
thermophilic 80–81, 84, 108,
   277
waterborne 80, 82
Zymomonas 208
Zymomonas anaerobia 84
Zymomonas mobilis 84
Balling See Density
Barley 5, 11, 91, 92
   flaked 180
   four-row 10
   heads 5
   malting 8
   moisture content 5, 6
   nitrogen content 8–9, 11
   roasted 180
   six-row 5, 9–10, 92
   steely 93
   steeping 91
   two-row 5, 9
Barley kernel 8, 20
   aleurone layer 8, 19, 22, 23
   embryo 8, 21, 23, 91
   endosperm 8, 19, 91, 92
   husk 8, 20, 22
   pericarp 8, 22
   weight 267
Basalt 32
Beaker 224
Beer
   aroma 80, 82, 83, 117, 133–134,
     143, 144, 147–148, 168–169,
     202, 206, 208
   bitterness 169–170
   body 20, 21, 23, 111, 112, 208,
     278

clarifying 164-166
carbonation 142, 167-168, 203-204
character 192
clarity 21, 22, 49, 72, 74, 80, 81, 111, 112, 117, 120, 132, 135, 155, 157-158, 164, 168-169, 207, 208
color 22, 49, 136, 162, 168-169
draft 163, 204
flavor 22, 23, 49, 51, 52, 57, 60, 69-72, 74, 80-82, 97, 103, 113, 117, 128-130, 133-137, 139, 147, 150, 158, 163, 168-170, 207-208
fullness 170
haze 22
head 20, 21, 23, 208
oxidation 21
ruh 164, 277
stability 49, 120, 132, 155, 163, 168
sweet 117
Beerstone 211, 272
Bicarbonate 28, 45, 46-48, 52, 55
Big Book of Brewing, The 64
Bitterness Units 64, 181-184, 192
Bleach See Chlorine bleach
Blow-off tube 236
Bock 4, 183-184, 192
Boiling See Wort
period 193-194
Borate 45, 46
Boron 73
Bottle 203, 215
capper 242
cleaning 203
conditioning 167
filler 242
pressure 167, 203
rack 242
Bottling 166-176, 202-204, 249
volume 175
Brewing 89-166, 185-201
planning 171
procedure 185-204
log 209-210
Brush
bottle 240, 242
scrub 224
Buchner 70
B.U. See Bitterness Units

Calcium 28, 29, 35, 45-48, 49-50, 54, 55, 57, 73
bicarbonate 33, 46, 57
carbonate 33, 45-46, 47, 55
carbonate salts 106
chloride 45, 46
hydroxide 57
phosphate 49, 57, 110, 131
sulfate 45-46, 57, 73, 212, 216
Capacity 256-259
Caps-crown 242
Carbohydrates 15-20, 80, 103
Carbon 69
activated 29, 36
Carbonates 46-47, 52, 56, 57, 64, 272
Carbon dioxide 1, 52, 54, 69, 70, 73, 87, 89, 135, 142, 143, 148, 151, 156, 162, 167
Carbonic gas See Carbon dioxide
Carboxyl 88
Carboy 236, 239, 241, 248
Carlsberg 70
Cation 38, 44-46, 47, 272
earth 49-50
metal 45, 51-52
Caustic soda 167, 203, 212-214, 215
Cellulose 15, 20
Chalk 33
Chill haze 21
Chips, beechwood 142, 163, 165-166
Chloride 35, 45, 46, 52-53, 55, 57, 64
Chlorine 28, 206, 208
Chlorite 33
Christian, Jacob 70
Clay 32, 36
Cleansers
acid 212, 215-216
alkaline 215
Chlorine bleach 167, 203, 213, 214
Colloids 36, 56, 128, 130-132, 164, 272
Compound
carbonyl 143
covalent 39-40
hydrated 40
inorganic 44
ionic 38, 40, 45
organic 44

sulfuric 143, 158, 163
Conditioning *See* Lagering
CO_2 *See* Carbon dioxide
Copper 29, 35, 52
Cornflakes 180
Cup—measuring 220

Decarboxylation 148, 151
Density 2, 130, 139, 145, 151, 153–155, 156, 157, 162, 164, 261–262, 273
Detergent 212, 215
Dextrin 15, 18, 88, 103, 110, 114–118, 148, 162, 166, 273
    achroodextrin 18, 88, 117, 271
    a-limit 88, 114, 118
    amylodextrin 18, 80, 117, 272
    B-limit 89
    erythrodextrin 18, 80, 117, 273
    small 18
Dextrocheck 157, 164, 200, 240, 248–249
Dextrose 167, 180
Diacetyl 74, 81, 147, 152–153, 155, 157, 158, 163, 208
Diketone 273
Diols 153
Disaccharides 15, 72, 273
DMS 143
Dolomite 49
Dopplebock 4, 184, 192
Dortmunder 3, 1616, 182, 192
Dreher, Anton 70

E.D.T.A. 47
Element 37
    alkaline earth 44–45
EMP pathway 146, 151
Enzymes 1, 22, 42, 43, 49, 69, 72–74, 87-90, 91, 94, 103, 146–148, 273
    a-glucosidase 72, 89, 90, 113, 114–115, 117, 148
    alcohol dehydrogenase 151
    alpha amylase 49, 52, 88, 110, 114, 116–117, 116
    Beta amylase 88–89, 110, 114–115
    cellulase 88
    collagenase 88
    constitutive 87, 91
    cytase 113

debranching 89
diastatic 19, 57, 87, 88, 109, 111, 119, 273
extracellular 87, 90, 148
glucase 90
heat-labile 113
hemicellulase 88
hydrolytic 91
inducible 87, 93, 148
intracellular 87, 90
invertase 72
limit—dextrinase 89, 113
malt 91–92
maltase *See* a-glucosidase
pectinate 88
peptase 88, 113
peptidase 88, 113
peptonizing 88
phosphatase 88
phytase 88, 106–108, 113
preservation 104
protease 88, 113
proteinase 88
proteolytic 20, 21, 87, 88, 90, 110–112, 119, 166
pyruvate decarboxylase 151
sucrase *See* invertase
viability 116, 166
zymase 69, 70, 87, 89–90
Epsom salts 57
Equipment 171, 217–243
    cleaning 211–215
    sterilizing 211–215

Esters 72-73, 87, 130, 144, 147–148, 157, 158, 163, 273
Esterization 143, 147
Ethanol 82, 84

Ethyl acetate 147
Extract 273
    apparent 156, 166
    efficiency 195
    fermentable 103, 162
    high-maltose 110
    potential 179–180
    real 156, 166
    reduction 145, 151, 154–157, 162, 166
    requirement 177–179
    rest 103
    unfermentable 166
    yield 13

False bottom 224-227
Fermentation 69, 89-90, 137-166, 197-202
  aeration 82
  anaerobic 149
  apparent attenuation 156
  Burton Union 236
  closed 150, 159, 161, 273
  contamination 74, 139-140, 150, 161-162
  density 198, 200
  diacetyl rest 155, 200
  duration 198, 201
  head 129, 133, 135, 148-150, 153-155, 206-207
  high kraeusen 153-154, 198
  kraeusen 77
  lag phase 83, 90, 141, 145-149, 198, 206-207
  lock 143-144, 159, 161, 201, 214
  low kraeusen 149-153, 198
  one-third gravity 156, 162
  pH 70, 74-75, 145, 154, 162, 198, 200, 206-207, 248
  post-kraeusen 154-155, 200
  primary 144, 145-156, 197-200
  racking 82, 132, 142, 156-158
  real attenuation 156, 166
  ropy 80, 277
  secondary 155, 158, 161-162, 201
  skimming 151, 154, 159, 198
  temperature 70, 74-75, 142, 144-145, 151, 153-155, 161-163, 197, 202, 206-207
  temperature control 198-200, 248
Fermenters 214, 220, 236-237, 238-240, 241
  capacity 172-173
  primary 151, 236, 237
  secondary 157, 163-164, 172-173, 238-240
  topping-up 142, 150, 157
Filterbag 224-227
Final density 2
Fining 164-165, 202, 248, 274
  temperature 165
Fission fungi 79
Forcing test 84, 208
Formulas 268-269

Fructosant 18
Fructose 16, 17, 70-72, 80, 84, 90

Galactose 16, 17, 20, 70-72
Gelatin 164-165, 202
  brewers 165
  vegetable 75, 76, 165, 236
  wort 75, 278
Glucodifructose 18
Glucose 16-20, 70-72, 80, 81, 84, 88-90, 106, 114, 146, 148, 152, 180
  chains 18, 108
Glycerol 23
Glycogen 146-149, 163
Glycosis 146
Gneiss 32
Grain mill 97-98
Graminae 5
Granite 32
Gravel 32
Gravity See Density
Gypsum 49, 56, 57, 187

Hammer mill 97-98
Hanson, Emil 70
Hemicellulose 15, 19-20, 91, 103
Hops
  A.A.U. See Alpha Acid Unit
  adhumulone 59
  adlupulone 60
  alpha acid content 60, 64, 65, 129
  Alpha Acid Unit 64, 192
  alpha resin 59, 62, 128
  analysis 62-67
  aroma 60, 62-63, 64, 128, 133-134, 165, 202
  aromatic 60
  bales 62
  Beta acids 207
  Beta resin 59-60, 62
  bittering 60, 64
  bittering principles 59, 62, 113
  bitterness 129-130
  boiling 60, 127-129
  bracts 59
  bracteoles 59
  cohumulone 59
  color 62, 64, 65
  colupulone 60
  cones 62

cultivation 60–62
deteriorated 192
dry-hopping 133
essential oils 59, 60, 62, 65, 127–130, 273, 277
extract 65, 133
finishing 129, 130, 133–134, 192, 194, 246
flavor 60, 62
foil-mylar packaging 64
gamma resins 59
hard resins 59, 62
harvest 62
humulone 59
iso-a-acids 59, 64, 128
isohumulone 81, 82
isomerization 64, 128–129
lupulin 59, 64
nitrogen 59, 65
oxidation 60, 64
pellets 64, 194, 245
polyphenols 59, 60, 113
quality 65
rates 64, 128, 129–130, 133, 181–184, 192
size 62–63, 65
soft resins 59
solubility 129
sparging 133–134, 194–195
strobiles 59
tannin 59, 60, 65, 113, 127, 130–131, 135–136, 165
Humulus lupulus 59
Hydrated lime *See* Slaked lime
Hydrogen 42, 43
buildup 151
Hydrogen carbonate *See* Bicarbonate
Hydrogen peroxide 215, 216
Hydrogen sulfide 84, 143, 208
Hydrolysis 17, 19, 20, 32, 33, 72, 107, 157
Hydrometer 156, 224
correction 263–264

Immersible heating element 214, 222
Iodine 18, 88–89, 100, 116–118, 124
testing 188, 251, 254
Ion 37–38, 40, 44, 57
hydronium 40–41, 42, 46

hydroxide 40–41, 42, 46
Ionic bond 38
Iron 29, 33, 35, 45, 51, 54, 56, 206
oxide 32, 33
Isinglass 165
Isomaltose 72, 166

Jars 233–234

Keg 204, 241
Cornelius 201, 241
Ketones 130, 143
Kettle 171, 211, 214, 217, 230–232, 245
capacity 174
decoction 187, 224
surface etching 214
Kraeusening 140, 141–143, 157, 163–164, 167, 196–197, 201, 202–204, 274

Lactobacillus *See* Bacteria
Lactose 17, 72
Lager 275
U.S. 192
Lagering 163–166, 201
duration 161, 164
period 201
pressure 164, 202
temperature 161, 163
Lauter tub 120, 123–124, 171, 189, 214, 224–230
diameter 120
false bottom 120
flushing 190
Lechithin 49
Lime 32
oxalic 212
Limestone 33, 49
Line, Dave 64
Lipid 22–23, 119, 147, 275
Litmus paper 42
Loop–s.s. 76, 236

Magnesium 29, 33, 35, 45–48, 50–51, 54, 55, 57, 73
bicarbonate 46, 57
carbonate 47, 55
chloride 46
sulfate 46, 56, 57, 73
Magnetite *See* iron oxide
Malt 1, 11, 13, 81, 94–96, 97, 103

acidity 94
acrospire 13, 14, 271
acrospire growth 91–92, 93, 185
aleurone layer 103, 104, 113, 272
amber 95
American 91–92
analysis 12
black 00
Bohemian 95
British 87–88, 91–92, 106
British Pale 95
character 14
chit 93
chocolate 15, 95, 180
Continental 91–92
color 13, 14
crushed 00
crushing 97–101, 118
crystal/caramel 15, 95, 180
Czechoslovakin 95
dark 15, 105, 106, 109, 185, 186
diastatic strength 110
Dortmund 15, 95
embryo 113
endosperm 104
enzymatic 95
enzyme-poor 105, 106
evaluation 13–15, 185
extract 180
extract syrup 245
hard-tipped 98, 105
hemicellulose 113
husk 13, 97, 119–122
lager 15, 92, 95
measurement 185
mill, six-roll 97, 213–214, 220–221
milling See Crushing
modification 13–14, 91–92, 93–95, 275
Munich 15, 95, 179
nitrogen 114
nitrogen content 13
oxygen uptake 92
pale 15, 43, 44, 107, 179
particles 110
Pilsner 15
polyphenols 163
protein content 14
requirement 174, 181

roasted 56, 163
six-row 95, 124, 179
size 14
smoked 95
starch 114–119
steely 185
two-row 179
U.S. pale 95
Vienna 15, 95
weight 267
well-modified 91, 100, 106, 251
Malted barley See Malt
Malting 89, 91–96
aeration 92
floor 93
germination 93–94
kilning 88, 94–96
kiln temperatures 23
respiration 92
steeping 92–93
temperature control 93
Maltose 16–17, 18, 19, 70–72, 80, 88–89, 139, 148, 149, 275
Maltoletraose 18, 116
Maltotriose 18, 70–72, 115, 117, 148, 162, 166
Manganese 29, 35, 45, 51, 54, 56, 73
Mannose 16, 70–72
Marble 32
Marl 33
Mash 204–205, 251, 253–254
albumin rest See protein rest
acidity 23
acid rest 106–109, 186–187
acidulation 81, 88, 106–108, 113, 186–187
boiled 109, 110
cold settlement 112
decoction 13, 87, 88, 97, 105, 106–107, 109–120, 128–129, 273
decoction volume 111
doughing-in 99, 103–106, 109, 118, 186, 251
extract efficiency 125, 195
filter-bed 110, 120–122, 124
first decoction 111–112, 187
first thick mash 187
infusion 109, 128, 251–252
lactic acid 108, 187–187
lauter 109, 275

lauter decoction 189
lauter rest 189, 252
pH 21, 42-44, 48, 49, 106,
    106-108, 110, 113, 187-188
protein rest 92, 109, 112-114,
    132
rancid 109
remixing 112-113, 187, 188
runoff 124-125
saccharification 188-189
second decoction 114, 188
second thick mash 188
set 122, 124, 205
step 251-252
strike temperature 112, 181-
    184, 186-188, 277
temperature maintenance 106,
    112
thinning 189
three decoction 111-120, 185-
    189
treatment 56
tub 214, 221, 222, 253
tub, lactic acid 221
two decoction 111
Mashing 103-120, 185-189, 275
Measure
    cubic 258
    dry 258
    linear 259
    liquid 256-258
    square 259
Melanin 20, 22
Melibiose 17, 72
Mercaptans 143
Metabolic pathways 69
Mineral oil 76
Microscope 236-284, 286
Mineral, trace 23
Mineral salts 29, 45, 56, 57-58, 106
    carbonate 193
    solubility 45-46
Mitcherlich 70
Mixing 112, 172
Monosaccharides 15-16, 18, 148,
    275
Munich, Dark 3, 15, 182-183, 192
Munich, Light 4, 183, 192

NAD 152
Neutron 37
Nitrate 28, 45, 46, 206

Nitrogen 22, 35, 69, 147, 166
Nucleic acid 22

Oligosaccharides 16, 18, 20, 88,
    115, 148, 166, 275
Original gravity (O.G.) 2, 164,
    181-184, 200, 201, 202
Oxaloacetate 147, 151
Oxidation 51, 157, 163, 167
Oxygen 69
Oxygenation 172

Paddle 222
Pasteur 70
Pectin 16, 113, 275
Pentosans 20, 275
Peptide 21, 22, 69, 88, 128
    links 21, 88, 113
Peptone 21, 49, 88
Percentage solutions 268
Permeases 148
Petri dish 76, 84, 234-236
pH 35, 36-37, 40-41, 42, 45-46,
    54-55, 57, 117, 123, 171
    meter 217
    paper 217
    scale 42-43
Phenol 96, 276
Phosphates 22-23, 45, 46, 50,
    147, 276
    alkaline (secondary) 49
    malt 49, 107-108
    triose 146, 152
Phosphorous 33, 73
Phytate See Phytic acid
Phytin 23, 107, 113
Pilsener 3, 116, 181, 192
Pilsner Urquell 3
Plate, porcelain 224
Plato See Density
Polypeptide 22
Polyphenol 22, 143
Polysaccharides 16, 18-20, 91,
    276
Potash 33
Potassium 29, 35, 45, 46, 51, 73
Potassium
    choride 48, 56, 57
    iodide 117
    metabisulfite 57, 212-213, 216
    phosphate 49, 131
Pressure 264-265

Primary fermenter 197
Protein 20, 21, 22, 42, 43, 44, 49,
    60, 73, 87, 88, 91, 103, 118–
    119, 122, 127–132, 135, 143,
    147, 276
    albumin 21
    flocculation 49, 52, 130–131,
        135, 274
    flocks 192–194
    globulin 21
    glutelin 21
    gum 110–111, 119
    haze 20, 92, 123, 157, 163–165
    hordein 21
    membraneous 113
    reduction 109, 110, 112–114
    sludge 122, 150, 190
    stability 22
    trub 110, 131, 134, 143, 155,
        157, 194, 208, 277
Proteolysis 132, 276
Proteose 21, 60, 88
Proton 37
Proteose 21, 60, 88
Proton 37
Pyruvate See Acid, pyruvic

Quartz 32

Racking 201, 276
Raffinose 18, 72
Recipes 181–184
Refrigeration 237
Rock
    conglomerate 33–34
    igneous 32
    metamorphic 32
    sedimentary 32–33

Saccharomyces 69
    carlsbergensis 18, 70–72, 74
    cerevisiae 18, 70–72, 74
    uvarum 70
Salt 57
Salts See Compounds, mineral salts
Sand 32, 212
Sandstone 32–33
Sanitization 79, 157
Scale
    balance 219
    gram 56, 218–219
    hop 232

malt 220
Schizomycetes 79
Screens 213–214, 221
Secondary fermenter 201, 248
Sedimentation 28–29
Sedlmayer, Gabriel 70
Shale 33, 49
Silica 23, 53
Silicate 43, 46, 53, 119, 123
Slaked lime 48, 57
Sodium 35, 45, 46, 51, 44, 47, 73
Sodium
    bicarbonate 46, 213–214
    carbonate 213–214
    chloride 46, 48, 56, 57
    hydroxide See Caustic soda
    hypochlorite See Chlorine
        bleach
    metabisulfite 78, 212, 213, 216
    phosphate 131
    sulfate 46, 48
Soapstone 33
Specific gravity See Density
Sparger 230
    hop 233
Sparging 1, 23, 99–100, 122–125,
        189, 190, 279
    rate 124
    temperature 122, 125
Sponge 224
Spoon
    slotted 237
    stainless steel 222
    long handled 237
Starch 15, 18, 49, 52, 88, 109,
        110, 120
    balled 97, 99, 103, 204
    flour 18, 97, 103
    gelatinized 115–117, 122
    gum 16, 119
    native 18, 114–115, 118, 122
    soluble 103, 114, 117–118
    unmodified 110, 116
Sterilants
    acid 216
    alkaline 216
Stoppers 236, 239, 242
Sucrose 17, 70–72, 80, 90, 148, 180
Sugar 15, 103
    analysis 157, 165
    analysis kit 240
    corn 148, 180

hexose 20, 274
pentose 20, 275
priming 202, 204, 248-249
simple 117
Sulfate 33, 35, 45, 46-47, 52, 55, 57
Sulfur 73
Sulfuric acid 212, 216
Sulfurous acid 212, 216

Tannin 20, 22, 43, 129, 163, 277
Temperature 2, 260-261
ambient 272
Terminal gravity (T.G.) 2, 166, 181-184, 277
Tetrad 80
Thermometer 223-224, 267
Thiols 143
Triacyl glycerol 23
Trial tube 224
Triglycerides 23, 147
Trisaccharides 18, 277
Trisodium phosphate 213-214, 215
chlorinated 213, 215
Trouble shooting 204-208
Trub 80, 277
TSP See Trisodium phosphate
Tub, priming 241
Tubing 236, 239, 242
Turbulence 80, 277

Valence 40, 45, 46, 277
VDK 147, 152-153, 155
Vicinal diketones See VDK
Vienna 3
Vinegar 80
Vitamins 22, 69, 73, 107
B-complex 73
myo-inositol 107
Volume 2
brewing vessels 172-177
Volutin 73

Water 25-26, 156, 266
acidity 36-37
alkaline 92
alkalinity 20, 35, 37, 44-48,
alkalinity as $CaCO_3$ 35, 47-48, 57
analysis 34-55, 35, 48, 49-55
boiling 48, 55-56, 106
boiling point 266

carbonate 36, 55, 106, 123
character 181-184
color 35, 36
composition 29, 34
deep well 29
Dortmind 55
filtration 56
hardness 32-33, 35, 44, 48, 49, 54-55, 64, 265
hardness as $CaCO_3$ 35, 47-48, 55
hardness test kit 217
ion exchange 56
mineral 29
Munich 55
municipal 28-29
odor 35, 36
permanent hardness 33, 46-48
pH 187
Pilsen 55
purity 28, 34, 53
rain 28
sediment 35, 36
shallow well 29
soft 32, 34, 106
softeners 56
sparge 122-123
spring 29
sulfate 106, 108
surface 28
table 29, 30-31
temporary hardness 33, 46-48
testing 34
test kits 217
total dissolved solids 44, 48, 54, 55, 57
treatment 36, 53-56
turbidity 35, 36
underground 29-34
Vienna 55
Weight and measures 255-269
Wine thief 232
Wort 1, 82-83, 278
aeration 131, 135-136, 143, 197, 206
bitter 134-136
boiling 64, 127-134, 190-194, 245-246
character 193, 197
clarity 56, 132, 193
cold break 132, 135-136, 142, 193-194, 205, 246

composition 137
contamination 136
cooled 134, 135, 140–141, 197
cooler 233
cooling 135–136, 193–194, 247
density 2, 116, 130, 139, 193, 195, 196, 200, 202, 205, 245–246
dextrinous 115–116
evaporation 127, 130–131
filtering 133–134
hopping 125
hot break 131–132, 192, 205
maltose rich 115–116
mineral content 88, 107
movement 131
nitrogen 21
pH 44, 127, 131–132, 136, 192–193, 195, 205, 245–246
sweet 124–125, 130, 190
volume 130–131, 134, 195

Xylose 20
Xylulose 70–72

Yeast 1, 42, 49, 57, 69–71, 81, 89–90, 137–140, 157–159, 164–165, 206–208
ale 145, 153
autolysis 139, 144–145, 147, 208, 272
barm 159
binary fission 73
bouquet 207
break 158
bottom fermenting 70, 145, 153
Bruchhefen 158
budding 73, 277
Candida 74
carbon metabolism 70
cell membrane 146–148
character 139–140, 159
colonies 76
composition 73
culture 139–140, 142, 147–148
culturing 75–77
culturing equipment 234–236
dusty 72, 139–140, 141, 158, 161, 206
examination 75–76
Frohberg 72
frozen 77, 78, 140, 159

granulated 77, 140, 148
growth 113, 139, 149–151, 153–154, 162
lager 145, 153
metabolism 146–149, 151–155
mutation 74, 145
nutrients 21–23, 107, 114, 162
oxo-acids 146, 147, 151–152
oxygen required 135–136, 139, 146–148
Pichia 74
pitching 142–143, 159, 276, 196–197
pitching rate 139
plasma 73, 276
pure culture 70, 75–77, 197
reproduction 73, 74
respiration 135, 141, 147–149
rinsing 159
Saaz 72
sediment 158–159, 161, 168
sedimentary 72, 158
seed 158–159, 201
slant 76–77
starter culture 77, 134, 140, 141, 142, 194, 196–197, 245
staubhefen 158
storage 77–78, 159
strains 70
streaking 76
subculturing 78
top fermenting 70–72, 145, 153
Torulopsis 74
vacuoles 73
washing 78, 159
wild 74–78, 140, 141, 158, 207, 208

Zinc 29, 35, 52, 54, 73

BOOKS for Brewers and Beer Lovers

Order Now ... Your Brew Will Thank You!

These books offered by Brewers Publications are some of the most sought after reference tools for homebrewers and professional brewers alike. Filled with tips, techniques, recipes and history, these books will help you expand your brewing horizons. Let the world's foremost brewers help you as you brew. So whatever your brewing level or interest, Brewers Publications has the information necessary for you to brew the best beer in the world — your beer.

Please send me more free information on the following: (check all that apply)

◇ Merchandise & Book Catalog
◇ American Homebrewers Association

◇ Institute for Brewing Studies
◇ Great American Beer Festival℠

Ship to:

Name _____

Address _____

City _____ State/Province _____

Zip/Postal Code _____ Country _____

Daytime Phone (_____) _____

Payment Method

◇ Check or Money Order Enclosed (Payable to the Association of Brewers)
◇ Visa   ◇ MasterCard

Card Number ____ – ____ – ____ Expiration Date _____

Name on Card _____ Signature _____

Brewers Publications, PO Box 1679, Boulder, CO 80306-1679, (303) 546-6514, FAX (303) 447-2825.
BP-O93

BREWERS PUBLICATIONS ORDER FORM

PROFESSIONAL BREWING BOOKS

QTY.	TITLE	STOCK #	PRICE	EXT. PRICE
_____	Brewery Planner	440	80.00	_____
_____	North American Brewers Resource Directory	451	80.00	_____
_____	Principles of Brewing Science	415	29.95	_____

THE BREWERY OPERATIONS SERIES
from Micro and Pubbrewers Conferences

QTY.	TITLE	STOCK #	PRICE	EXT. PRICE
_____	Volume 4, 1987 Conference	424	25.95	_____
_____	Volume 5, 1988 Conference	428	25.95	_____
_____	Volume 6, 1989 Conference	430	25.95	_____
_____	Volume 7, 1990 Conference	433	25.95	_____
_____	Volume 8, 1991 Conference, Brewing Under Adversity	442	25.95	_____
_____	Volume 9, 1992 Conference, Quality Brewing — Share the Experience	447	25.95	_____

CLASSIC BEER STYLE SERIES

QTY.	TITLE	STOCK #	PRICE	EXT. PRICE
_____	Pale Ale	431	11.95	_____
_____	Continental Pilsener	434	11.95	_____
_____	Lambic	437	11.95	_____
_____	Vienna, Märzen, Oktoberfest	444	11.95	_____
_____	Porter	443	11.95	_____
_____	Belgian Ale	446	11.95	_____
_____	German Wheat Beer	448	11.95	_____
_____	Scotch Ale	449	11.95	_____
_____	Bock (available Spring 1994)	452	11.95	_____

BEER AND BREWING SERIES, for homebrewers and beer enthusiasts,
from National Homebrewers Conferences

QTY.	TITLE	STOCK #	PRICE	EXT. PRICE
_____	Volume 8, 1988 Conference	427	21.95	_____
_____	Volume 9, 1989 Conference	429	21.95	_____
_____	Volume 10, 1990 Conference	432	21.95	_____
_____	Volume 11, 1991 Conference, Brew Free Or Die!	435	21.95	_____
_____	Volume 12, 1992 Conference, Just Brew It!	436	21.95	_____

GENERAL BEER AND BREWING INFORMATION

QTY.	TITLE	STOCK #	PRICE	EXT. PRICE
_____	Brewing Lager Beer	417	14.95	_____
_____	Brewing Mead	418	11.95	_____
_____	Dictionary of Beer and Brewing	414	19.95	_____
_____	Evaluating Beer	456	25.95	_____
_____	Great American Beer Cookbook	455	24.95	_____
_____	Winners Circle	407	11.95	_____

Call or write for a free *Beer Enthusiast* catalog today.
- U.S. funds only.
- All Brewers Publications books come with a money-back guarantee.
- **Postage & Handling:** $3 for the first book ordered, plus $1 for each book thereafter. Canadian and foreign orders please add $4 for the first book and $2 for each book thereafter. Orders cannot be shipped without appropriate P&H.

SUBTOTAL _____
Colo. Residents Add
3% Sales Tax _____
P & H * _____
TOTAL _____

Brewers Publications, PO Box 1679, Boulder, CO 80306-1679, (303) 546-6514, FAX (303) 447-2825.

BP-O93